"Every so often there comes a book th[...]
it is useful. In *How to Raise Kind Kids*, Thomas Lickona has given us just
that. Not only does this wonderful book raise interesting issues of morality, it also provides a practical guide to ensure that children are brought
up to be kind and good citizens. In uncaring and confusing times, what
could be a more worthwhile project?" —ALEXANDER MCCALL SMITH,
author of *The No. 1 Ladies' Detective Agency Series*

"Tom Lickona is an American hero. I don't know anyone who has done
more to help parents and educators raise children who care about the
greater good. In this wonderfully wise, engaging book, he nimbly draws
from many disciplines to inform the 'art' of parenting to cultivate kindness, bravely wading into the muddy challenges parents face today, including our toxic political culture, addiction to screens, and a parenting
culture that can fuel entitlement." —DR. RICHARD WEISSBOURD,
co-director of Harvard University's Making Caring
Common program and author of *The Parents We Mean to Be*

"Parents, educators, and perhaps all of society owe Tom Lickona a debt
of gratitude for this latest contribution in his lifelong quest to develop in
young people the ability to know the good, want the good, and do the
good. He combines the skills of a first-class scholar and an adept story-
teller to present a blueprint for instilling in children the vital virtues of
compassion, empathy, and social responsibility. It should be a basic text
for all those who take the job of parenting seriously." —MICHAEL JOSEPHSON, founding president of the
Josephson Institute of Ethics

"Today's children are faced with a plethora of distractions, especially
from electronics, which can affect their ability to listen and be sensitive
to the presence of others. Dr. Lickona reminds us that kindness begins
in the home with positive parenting but also depends on leaders who are
positive role models." —DAVID P. SORTINO, author of *A Guide to How
Your Child Learns: Understanding the Brain
from Infancy to Early Adulthood*

"A treasure trove of traditional wisdom backed by modern science that should grace every parent's nightstand."
—MICHELLE CRETELLA, MD, FCP, president of the American College of Pediatricians

"Over the last thirty years, no one has surfaced more useable research and practical wisdom on character formation than Tom Lickona. Now he brings together the best of his insights in a book filled with helpful information and real-world advice. This is the ideal book for thoughtful parents and teachers."   —KEVIN RYAN, director emeritus of Boston University's Center for Character and Social Justice

"Reading this essential book was addictive. It addresses the character issues we must face if we hope to build a better, more productive, and happier society."   —DOUG KARR, president and CEO of Character.org

"A gold mine of practical suggestions for bringing out the best in our kids."   —HAL URBAN, author of *Life's Greatest Lessons*

"This wise and practical book reminds us that in a world where children often lack a shared moral lexicon, the indispensable virtue of kindness has the power to increase their life satisfaction and bring many benefits both to them and their parents."   —JAMES ARTHUR, director of the Jubilee Centre for Character and Virtues

"*How to Raise Kind Kids* masterfully weaves Dr. Lickona's deep human sensitivity together with strands of age-old wisdom, practical experience, and compelling findings from twenty-first-century research. A rich parental resource for nurturing kindness—and character—in kids."
—DAVID STREIGHT, former executive director of the Center for Spiritual and Ethical Education

PENGUIN BOOKS

HOW TO RAISE KIND KIDS

THOMAS LICKONA, PhD, is a developmental psychologist and the founding director of the Center for the 4th and 5th Rs (Respect and Responsibility) at the State University of New York at Cortland, where he won national recognition for his award-winning work as a professor of education. He has been called "the father of modern character education." His eight books on character development include *Raising Good Children*, *Educating for Character: How Our Schools Can Teach Respect and Responsibility* ("the bible of the character education movement"), and *Character Matters*. He received the Sanford N. McDonnell ("Sandy") Award for Lifetime Achievement in Character Education. A past president of the Association for Moral Education, he is an adviser to Harvard's Making Caring Common project and partners with the University of Leeds on the Narnian Virtues character education project. He speaks around the world to secular and faith-based groups on the subject of fostering good character in families, schools, and communities, and writes a blog for *Psychology Today* called *Raising Kind Kids* (www.psychologytoday .com/blog/raising-kind-kids).

Also by Thomas Lickona

Character Matters:
How to Help Our Children Develop Good Judgment, Integrity,
and Other Essential Virtues

Educating for Character:
How Our Schools Can Teach Respect and Responsibility
(winner of a Christopher Award)

Raising Good Children:
Helping Your Child through the Stages
of Moral Development—From Birth through the Teenage Years

Smart & Good High Schools:
Integrating Excellence and Ethics for Success in School,
Work, and Beyond
(with Matthew Davidson)

Character Quotations: Activities
That Build Character and Community (with Matt Davidson)

Sex, Love, and You:
Making the Right Decision
(with Judith Lickona and William Boudreau, MD)

Moral Development and Behavior:
Theory, Research, and Social Issues (editor)

Character Development in Schools and Beyond
(coeditor with Kevin Ryan)

How to Raise
Kind Kids

AND GET RESPECT, GRATITUDE,

AND A HAPPIER FAMILY

IN THE BARGAIN

THOMAS LICKONA

PENGUIN BOOKS

PENGUIN BOOKS
An imprint of Penguin Random House LLC
375 Hudson Street
New York, New York 10014
penguin.com

ISBN 9780143131946 (paperback)
ISBN 9780525503736 (e-book)

Printed in the United States of America
1   3   5   7   9   10   8   6   4   2

Set in Minion Pro

Three things in human life are important. The first is to be kind.
The second is to be kind. And the third is to be kind.

—Henry James

No act of kindness, however small, is ever wasted.

—Aesop

We are called to do small things with great love.

—Mother Teresa

If you want others to be happy, practice compassion. If you
want to be happy, practice compassion.

—Dalai Lama

Contents

to

everyone

who is working

to create

a kinder world

Acknowledgments

I WOULD LIKE TO express my heartfelt gratitude:

To Joy de Menil, my editor at Penguin, for her commitment to the cause of creating a kinder world for our children to grow up in; for encouraging me to write a book that would help guide parents in their efforts to raise kind kids; for her close reading, rereading, and thoughtful critique of every chapter and her pointed questions and challenges, prompting entirely new chapters that reshaped the book; for bringing to bear her experience and insights as an engaged and observant mother; for spot-on, line-by-line editorial improvements throughout the text; in short, for as intense and supportive a collaboration as any author could possibly hope for—all of which made this a far better book than it would have been without her good counsel and help.

To Robin Straus, my agent for nearly four decades, for her unflagging support and for finding me a wonderful editor and publisher.

To Kathryn Court, Patrick Nolan, and everyone else at Penguin who believed that a book on raising kind kids was needed in these trying times.

To those on the Penguin team who played a part in the editorial process, design, production, and launch of the book: Haley Swanson, Joy's assistant, for her quick and kind help on myriad matters; Jenny Carrow for the delightful cover art; Katy Riegel, for the pleasing interior design; Erica Ferguson, for going the extra mile in her invaluable work as copy editor; Louise Braverman and Carolyn Coleburn for their commitment to this project and all of the unseen labor involved in calling attention to a new book; and the Penguin sales team for everything they do to get good books into the hands of readers.

To the many parents I have worked with and learned from over the past half-century, for sharing their stories; and to all parents who have embraced the demanding, quietly heroic, and profoundly important work of raising a caring family. If it is true that as the family goes, so goes the nation, we are all in debt to those who commit heart and soul to raising the future citizens on whom our common good depends.

To the many dedicated researchers and authors whose findings and wisdom about parenting, child development, and the formation of character have generated a knowledge base on which I've been grateful to build; and to my academic and practitioner colleagues in the increasingly international character education and social-emotional learning movements, for their tireless efforts to create schools of character that extend what parents are doing at home to foster good character in children.

To the State University of New York at Cortland, for its continuing support of the work of our Center for the 4th and 5th Rs (www.cortland.edu/character) and to the John Templeton Foundation, Sanford and Priscilla McDonnell Foundation, and Dr. Hal Urban for their ongoing financial support of the Center's work. To Professor Mark Pike at the University of Leeds, for inviting our Center to partner on the Narnian Virtues character education project, and to Marthe Seales, the Center's Office Manager, for her many contributions to our work and in particular for her help with the character quotations in Appendix A.

To my family: Mark and Matthew for their love and encouragement and for teaching me about being a father (with special thanks to Mark for using his creative talents to design a website for his tech-dinosaur dad); to Lisa and Deirdre, who with our sons have blessed us with fifteen grandchildren; and to our grandchildren, for the special joys and new learning they have brought into our lives.

To my dear wife Judith, for her help in assembling the list of recommended books for young readers; for serving once again as my first (and always tough) editor; for bringing me delicious dinners at the computer during the long push to the book's completion; for being a discerning and devoted mother and grandmother; and most of all for being, over the fifty-one years of our marriage, the soulmate who makes possible all that I do.

And to God, who makes all things possible.

Cortland, New York
October 2017

Author's Note

THE STORIES IN this book—of parents, children, students, colleagues, and others I've been grateful to know and work with—are true. In some cases, I have changed people's names to protect their privacy.

Introduction

THIS IS A book about kindness—how to teach it to your children, foster it at home, and spread it beyond your immediate family. You may have picked it up because you are just starting out as a parent and want to do everything you can, from the outset, to nurture kindness in your child. Or you may feel you have a child who *isn't* kind—or isn't as kind as you want them to be—and you'd like to try to change that. You may feel that all too often your family's interactions—between adults, parent to kid, and among the kids themselves—are not as respectful as you'd hope. You'd like to see more cooperation and less complaining.

Anyone who offers advice about parenting has to do so with great humility. You may have heard the story about the man who taught a class on childrearing called Ten Commandments for Parents. People came from far and wide to learn how to be better parents. Then he got married, and he and his wife had a child. A couple of years later, he renamed his class Five Suggestions for Parents. Then they had another child, and not long after, he renamed the class Three Tentative Hints for Parents. After their third child was born, he stopped teaching the class altogether.[1]

A humorous story but with a valid point: there's no secret formula for raising kids, no 10 easy steps that can guarantee the outcome. Raising human beings isn't like baking a cake or fixing a flat tire. As I watched a conscientious father valiantly trying to keep his cool while dealing with yet another conflict among his children, it seemed to me a more accurate title for the book you're about to read might be something like: *How, on Your Good Days,* to *Try to Get a Little Bit Better at Helping Your Kids Be a Little Bit Kinder.* But that was a lot to fit on the cover.

That said, I do believe there are important principles and practices—some drawn from the wisdom of the ages, others from contemporary advances in moral development and brain research—that can guide you in helping your child on the road to good character. We know that children thrive on a combination of support (lots of love) and challenge (high expectations and accountability). We know that good character involves knowing what's right, caring about what's right, and doing what's right—and that *doing* is the hardest part. Modern moral psychology confirms what Aristotle taught centuries ago: We become good by doing good. For that reason, a parent has to be a "character coach," teaching character skills like self-control and kindness in very deliberate ways and then helping kids practice them again and again, in everyday situations, until such behaviors become easier and more of a habit.

Being a character coach means giving your children opportunities for *moral action* in family life, such as doing chores; playing with, reading to, or caring for a younger brother or sister; helping without being asked; making amends after doing something wrong; and taking part in problem-solving sit-downs where everyone has a voice and responsibility to help to create a happier, more peaceful family. It also means talking to your kids about doing the right thing even when it's hard. It means helping your children to learn from their mistakes and to recognize the times when they may not have resisted temptation or peer pressure. You want them to know that being a good person and doing what's right often isn't easy, but that there's no other way to have self-respect or be truly happy.

The toughest part of being a character coach is doing so in the heat of the moment, when you're tired, frustrated, or running late and your kids are not doing what you ask or are on the verge of a meltdown. In the rough and tumble of family life, you usually have to do something on the spot to deal with the problem at hand. At the same time, you want your immediate response to have long-term benefits that can help to prevent variants of the scenario from happening again. You want to address undesirable behavior in a way that helps your children grow in maturity. You want to help them make progress toward becoming a person of character—someone who is self-controlled, glad to be helpful, respectful and kind, and brave enough to do what's right regardless of what others are doing.

~

Much of what I've learned about parenting has come from my experiences in the trenches as a father of two boys and now as an observing and involved grandfather of fourteen children between the ages of five and twenty-two. I am, by training, a developmental psychologist with a specialization in the moral development of children and adolescents. My first book for parents, *Raising Good Children*, was a guide to helping children develop through the stages of moral reasoning, the process of understanding why some actions are right and others wrong. But moral reasoning is only one part of character—the "head part." Good character also involves "the heart" (caring about what is right) and "the hand" (putting into practice what you know to be right). In my work with parents over the past fifty years, my focus has become character in the full sense: head, heart, and hand—knowing the good, desiring the good, and doing the good.

During that same period, I was a professor of education at the State University of New York at Cortland in upstate New York, helping to prepare the next generation of teachers. A central pillar of my professional career has been training teachers to be character educators, and I continue to direct the character education center that I founded there. Most people who go into teaching want to make a difference in a child's life. There's no better way to do that than to help them develop good character.

Character education is not a new idea—it's actually one of the oldest missions of American schools. In the early days of the republic, all kids had to go to school to learn two things: literacy and virtue. If there was to be government by the people, then the people would have to be committed to democracy's moral foundations: respect for the rights of individuals, voluntary compliance with the law, participation in public life, and concern for the common good. Benjamin Franklin said, "Nothing is more important for the public good than to train up youth in wisdom and virtue."

Ben Franklin might be discouraged if he were around today. That's not to say that there weren't problems in his day, but at this point in our nation's moral journey, it can sometimes seem like we're going backward. In public opinion polls, a majority of adults say they think most Americans are less moral than they used to be. They think that our political system is broken and that the government doesn't listen to or care about people like them.

But there are signs of a movement afoot, even in our current culture, to change this. To be sure, it remains an uphill battle, and it will take the two great formative institutions—the family and school—working together to turn things around. Of those two institutions, the family has the job of laying down the first building blocks of morality and character. In principle, schools build on that base and extend it, but many families have been so dissatisfied with what they have found at school that they have chosen to take on the task of educating their children themselves at home. Just as often, schools feel that parents aren't doing their part to teach things like respect and kindness, leaving teachers to take up the slack.

In the early nineties, national organizations such as the Character Education Partnership (now Character.org) and Character

Counts! came on the scene to promote the goal of comprehensive character education in every school. A strong partnership with parents is a key part of this movement, whose ultimate aim is for all children to attend a school where they will be valued and cared for in a productive learning environment and taught the virtues that make up good character. We're a long way from achieving that goal, but the vision is out there.

At the same time that character education was gaining momentum, we launched the Center for the 4th and 5th Rs (Respect and Responsibility) at SUNY Cortland. I had been gathering best practices in character education for many years, working with teachers and studying exemplary schools across the United States and Canada. Drawing on those practices, I published *Educating for Character: How Our Schools Can Teach Respect and Responsibility*, which caught the wave of the growing interest in character education. Soon after that, our Center began training principals and teachers in the comprehensive approach that *Educating for Character* described. Today, initiatives like Harvard's Making Caring Common, Boston University's Center for Character and Justice, St. Louis's Leadership Academy for Character Education, and the University of San Diego's Character Education Resource Center are providing fresh impetus for the character education movement.

From the perspective of character education, every moment of the school day is a "character moment." Every experience, every interaction—in classrooms, in corridors, on the playground—has the potential to shape the values and character of a child. That's even more true of the interactions you have with your child at home. You are your child's first and potentially most powerful character educator. I hope this book will offer you hope, affirm the good things you're already doing, and give you some new strategies for your toolbox that will help you support your child's character development and create a culture of kindness and respect in your home.

The Challenge

Parenting remains the hardest job on the planet. It taxes our energies and tests our character. We often see our own faults—pride, impatience, a strong will, a short temper—reflected or magnified in our children. "God gives us children to teach us humility," sighed a young mother of a four-year-old boy.

Every child is different. Temperaments vary widely. Some kids are calm, some hyper. Some are focused and organized, others impulsive and distractible. Some are very sensitive and dissolve into tears at the slightest scolding. With others, our words seem to go in one ear and out the other. Some seem to come naturally by sharing and generosity. Others struggle to acquire such behaviors. Some seem born to be cooperative and obedient; others are stubborn and always testing the limits. Many are relatively easy during the childhood years but tougher in the teens. With others, just the opposite is true. Boys and girls present different challenges, and not necessarily in predictable patterns.

All of this makes parenting an art, not a science. From infancy on, we have to try to understand our children's individual personalities, pay attention to how they respond to what we do and to the world around them, find out what works best in eliciting their strengths, and help them with their difficulties. And no matter how much we learn from living with them or from reading books or taking courses on parenting, there will still be aspects of our children's individual personalities and our relationships with them that we may never fully understand.

Nevertheless, we should begin to think now about the kind of people we hope our children will be when they are grown men and women. Wise parents see themselves as "raising adults."[2] Will they be responsible adults who live by high moral standards? Will they make faithful husbands and wives and loving mothers and fathers?

Will they contribute meaningfully to their community and to society?

This is not to say we control the outcome. Some years ago, after I spoke to parents at a high school, a mother came up to me and said: "I have three sons. The first two are hardworking and responsible. The third says he's a hedonist. He's twenty-six and says his sole purpose in life is to have a good time. Where did I go wrong?"

After a lighthearted reassurance that "two out of three isn't bad," I reminded her that there is not a one-to-one correspondence between our efforts as parents and how our kids turn out. We do not create the person our child becomes. That is influenced by a host of factors, including their genes and innate temperament; the idiosyncrasies of their brains; the ever-changing world they're growing up in; their teachers, coaches, and schools; the presence or absence of a spiritual support system in their lives and a belief in something larger than themselves; the company they keep and the popular culture, social media, and other influences they take into their minds, hearts, and souls.

To a large degree, our children create their character by the choices they make every day. Or, as the new brain research would put it, they "wire and rewire their brains" constantly by what they choose to do and experience. Fourteen-year-old Anne Frank, before the Gestapo captured her family, put it this way in her diary: "Parents can give good advice and put their children on the right path, but the final forming of a person's character lies in their own hands."[3]

Our role as parents is to do the best we can. It's to make the most of the countless opportunities we have to contribute to our children's growth in character. In doing that, we need to take the long view and work to lay the best possible foundation for growth. If your children are already teens and you feel you've made mistakes, have the confidence that it's never too late to make a fresh start. We can't change the past, but we can choose the future. Our children are a work in progress; so are we as parents.

Make a list of what you already do well as a parent and build on those strengths as well as working on what you can do better. Get support by talking with your spouse. If you're a single mother or father, or if your spouse is not receptive, find at least one other parent to talk to about parenting.

Let's look now at the challenges of trying to raise kind kids in our current, often unkind culture. In today's world, creating a family culture of kindness and respect will in many ways be countercultural. But it's still possible. Parenting for kindness and respect will be harder with some children than with others, but we can help every child make progress on the road to good character.

How to Use This Book

I'd encourage you to read this book in whatever way you feel is most useful to you. The chapters follow a logical progression, but I've written them so they stand alone. You can read and make use of each one without having read the one before. Take a look at the table of contents and see what interests you most—perhaps what speaks to "where the shoe pinches." If you have questions about discipline, you might want to start with chapter 7. If you're concerned about how to give and get respect, go straight to chapter 6. For the 10 essential virtues that make up good character and how to foster them, read chapter 5. If you want to work now on building a family culture based on kindness and respect, chapter 4 will give you 6 key strategies. If you can't get your kids to do their chores, chapter 4 will help with that, too. If you feel screens have taken over your family, read chapter 9 for ways to get control of that. Never done a family meeting? The steps for a successful one are laid out in chapter 8. I encourage you to try that soon; approached in the right spirit, a family meeting will boost the happiness of your home in ways you can feel. Want some quick ways to have better family conversation? That's in chapter 11.

Is your kids' complaining driving you crazy? Chapter 12 explains how to teach and practice gratitude in family life. If you have teens or preteens and are concerned about the hypersexualized world they have to grow up in—including the new challenges posed by the worst aspects of social media and ubiquitous Internet pornography—I hope you'll find support and practical help in chapter 15. If you wonder what you can do to try to create a more positive societal culture instead of the increasingly angry one we're now struggling with, chapter 2 speaks to that. And if you want a glimpse of "schools of character" (I hope your kids are able to go to one) that make teaching kindness and respect a top priority, you'll find that in chapter 14.

If you enjoy inspiring quotes, are looking for children's books that build character, or want some fun family projects that foster kindness and purpose, those are all in the appendices.

Okay—roll up your sleeves and dig in!

CHAPTER 1

Why Kindness Matters

It is a bit embarrassing to have been concerned with the human problem all one's life and find at the end that one has no more to offer by way of advice than "try to be a little kinder." —ALDOUS HUXLEY

A grandfather to his 7-year-old granddaughter, Winnie: "How can parents teach their children to be kind?"

Winnie: "They should be kind to them."

IN A WORLD WHERE ANGER, cruelty, and violence are all around us, we are grateful when our attention is turned to kindness. In 2013, at Syracuse University, the American short story writer George Saunders gave a commencement speech that soon went viral. He asked the graduates, "Who, in *your* life, do you remember most fondly—with the most undeniable feelings of warmth?" Then he answered his own question: "Those who were kindest to you, I bet."[1]

We never forget acts of kindness. They touch something deep in our souls. When we are struggling, kind words help—even from a stranger. Beth Elfrey, a Connecticut attorney with two sons, shares this story:

When our son Luke was born, my husband, Joe, and I learned that he had multiple disabilities. Luke, now 11, has to wear braces on his legs. He is nonverbal, and he is not yet toilet-trained. Developmentally, he is like a toddler. Not long ago, we took our older son, Sam, who is a typical 13-year-old, and Luke to Disney World. I had been pushing Luke in the wheelchair, taking him to public bathrooms to change his diapers. I was exhausted and feeling a tinge of despair.

We went to see a live [*Finding*] *Nemo* show and sat in the handicapped row in the back to accommodate Luke's wheelchair. I told Joe I was concerned that Luke couldn't see the stage. A grandmother in front of us with her grandsons heard my concern and offered to switch seats with us. I think she also sensed my despair, because after the show she turned around and grabbed my hand. She told me that it was right to expose Luke to things because you cannot know what he gets out of them. She reassured me, "All you can do is your best and let God do the rest."

A feeling of love and calm washed over me. Tears streamed down my face. I thanked the woman for her kindness. I left the theater with a renewed sense of energy to get through the rest of the day. I silently prayed, thanking God for the love and kindness shown to me.[2]

Kindness mattered to this mother. It helped her to keep going.

Acts of kindness, big and small, keep us all going. Consider all the ways people do kind things for others. Someone holds a door for someone coming behind. Someone gives up a seat on a bus or subway. People stop to help a driver who's having trouble. A passerby gives money or food to a homeless person. A kid at school reaches out to a peer who seems to have no friends. Neighbors or church members make meals for a family that's just had a baby, is facing a serious illness, or has lost a loved one. People raise funds for a family that's facing unmanageable medical bills or has lost their home to a fire. People rescue abused animals. Volunteers staff soup kitchens and help in hospitals. Others provide counseling and support for women facing crisis pregnancies and single mothers who need help. People give blood. Thousands of citizens give money, goods, or hands-on help to victims of natural disasters.

Many labor on behalf of the victims of hunger, disease, or injustice, or work to safeguard the natural environment.

These are not "random" acts of kindness. They are quite deliberate acts that spring from a disposition to respond compassionately and generously to the needs of others. And nearly all of these acts of service are done quietly, out of the limelight, without any kind of public recognition. This list doesn't include the countless acts of kindness done daily for members of our own family or on the job as part of our work. Parents getting up in the night to care for a sick child. Adults caring for elderly parents who can no longer take care of themselves. Teachers going the extra mile to meet every student's needs. Doctors, nurses, and hospice personnel working tirelessly to help a very sick patient. Even if we are paid for such work, it's the kindness with which we do it that makes our work an act of love. Try to imagine a world without kindness.

Acts of kindness renew our sense of the goodness that human beings are capable of. They can also renew our resolve to be kinder in our own lives. Many of us will remember moments when we could have been kind but instead did nothing. The writer Martha McVeigh remembers when she was 7 years old, in 2nd grade, and there was a girl named Robin who had seven siblings.

Her family was quite poor. My mother packed up clothes my sister and I had outgrown and gave them to the family. One day I saw Robin wearing a dress that I'd worn the previous year. Because Robin was poor, most of the kids wanted nothing to do with her. Some said she smelled (she didn't) and was stupid (she wasn't). I was torn. Stick with my friends who didn't want Robin in our group, or play with the one girl who stood alone on the school yard? I played it safe and stayed with my friends. I rationalized that Robin would be okay without me.[3]

More than thirty years later, McVeigh still thinks about Robin. It's natural as a kid to want to play it safe. So what can we do as parents to nudge our children out of their comfort zone when being kind takes courage?

The Most Important Question

What is the most important question we can ask ourselves as parents? It's this: *What kind of person do we want our child to be?*—now, as we're raising them, and later, as an adult. If you are like most parents, you will say that you want your child to be a good person. Of course, you also want them to be happy. You want them to have friends. You want them to discover and develop their talents, find meaning in life, and enjoy a measure of success at whatever they feel called to do. But success will be hollow if they don't have good character.

Of all the virtues that make up character, love has been considered by many philosophers to be the wellspring of all the others. No virtue is more central to love than kindness. But what does it mean to be kind?

Webster's New Collegiate Dictionary defines "kind" as:

- having feelings befitting our common nature
- benevolent—disposed to promote the happiness of others
- and proceeding from, and characterized by, goodness.

This suggests that kindness has three components: (1) feelings for other people, (2) a desire to promote their happiness, and (3) an inner goodness as its source. In other words, kindness is not simply external actions that are helpful, but actions motivated by a certain *inner attitude*—a concern for another's happiness. Kindness comes from a loving heart.

Some years ago, I taught one of the religious education classes for teens preparing for confirmation at our Catholic church. Not long ago, I was asked to speak to a friend's 8th-grade confirmation class. Eighth graders can be a tough audience. I decided to start with a story about kindness—one that I hoped would take them out of themselves. It's the story of Daniel DeLoach, who, in his first 18 years of life, had experienced extraordinary adversity—including extreme cruelty—but also great kindness, especially from his older sister, Kathleen.[4]

At birth, Daniel DeLoach weighed fourteen pounds. Half of that was tumors. He was born with Proteus syndrome, a very rare disease made more widely known by the film *The Elephant Man*. "Daniel had webbed feet, all sorts of deformities," his sister, Kathleen, says. By the time he was 18, Daniel had had ninety surgeries. But the most difficult thing to endure was not the physical suffering but the cruelty of others. Kathleen explains: "Daniel is Mr. Social, so when people get to know him, it doesn't take them long to get past differences. But every time we go on vacation, people stare, they ridicule. They tap each other and say, 'Did you see that ugly kid?'"

Because of Daniel, Kathleen got a master's degree in bioethics. She self-published a book about her brother and has worked with her mother to raise money for a foundation for kids with Proteus syndrome. And she has joined Operation Respect, an organization dedicated to preventing the kind of cruelty her brother experienced. Kathleen says that Daniel was an inspiration to the whole family. Her experiences with her brother, she says, "have made me realize that everyone has hurt, and everyone deserves respect."

Daniel himself said he drew strength from his faith in God. "This disease has actually forced me to have a good outlook on life," he remarked. He hoped that "other people with little illnesses or small surgeries can think of me and draw courage." He said he'd learned a "deep lesson" from his disease: "It's not the way people look but the way they act toward others that counts."[5]

I gave the class a couple of minutes to think about what

Daniel's story meant to them, and to write a sentence: "After listening to Daniel's story I . . ."

They were clearly moved by the story. They said they admired Daniel's courage, his faith, his amazingly positive attitude toward life despite all the trials he'd endured, and his compassion for the suffering of others. They admired his sister Kathleen's great love and devotion to her brother and all that she had done to try to create a world where everyone receives the love and respect they deserve.

Finally, I asked these 8th graders, "What is one thing you'd be willing to do in the next week to practice one of the character qualities you admired in Daniel and Kathleen?" Several said they were going to try to complain less; if Daniel could keep a positive attitude despite all that he'd been through, they should be able to deal with the problems they faced.

The Choose Kind Movement

My 8th graders' response to the life of Daniel DeLoach shows the power of a good story and the attractiveness of virtue. Let me give a more recent example of this. In 2012, a graphic designer and illustrator by the name of R. J. Palacio wrote her first book, *Wonder*, a novel for kids 8 and up (a subsequent picture book, *We're All Wonders*, is now available for younger readers). *Wonder* became a #1 *New York Times* bestseller, won a hatful of best-children's-book-of-the-year awards, and has since sold more than five million copies and been made into a movie. It has even launched a movement that challenges all of us, young and old, as we go through our day, to be more aware of our decisions and actions and to "choose kind." *Wonder* has provided a powerful tool that both parents and teachers can use to teach kindness. As it happens, this captivating fictional story has many parallels to the true story of Daniel DeLoach. *Wonder*'s protagonist, 10-year-old

Auggie, has a severe facial deformity that caused him to undergo multiple surgeries. After homeschooling him, his parents decide to send him to the local public school for the first time as a 5th grader. He experiences cruelty from a lot of kids, but with the support of friends and family and his own plucky resilience, insight into people, and sense of humor, he manages to triumph. His presence and character help those around him learn what it means to be courageous and kind.

Recently the editors of Brightly's Book Club for Kids (www .readbrightly.com/book-club/) interviewed R. J. Palacio about the Choose Kind movement. She began by speaking honestly about the difficulty of being kind on an everyday basis and why it's worth the effort.

I'm a born-and-bred New Yorker. . . . Everyone's always in a rush. Tempers can flare easily. If you keep that refrain, "Choose kind," in your head at all times, though, it has a way of changing your relationship with the world. . . . The precept that resonates the most with me now is Ian Maclaren's: "Be kind, for everyone you meet is fighting a hard battle." . . . If you remember this . . . you can view everyone with a little extra compassion. It makes you feel a genuine tenderness for other human beings, which helps in choosing kindness.[6]

Asked by Brightly's interviewer what she hoped kids and parents would take away from reading Wonder, Palacio stressed the importance of maintaining high expectations.

Don't buy into that nonsense that "all kids go through a mean phase" in middle school. That's absurd. . . . Of course, kids that age are finding themselves and testing boundaries, but it doesn't mean they get to be mean about it. Making new friends doesn't mean you get to treat your old friends like

yesterday's news. . . . [P]arents need to remind their kids . . .
the Golden Rule still applies in middle school. Expect them
to be kind in all their social dealings.[7]

Kindness obviously matters a great deal in schools, where children
can experience either acceptance and friendship or rejection and
abuse, depending on whether a culture of kindness prevails in
classrooms and the school as a whole. As Palacio points out, we
should remind our children that we expect them to treat all of their
schoolmates with the same kindness and respect they themselves
want to receive. But children's natural social development can
include tendencies—to form cliques, for example—that work
against kindness. By 5th and 6th grade, and sometimes sooner,
students (especially girls) tend to create tight little status-conferring
social groups that often war with one another and leave some kids
out in the cold. But it doesn't have to be that way. If we really care
about kindness, we'll find a way to provide what I call "support
structures" that help kids overcome negative social tendencies and
develop a caring classroom community where no one is left out.

Let me give an example of a teacher who did this. Janet Fagal,
a former student of mine, struggled with cliques in her first year
as a 5th-grade teacher. "They were destroying any sense of community," she says.

At the start of the new school year, she decided to try to prevent cliques from having a chance to form by holding a weekly
"seat lottery." She put the desks in the shape of a horseshoe, with
all desks facing the center and kids elbow to elbow, so they could
easily converse and work with a neighbor. She gave each desk a
number. At the end of the week, students each drew a number from
a hat; that number designated their desk for the next week. A new
desk meant new neighbors—and the possibility of making new
friends.

"It changed the social chemistry of the class," she says. "Kids still had 'best friends,' but there were no longer exclusive cliques. Because they had to change seats every week, many kids became friends with people they had never gotten to know before—and in some cases, had even disliked." We should keep the bar high—at school and at home—and give kids the support structures they need to be their best selves.

Being Good Is Good for You

Being kind—at school, in the family, and in every other social environment—not only makes other people happy; it makes us happy too. New studies are finding that even very young children are happier when they act in kind and helpful ways. A study of 2-year-olds carried out by psychologist Lara Aknin and colleagues at the University of British Columbia's Centre for Infant Cognition was the first to demonstrate the feeling of elation that even young children can experience from being kind.[8] Brain researchers have called this phenomenon "helper's high": doing a kind act lights up the part of the brain that lets us experience joy.[9] In the study, 2-year-olds appeared happier when they gave a treat (to a monkey puppet) than when they received a treat. Moreover, they acted *happiest* when they gave the monkey *one of their own treats* ("costly giving," as the researchers termed it).

Feeling happy because we've made another person happy, even when it involves a sacrifice, is the essence of kindness. As parents and teachers we can capitalize on this—by providing regular opportunities for kids to experience the intrinsic rewards of being helpful and generous. We can prompt that by using the language of virtue: "This is a chance to be generous. Remember how good it felt to be generous yesterday when you shared your Skittles with Bobby?" "Remember how happy you were when you helped me get dinner ready last night?"

Being altruistic is not only intrinsically rewarding; it fosters emotional and physical health across the life span. In *Why Good Things Happen to Good People*, Stephen Post, MD, summarizes the growing evidence that being good is good for us:

> Give daily, in small ways, and you will be happier. If you engage in helping activities as a teen, you will still be reaping health benefits 60 or 70 years later. Generous behavior is closely associated with reduced risk of illness, lower rates of depression, and traits such as social competence, empathy, and positive emotions. By learning to give, you become more effective at living itself.[10]

We're hardwired to be happier and healthier when we do good. Our children should know this.

What Good Parenting Looks Like

We know a lot about what good parenting looks like from the accumulated wisdom of the ages and from more than a half century of parenting research.[11] The family is the cradle of learning. Kids do better in school, studies find, when there are two parents in the home (though some single parents heroically manage to shoulder the whole load, and their children thrive); when kids are well cared for and feel secure; when the family environment is intellectually stimulating; when parents encourage self-discipline and perseverance; and when they limit TV, monitor homework, and ensure regular school attendance.[12]

The family is also the first school of virtue. It is where most of us first experience love and learn to give it in return. Research finds that children's character development is best supported when parents provide a stable and loving family environment; when they stress the importance of being a good person and also set a good example; when they teach respect for legitimate authority, including theirs as parents; when they not only teach kindness and respect but also hold their children accountable to those expectations through appropriate correction and discipline; when they help their kids understand how their actions affect other people; when children have meaningful responsibilities in family life; and when they grow up with a vision of life that gives them a sense of purpose and an ultimate reason for trying to lead a good life.[13] Much of good parenting is a matter of recovering this wisdom, which used to be more reliably passed on from one generation to another. A landmark study that helps reveal how caring parents go about trying to raise caring children, Samuel and Pearl Oliner's *The Altruistic Personality* draws on the most extensive research ever carried out on people who rescued Jews from the Nazi Holocaust.[14] Rescuers risked their lives to save strangers, people to whom they did not have personal ties. Why did they do it? How were their families different from those of others who lived in the same Nazi-occupied countries but did *not* get involved in rescue work?

The Oliners found that rescuers were more likely to describe growing up in close families where parents modeled and directly taught caring moral values. Their parents were more likely to emphasize the obligation to help others generously, without concern for getting anything back. Said a woman who rescued: "My mother always said to remember to do some good for someone at least once a day." A man said, "My parents taught me to serve others. If somebody was ill or in need, my parents would always help." Another said, "We are our brother's keeper. When you see a need, you have to help."

Non-rescuers more often described their parents using physical punishment to discipline them. As children, they usually experienced punishment more as a cathartic release of the parent's anger than anything related to what they had done. "He hit me with a wet strap," said one non-rescuer of his father, "mostly when he was in a bad mood." By contrast, rescuers remembered their parents as more often "explaining things," telling them that they had "made a mistake" or hadn't understood the other person's point of view. "When I came home from school full of criticisms of some friend," recalled one man, "my father would bring up both sides. 'Moral education' is the best expression for what he did."

The parents of rescuers were also more likely to explicitly teach tolerance—positive attitudes toward other cultures and religions. Said one rescuer: "My father taught me to love God and my neighbor, regardless of race or religion. And at my grandfather's house, when they read the Bible, he invited everybody in. If a Jew happened to drop in, he would ask him to take a seat. Jews and Catholics were received in our place like everybody else." It was no accident, this study concludes, that when the lives of Jews were threatened, those who had been brought up to respect and care about all people, responded by reaching out. Saving Jews from the Holocaust grew out of the ways in which the rescuers had ordinarily related to other people. Kindness had become part of their character.

The findings of the Oliners are strikingly similar to those of an earlier study of rescuers carried out in the 1960s, soon after the trial of Nazi concentration camp commander Adolf Eichmann revealed to the world the full horror of the death camps.[15] That earlier study also found that rescuers remembered their parents as strong, good people who both preached and practiced morality. One rescuer had once been a wealthy German businessman. He described how he first became involved in rescue:

> I was believing in 1942 that the war will be another year. . . .
> I was then a rich man. I had about 300,000 or 400,000 marks,
> and I started with one person, then six people, from there to
> 50, then 100 . . . People came to me . . . asking me very bluntly
> and very frankly, "Will you save me?"

By the war's end, he had spent four years and all of his fortune to save more than two hundred Jews. This is what he said about his family:

> I come from a poor family. . . . You inherit something from your parents, from your grandparents. My mother said to me when we were small, and even when we were bigger . . . "Regardless of what you do with your life, be honest. When it comes to the day you have to make a decision, make the right one. It could be a hard one. But even the hard ones should be the right ones."

He went on to talk about his mother in glowing terms, how she had taught him how to live and had exemplified morality for him. "Always in life she gave me so much philosophy. She didn't go to high school, only elementary school, but so smart a woman. Wisdom, you know."[16]

~

Kindness matters for many reasons. We make others happy when we treat them kindly, and are happiest ourselves when we do so. We are most fully human when we are kind; it's the heart of good character. We'll have safer, more welcoming schools—ones our children will look forward to going to—when kindness is the norm. We'll have happier homes. Let's turn now to the challenges we face as we try to raise kind kids—and how we can meet them.

CHAPTER 2

Does Our Culture Cultivate Kindness?

O beautiful for spacious skies,
For amber waves of grain,
For purple mountain majesties,
Above the fruited plain!
America! America!
God shed His grace on thee,
And crown thy good with brotherhood
From sea to shining sea!
— KATHARINE LEE BATES,
"AMERICA THE BEAUTIFUL"

THIS FOURTH OF JULY, singing those familiar words at morning Mass stirred strong feelings. But the "brotherhood" for which Katharine Lee Bates prayed seems less and less to describe our country. As I write, I'm looking at our hometown paper's front-page headline: "Doctor Shoots 7 in NYC Hospital." The opening paragraph reads: "A doctor forced from a New York hospital because of sexual harassment accusations returned Friday with an assault rifle hidden under a lab coat and shot seven people, killing one woman in an attack that left several doctors fighting for their lives."[1]

We've been battered by news of other horrific shootings, with a much greater loss of life—in an elementary school, a nightclub, a community center, a movie theater, the workplace, a church, a music festival. But by a doctor . . . in a hospital . . . where you go to be taken care of? What's happening to our country?

If we want a kinder society—if we hope to build a wider culture of kindness and respect in which to try to raise kind children—we will have to begin by taking a hard look at where we are today.

Human behavior has always been influenced by the interaction of character and culture. Think of character as what's on the *inside*—the capacities and dispositions that influence how we act and react. Culture is what's on the *outside*—all the factors in our environment, including social norms and expectations, what is valued or devalued by others, how people around us are behaving, everything that makes up the "social ecology" we inhabit. This includes our family, and its values and expectations. All these environmental factors operate, over time, to form our inner dispositions, and then, in any given situation, the outside influences bring out either the best or the worst of our character.[2]

In considering how we can prioritize and promote kindness in our families, I'd like to examine four important, character-influencing changes in American culture, how they make the work of raising kind and respectful children more challenging than ever, and what we can do as parents to meet those challenges. Those four cultural changes are: (1) America's increasingly toxic political culture, (2) the emergence of a culture of entitlement that has made kids more demanding and self-centered and has delayed their progress toward becoming responsible, contributing adults, (3) the dominance of electronic screens in family life and the negative effects of too much screen time, and (4) the sexualizing of our culture and children that is currently exacerbated by ubiquitous pornography and the worst aspects of social media.

This chapter examines the first two of those cultural changes; the second two will be addressed in chapters 9 (on screens) and 15 (the sexual culture). We have to be aware of how these cultural forces are affecting our kids—and intentional about creating a family culture strong enough to resist the unhealthy influences of the wider culture. Increasingly, that means pushing back—making choices and standing for values that are not supported by prevailing norms.

Our Toxic Political Culture

I think most Americans, no matter what their politics, have been shocked and dismayed by how toxic, angry, and vicious our political culture has become. A nation that only a few years ago elected and then reelected its first black president is looking more and more like something out of the pre–civil rights era. Many people who used to be able to discuss their political and ideological differences with friends and associates now say that's much harder, if not impossible, to do.

I joined my grandsons in watching the 2017 NBA playoff games between the Cleveland Cavaliers and the Golden State Warriors. Just before the finals began, it was reported that the Los Angeles home of LeBron James, the Cavaliers' veteran superstar, had been spray-painted with the N-word. James is not only admired for his basketball prowess: in 2017, he won the league's J. Walter Kennedy Citizenship Award for helping to improve educational opportunities for youth in his hometown of Akron, Ohio. At a press conference, he spoke calmly, but with obvious emotion: "Hate in America, especially for African-Americans, is living every day. . . . No matter how much money you have, no matter how famous you are, no matter how many people admire you . . . being black in America . . . it's tough."

A few days before, in Washington, DC, a noose was found hanging outside the National Museum of African American History and Culture—the second such incident within a week. In the same month of May, a black college student in College Park, Maryland, was fatally stabbed by a self-professed white supremacist days before he would have graduated.[3]

According to California State University's Center for the Study of Hate and Extremism, hate crimes during the 2016 election year rose by 6 percent in twenty-five of the nation's largest cities. In June 2017, the federal Bureau of Justice Statistics released a report estimating that 250,000 hate crimes are committed in America every year.[4] Of those reported (an estimated half are not), 48 percent involve racial bias. In the most recent year, Hispanics were victimized at the highest level, followed by blacks.

After the 2016 presidential election, the nation's schools became an increasingly common location for hate incidents. Harassment of Muslim and other minority students increased significantly. College campuses saw an increase in the posting of white supremacist flyers,[5] and many Hispanics reported that people have told them to "go back to Mexico"—even when they are US citizens or not even from Mexico. One woman, whose family has lived in California since before it was a state, said that as she was talking on her phone in Spanish, a woman walked by her and said, "I can't wait for them to deport you."[6]

In February 2017, in an Olathe, Kansas, bar, a man angrily demanded to see the visas of two Indian men, who were in fact educated in and working legally in the US. Shouting, "Get out of my country!" the antagonist stormed out of the bar, then returned to shoot both men, killing one and injuring the other.

As summer approached, violence began to invade politics. In June, Fox News filmed a Montana congressman-elect body-slamming and then punching a reporter in an unprovoked attack. The next day, a Montana voter threatened a CNN crew, "You're lucky someone doesn't pop one of you."[7] Two Democratic political candidates, citing repeated death threats, withdrew their challenges to Republican incumbents. One such withdrawal happened in the small city of Binghamton, not far from where I live in central New York. Democratic mayoral candidate Michael Treiman, the manager of a solar company, announced he was ending his race against Binghamton's Republican mayor after getting emails threatening to do "heinous things" to his wife and three children. That day, an unidentified man in a truck had driven by his house; yelled, "Liberal scumbag"; and thrown a full soda can that hit Treiman in the back as he held his infant child.

Incivility and violence can be found on both sides of our growing political divide. A shooting later that same week stunned the country. On a ballfield across the Potomac from the Capitol in Washington, DC, Republican congressional representatives were practicing for the next day's annual Democrat-Republican baseball game, a charity fund-raiser and traditional respite from partisan politics. An unemployed 66-year-old Illinois man—who had written letters to the editor of the *Belleville News-Democrat* denouncing Republicans' "favoring the rich" and posted social media messages such as "It's Time to Destroy Trump & Co."—aimed a rifle through the field's chain-link fence, opened fire, and wounded four of the representatives, one critically, before being fatally shot by Capitol police.

For some people, the attack only fueled their anger. The day after the shooting, Claudia Tenney, a newly elected Republican congresswoman from central New York, got an email with the subject line "1 down, 216 to go . . ." and an email message that read in part, "Do you NOT expect this?" Tenney's spokeswoman said her office receives similar threats all the time. On the congresswoman's official Facebook page, someone had made a Memorial Day post about her son, a US Marine now serving in the Middle East: "Waiting on your son to come back bagged."[8]

All this ugliness has taken place in a bitterly polarized political culture where each side has accused the other of growing intolerance, name-calling, and closed-mindedness.

How did we get to this point?

Critics of President Donald Trump attribute the deteriorating state of our public life to things he said and did—such as stirring up animosity toward immigrants, making degrading comments about women, firing off angry tweets at anyone who criticizes him, and urging supporters to rough up anti-Trump protesters—lowering the bar of American politics and unleashing the worst instincts in the body politic. Many voters who supported Donald Trump politically have been upset by and publically critical of such actions. Other commentators have criticized intolerance on the left and cited it as contributing to Trump's election and our cultural civil war. Increasingly on college campuses, conservative speakers have had their invitations canceled because some students and faculty objected to their views, have been shouted down if they came, or have been kept away by threats of violence. In a September 2015 *Atlantic* article, "The Coddling of the American Mind," constitutional lawyer Greg Lukianoff and social psychologist Jonathan Haidt noted that since 2000 more than 240 campaigns have been launched at US universities (most of them since 2009) to prevent public figures from speaking at campus events. In many quarters of society, political correctness has stifled open debate about controversial issues about which people should be able, in good conscience, to disagree. Often, people have been treated as bigots if their moral or religious beliefs didn't meet with others' approval.

We should talk about these things with our children, in ways that are appropriate to their ages. Ask at the dinner table, "What behaviors are you seeing at school?" "How are kids treating each other?" "Do you talk at all about what's in the news?" What would we do if we heard or saw someone being harassed, like the Hispanic lady to whom a passerby remarked, "I can't wait for them to deport you"?

Discuss with your kids: "What can each of us do to try to show respect, self-restraint, and open-mindedness, especially when we disagree with somebody?" "How can we show respect for people who think differently?"

How can we foster greater civility and respect for differences—in our schools, on our campuses, in the workplace, on the Internet, and in our homes, where angry words and tuning out may be all too common?

We want our kids to feel that being a citizen in a democratic society means caring about questions like these. We want to convey a sense that we're at a critical juncture in our democracy's history, where the quality of our public life will either get better or continue to get worse. As parents and teachers, we have a responsibility to try to influence that in whatever ways we can.

Let me give just one example of the positive possibilities—this from the classroom of a thoughtful character educator. Tim Leet is 50 years old, teaches ethics to the upper-school students at Columbus Academy near Columbus, Ohio, and recently published the e-book, *Ethics and Identity.* He was deeply troubled by what he saw as new lows in respect for civility and truth during the 2016 presidential campaign and worried about what it meant for our democracy. He wanted to address this issue and to provide a forum for a spectrum of views for all students in the school. He emailed me to share what he, some colleagues, and student leaders came up with—an approach I think we can all learn from:

> We are sponsoring a series of cafe-style conversations with students on topics of interest related to the election and the new political leadership. The first one was titled, "Listening to Differences." We had two four-person panels, and each of the eight students was asked simply to explain why they were either supportive of our new leadership or opposed. The challenge for us all was to listen respectfully, not to debate or offer rebuttal of any kind. It was quietly, incredibly powerful. Events like this usually draw only 15–20 kids—this forum drew 150!

In discussing with our families the challenges our democracy is now facing, we should put our struggles in global perspective by considering what many other societies have to deal with. "Us" and "them" hatred continues to plague humanity. In many countries, imprisonment and torture are still methods of political control. Wars cause unspeakable suffering. Terrorism is a constant threat. People are bombed, beheaded, buried alive, or otherwise persecuted and oppressed because of their ethnicity, religion, sexual orientation, political beliefs, or other differences. The battle against such evils is never-ending.

Finally, lest we underestimate the challenge of lifting the level of civility and human decency in America today, we should not make the mistake of thinking that all was well in the pre-Trump era. Before the 2016 presidential primary campaigns even got under way, there were plenty of signs of dark forces growing stronger. Early in 2015, the Pew Research Center reported that while millennials as a whole are more racially tolerant, colleges across the country were experiencing chilling displays of racist attitudes not seen in decades.[9] Anti-Semitism was also raising its ugly head. On November 7, 2013—on the eve of the seventy-fifth anniversary of Kristallnacht, the violent anti-Jewish pogrom that took place in Nazi Germany in 1938—the *New York Times* published a front-page account documenting rampant anti-Semitism in a rural school district where Jewish families were a small minority.[10] There were swastikas everywhere—on walls, desks, lockers, textbooks, computer screens, a playground slide, often with "die Jew."

When and how should you talk to your children about these things? Some parents try to shield their children from this ugliness. That's understandable; we don't want them to think that the bad news that makes the headlines represents how most people lead their daily lives. But kids often pick up more than we may realize and need our help in processing that. From the age of 6 on, children are capable of engaging in thoughtful discussions about cruelty and persecutions; 9-year-olds can have a surprisingly sophisticated understanding of conflicting social pressures. Draw them out; ask them what they are thinking. Help them make sense of what they see and hear.

The bottom line: whether we reverse the destructive trends that are bringing out the worst in many Americans, and make progress toward a kinder, more respectful society, depends on each and every one of us—and starts at home. With your family, check out the new national initiative, Better Angels (http://better-angels .org/), to "help Americans move past the insults and bring people together across the political spectrum to find common ground."

A Culture of Entitlement: "We've Spoiled Our Kids"

The angry politics and bigotry swirling around us pollute the moral atmosphere we all breathe. But even more impactful on our children's character development is what's happening day to day under our own roofs. That brings us to a second big change in our society: the emergence of a culture of entitlement and the consequent stunting of our children's development of a sense that they have a responsibility to contribute to the welfare and happiness of others, beginning in their own family.

Responsibility—in the literal sense of "response-ability"—has everything to do with kindness. To the degree that kids practice kindness, they'll think of others, not just of themselves. They'll make an effort to be helpful and considerate of others' needs and feelings. They'll need reminders, and they'll have better and worse days, just as we all do. But if we make choosing kindness a priority in our family culture, they'll show progress in their capacity to take pleasure in doing things for others—in performing actions, however small, that make life more pleasant for those around them.

Unfortunately, American families appear increasingly to be producing just the opposite: self-centered, entitled kids, the product of family cultures where adults do all the giving and kids do all the taking. If we want to develop kind kids, we're shooting ourselves in the foot.

There were warning signs decades ago. In 1975, Harvard anthropologists Beatrice and John Whiting published *Children of Six Cultures*, their cross-cultural study of children's altruism (defined as doing things for others without the expectation of any reward).[11] From the Whitings' observations came a clear finding: the degree to which children were helpful to people inside and outside the family depended on the degree to which they were assigned responsibilities that contributed to the maintenance of their family. The more children had to take care of younger children, tend to animals, help grow and harvest food, do household chores, assist with meals, and the like, the more altruistic was their behavior in general, not just toward family members but toward others as well.

Which of the six cultures had the most self-centered, least helpful children? Ours. What family responsibilities did American kids have? Typically just keeping their room in order. Today, even that is often not expected. The Whitings' findings were confirmed by subsequent research. Children who have household chores—jobs they're not paid to do but ones they're expected to do as contributing family members—develop a greater concern for others.[12]

We may be waking up to the character consequences of not expecting our children to share in the responsibilities of family life. A few years ago, *The New Yorker* magazine featured an article by Elizabeth Kolbert provocatively titled, "Spoiled Rotten: Why Do Kids Rule the Roost?"[13] It cited a poll commissioned by *Time* and CNN reporting a surprising self-indictment by American parents: two-thirds said they think they've spoiled their children. The article began by taking us out of our own culture—as the Whitings' study did—to give us a sense of what is expected of children in other cultures. In 2004, Dr. Carolina Izquierdo, an anthropologist at the University of California, Los Angeles, spent several months with the Matsigenka, a tribe of about twelve thousand people who live in the Peruvian Amazon. The Matsigenka roof their houses with *kapashi* leaves harvested from a particular kind of palm tree. At one point, Dr. Izquierdo joined a local family in traveling down the Urubamba River to gather such leaves.

A member of another family, a girl named Yanira, was allowed to come along. During the five days on the river, Yanira had no assigned role but she found many ways to make herself useful. Twice a day, she swept the sand off the sleeping mats. She helped stack the *kapashi* leaves so they could be transported back to the village. Later in the day, she fished for crustaceans, which she then cleaned, boiled, and served to the others. Dr. Izquierdo was very much impressed by Yanira's self-possessed manner and her competence at the many things she did to help—because at the time of the trip, Yanira was just 6 years old. While we might react with astonishment at this degree of spontaneous and competent helpfulness on the part of a 6-year-old child, the Matsigenka adults did not.

Now shift the scene to twenty-first-century Los Angeles. There, the *New Yorker* article goes on to report, Dr. Izquierdo and her colleague Elinor Ochs had recruited thirty-two middle-class families in order to study a slice of American family life. These families agreed, bravely, to be filmed "as they ate, fought, made up, and did the dishes." In these thirty-two Los Angeles families, *no child* routinely performed household chores without being instructed to. Here are just two examples of what the researchers found:

> Often, kids had to be begged to attempt the simplest tasks; often, they still refused. In one fairly typical encounter, a father asked his 8-year-old son five times to please go take a bath or a shower. After the fifth plea went unheeded, the father picked the boy up and carried him into the bathroom. A few minutes later, still unwashed, the boy wandered into another room to play a video game.

In another representative encounter, an 8-year-old girl sat down at the dining table. Finding that no silverware had been laid out for her, she demanded, "How am I supposed to eat?" Although the girl clearly knew where the silverware was kept, her father got up to get it for her.[14]

Such vignettes give us a yardstick by which to measure our own family. How often, without intending to, do we slip into similar patterns—doing things for our kids that they could do for themselves and not asking them to help around the house— perhaps because of the busyness of our lives, or the urgency of their homework and after-school activities, or because we're thinking more about the next task we have to do than about what's really good for our kids? In my own work with parents, many have said they've given up trying to get their kids to do chores because it's more effort than doing the tasks themselves. If we fall into this kind of thinking, we avoid the short-term hassle but end up paying a long-term price.

The family patterns we establish early on are crucial. Matsigenka families teach their children how to do useful tasks at very young ages, and the skills children master build an authentic self-confidence. Toddlers learn how to heat their own food over an open fire. At age 3, children learn how to cut wood and grass with machetes and knives. At age 6, boys start to go with their fathers on fishing and hunting trips, and girls learn to help their mothers with the cooking. (Obviously, we can teach our daughters and sons both sets of skills. Our 9-year-old grandson, Ben, has helped his mother bake since he was 4—and now says he wants to be a chef.)

In first-world societies, the curse of affluence is a big part of the problem. Throughout history, cultures have seen their morality decline as their material success has increased. James Stenson, author of *Compass: A Handbook on Parent Leadership*, observes that most Americans today are rich by the standards of the past.[15]

Although prosperity is certainly not evenly distributed, many people don't earn a living wage, and lots of families struggle to make ends meet, as a nation we enjoy a level of prosperity—an abundance of food, drink, clothing, conveniences, recreational activities, and electronic devices like TVs, computers, smartphones, Xboxes, PlayStations, iPods, etc.—unprecedented in human history.

And yet our children are not happier. Endless entertainment doesn't make us happy. We become happy and find meaning in life by contributing to the happiness of others.

In *Slouching Toward Adulthood: Observations from the Not-So-Empty Nest*, Sally Koslow, a former *McCall's* editor in chief, shares what has become a familiar scenario for many American families. After college and two years on the West Coast, her son "moved back to Manhattan and settled into his old room in the family's apartment, together with thirty-four boxes of vinyl LPs. Unemployed, he likes to stay out late, sleep until noon, and wander around in his boxers."[16] Wondering why her son and so many of his peers seem stuck in permanent "adultescence," Koslow decided that the economy was one reason, but another was "parents like her." Our offspring, she says, have simply taken advantage of our "good intentions and overinvestment."

Why have so many well-meaning parents "overinvested" in their kids—done so much for them, while expecting so little in the way of contributing to family life? The obsession with getting kids into the best colleges may be part of the answer. The *New Yorker* article observes—correctly, I think—that in an increasingly competitive and insecure economy, many parents are driven to do more and more to give their kids a leg up on the competition. This includes not just taking care of all the household chores but also helping their children with their homework, hiring special tutors, and, if necessary, getting a lawyer if their child is punished for cheating in school or otherwise disciplined.[17] Kids get the message that academic achievement matters more than anything else.

Students tell researchers they often cheat to get top grades because of the pressure they feel from their parents.[18]

Many parents panic if their child gets a grade that might endanger their academic standing. A 5th-grade teacher at one school where I spoke told me she had just conferenced with two parents whose son had a 97 average in her class and who wanted to know "how we can help him do better." Outright bribery is probably rare, but at another school a 6th-grade teacher said that after she gave a student a C on an assignment, his mother made an appointment to see her. She said the mother, well-spoken and impeccably dressed, looked her straight in the eye and said very calmly, "You can go to any jewelry store and pick out anything you like—but I want that grade changed." In the words of one principal, "Today's parents are not just helicopter parents—they are a jet-powered turbo attack model."[19]

Ben Sasse's *The Vanishing American Adult* touched a nerve and became a *New York Times* bestseller at least partly because it articulated many of these realities. Sasse argues that we "are in the midst of a collective coming-of-age crisis without parallel in our history. We are living in an America of perpetual adolescence. Our kids simply don't know what an adult is—or how to become one. Many don't see a reason even to try." He points out that 30 percent of college students drop out after the first year. Only 40 percent graduate. A third of all 18- to 34-year-olds are living with their parents.

Our children won't become responsible unless they have responsibility. And like everything else, that starts in the home.

Responsibility that's motivated by a true spirit of kindness means much more than just doing regular chores, important as that is. It means sharing responsibility for creating a happier family by helping to avoid and solve conflicts, keeping the peace as much as possible, and being an active contributor to family problem-solving discussions where everyone thinks together about how to make the upcoming week go more smoothly (see chapters 4 and 8). It means not always waiting for a parent to ask you to do something but taking the initiative to ask, "Mom (Dad), how can I help?" ("Read a story to your little brother while I'm getting the dinner on." "Please set the table.")

We have to *teach* our kids to ask that, of course, and then have them practice; it won't come naturally. But they can learn to do it. You can point out, kindly, that parents do *lots* of things for kids without kids having to ask. When you'd like them to lend a helping hand, you can even say with a smile, "Please ask me, 'What can I do to help?'"

Finally, training in responsibility shouldn't be limited to our own family. Kids need the formative moral experience of helping others outside the home. Recall what the Holocaust research on rescuers found: their parents taught them to respect and care about all members of the human family. We can start with what's close at hand. One of my former students, now a mother, describes her early training in caring about people in their neighborhood:

> I come from a Quaker background. Somehow I always knew that whatever I did when I grew up, it would have to be, in some way, a service to others. Both my mother and my father were always involved in some kind of community work. I can remember coming home from school when I was just a little girl and my mother saying, "Susan, Mrs. Flannigan"—an old lady who lived down the street—"has been alone all day, and I'm sure she would enjoy visiting with you for a while." I remember asking sometimes why *I* had to do this and other kids didn't. She told me that what other kids did didn't matter—that I should do all that I was capable of doing.

Don't live in that kind of neighborhood? Find a way to do community service with your child. Ask your child's elementary or secondary school what service learning opportunities the school is providing. And let your child know you're just as proud of the caring ways they're contributing to their community as you are of their good grades—or even prouder. And say why that's so.

Seeing to it that our children have these opportunities to make regular and meaningful contributions to the welfare and happiness of others—in their own family and beyond—is harder than it was when many Americans grew up on the farm. But it's still possible—and vitally important. This is not a challenge we can dodge without a high cost to our children's character.

CHAPTER 3

Kids' Capacity for Kindness—and Cruelty—Is There from the Start

A N OLD FOLK STORY tells of a grandfather teaching his grandson about life. "A fight is going on inside of me," the grandfather says to the boy. "It is a terrible fight between two wolves. One is bad. He is cruelty, anger, resentment, arrogance, and selfishness. The other is good. He is kindness, peace, forgiveness, humility, and generosity. The same fight goes on inside you and inside every other person."

The boy asks anxiously, "Which wolf will win, Grandfather?"

The grandfather answers, "The one you feed."

Within every human being is the capacity for kindness and its allied virtues, and the capacity for cruelty and its ugly cousins. Our character, the kind of person we are, depends on which "wolf" is fed by the choices we make—and by the moral environment around us. Our job as parents is to consistently feed our children's capacity for kindness. At the same time, we must nurture other essential virtues—such as empathy, respect, courage, and self-control—that will dispose our kids to care about others and help them make kindness a habit.

Let's look first at the abundant evidence of the human capacity for kindness, even in very young children—and then at the sobering evidence of the coexisting capacity for cruelty. As you're doing the hard work of trying to raise kind kids, you'll be dealing with both.

The Internet gives us access to many inspiring acts of selfless kindness. One well-known example is the story of a little girl named Alex Scott and her lemonade stand. When Alex was just a year old, she was diagnosed with neuroblastoma, a type of childhood cancer. Doctors said that even if she beat the cancer, she probably wouldn't walk.

By her second birthday, Alex could crawl and stand up with leg braces. But at three, the tumors started growing again. At four, she received a stem cell transplant. Alex told her mother, "When I get out of the hospital, I want to have a lemonade stand. I want to give the money to doctors so they can help other kids like they helped me."

Later that year, with the help of her older brother, Alex and her lemonade stand raised $2,000. While she continued to battle her cancer, Alex and her family held yearly lemonade stands to benefit childhood cancer research. News spread of their efforts. People from all over the world, moved by her story, held their own lemonade stands and donated the proceeds to Alex and her cause. Kindness is contagious.

In 2004, Alex died at the age of eight. Her brothers, Patrick, Eddie, and Joey, and supporters around the world continue her legacy through Alex's Lemonade Stand Foundation. Check it out: www.alexslemonade.org.

Uplifting stories of character can be found in great abundance at the Giraffe Heroes Project (www.giraffe.org). It's the brainchild of Ann Medlock, a freelance editor and writer who started the project as an antidote to what she saw as the media's tendency to focus on negative role models rather than positive ones. The project has identified and honored more than thirteen hundred "Giraffe Heroes," kids and adults from around the world who have "stuck

out their necks for others." Schools have used the Giraffe Heroes
Project to inspire kids to find local Giraffes, interview them about
what they've done, and then take steps to become Giraffes themselves in their school, neighborhood, or community. Here, slightly
abridged, are just two Giraffe stories.

As a checkout clerk in a Los Angeles supermarket, Julie Leirich
saw that every day, the market threw away a lot of good food.
On the way home from work, she also saw a lot of hungry and
homeless people. She began quietly gathering up food the market was discarding and giving it to the homeless. When her
boss found out, he didn't fire her—he helped her do it better.
Customers who heard about Julie's efforts offered their help.
Soon Julie and her volunteer helpers were distributing six tons
of food a month to the hungry and homeless in Los Angeles.

At the age of 12, Toronto 7th grader Craig Kielburger was
outraged when he read about the murder of a Pakistani boy
after he escaped from slavery as a child laborer. Craig got
eleven other 7th graders to join him in starting an organization, now called WE (www.we.org), to end the exploitation of
child labor. He attracted international media coverage with a
fact-finding trip through five Asian countries. Now in his late
twenties, Craig explained on *60 Minutes* that WE sponsors
annual "We Days" at which thousands of youth from countries
around the world come together to share stories of what they
are doing to promote children's rights, schools for poor kids,
clean-water projects, health clinics, and economic cooperatives.

The Science of Love

How early in a child's life can we see evidence of a capacity for
kindness? Much sooner than child development experts once

believed. In 2006, *Science* magazine reported on a study showing that the capacity for altruism—indeed, a strong *inclination* to be altruistic—is evident as early as 18 months.[1] That conclusion was based on an experiment carried out by two researchers at Germany's Max Planck Institutes. Here's the ingenious method they used to reveal altruism in toddlers.

An adult performed a series of tasks in front of a toddler—such as hanging towels with clothespins, stacking books, or opening a cabinet in order to put away a heavy armload of books. With the toddler watching, the adult "accidentally" dropped a clothespin, knocked a book off the stack, or struggled unsuccessfully to open the cabinet. How would the observing toddler respond?

Every one of the 18-month-olds in the experiment reacted by helping—usually within seconds. A video shows one of the toddlers glancing at a dropped clothespin, then at the adult's dismayed expression, then quickly retrieving the clothespin and handing it with a smile to the adult. But the toddlers did *not* help if the adult deliberately threw the clothespin on the floor or knocked a book off the stack.

In another situation, the adult was unsuccessfully trying to get a spoon out of a box by squeezing his hand through a too-small hole in the box's lid. Each of the toddlers who observed the adult's plight promptly went over to the side of the box, lifted a cloth flap, retrieved the spoon, and happily presented it to the adult. In none of these cases did the adult *ask* for help. Nor did the adult even say "thank you" upon receiving the toddler's help, because the study wanted to see if the toddlers would display true altruism—helping without expecting or getting anything in return, even an expression of thanks.

Despite the absence of a request for help or any expression of gratitude for help given, *all* the toddlers spontaneously helped the adult in these scenarios. They did so whether or not their parent was present—showing that helping behavior was not a response to parental cues. And they did so even when helping meant they had to climb over an obstacle or stop playing with a toy.

Even at birth, there are signs of empathy. Newborns are more likely to cry—and cry longer—when they hear the sound of another baby's crying than when they hear another, equally loud nonhuman noise.[2] One-year-olds will often soothe other babies who are crying by touching or stroking them or offering a bottle or toy.[3]

The Moral Life of 3- to 8-Month-Olds

In 2012, the CBS News show *60 Minutes* went to Yale's Infant Cognition Center to film extraordinary manifestations of morality in the first year of life. As the program begins, Dr. Karen Wynn, the psychologist who directs the center, explains to *60 Minutes* interviewer Lesley Stahl that although babies can't talk, they can reveal what's going on in their minds through nonverbal responses such as looking or reaching.

Five-month-old Wesley is then shown a puppet morality play. Three dog puppets, each wearing a different colored shirt, are arrayed before him. The dog in the middle struggles unsuccessfully to lift the lid of a glass box and get the toy inside. Then the dog on the *right* (wearing a bright yellow shirt) helps the struggling puppet open the box and get the toy.

The same scene is then presented again: the same three puppets, with the one in the middle struggling unsuccessfully to lift the box's lid and get the toy. Only this time the puppet on the *left* (wearing a bright blue shirt) does a *mean* thing: he abruptly comes over and—*boom!*—he slams the lid shut so the middle puppet can't get the toy.

Next, a "blind" research assistant—who does not know which was the nice puppet and which the mean one—holds up both puppets and says to 5-month-old Wesley, "Wesley, do you remember these guys from the show? Who do you like?"

Five-month-old Wesley can't answer with words or even understand the experimenter's words, but he gets the idea—and he can reach. Smiling, he promptly extends both arms to take the nice puppet, the one who helped the middle puppet get the toy. Tellingly, more than three-quarters of the babies did the same thing—they reached for the *helpful* puppet rather than the mean one. A strong preference for prosocial behavior.

Wynn then tried the same experiment on even younger babies, *only 3 months old*. At this age, babies were on their tummies, holding themselves up with their hands as they watched the puppet drama unfold. When it came time for them to choose the puppet they liked, they couldn't show their preference by reaching—but they could vote with their eyes. They consistently fixed their gaze on the nice puppet, and hardly looked at the mean puppet at all.

Conclusion? At the tender age of 3 months, babies show a clear preference for good guys over bad guys.

There's more. The next experiment at Yale's baby lab revealed that even before one year of age, babies have a sense of justice. This experiment showed 8-month-old infants three bunny puppets who were rolling a ball back and forth to one another. But suddenly the bunny on the left, instead of rolling the ball back to the middle bunny, steals it and runs away. *Bad bunny.*

In the next scenario, the bad bunny is now in the middle, struggling unsuccessfully to lift the lid of the glass box and get the toy inside. The bunny on the right comes over and helps him lift the lid to get the toy.

Next scenario: The bad bunny is still in the middle and once again struggling to lift the box's lid and get the toy inside. Only this time, the bunny on the left comes over and *slams the lid shut.* The researchers intended this action to represent punishing the bad bunny for having previously stolen the ball.

Then the experimenter presented two bunnies: the one who

helped the bad bunny (by lifting the box lid for him), and the one who *punished* the bad bunny (by slamming the lid shut)—and asked the baby who had intently watched all this, "Which bunny do you like?"

Fully 81 percent of the babies reached for the puppet who had *slammed the box shut on the bad bunny.* They appeared to view that bad bunny as getting his just deserts.

Not only could these preverbal babies recognize bad behavior when they saw it; they wanted the culprit to pay for his crime.

Children's Capacity for Cruelty

We can draw inspiration and hope from all the studies and stories that testify to the human capacity for kindness. But recognizing and celebrating this capacity for goodness should not lead us to underestimate the dark side of human nature. "The line between good and evil," Alexander Solzhenitsyn said, "runs through every human heart."

In Yale's baby lab, the same research that revealed babies' preference for helpful puppets over mean ones also uncovered a disturbing dimension of human nature already operating before one year of age: the capacity for prejudice. The final segment of the *60 Minutes* program shows Karen Wynn and her fellow researchers giving 6- to 8-month-old babies a chance to choose a snack: Cheerios or graham crackers.

We watch 8-month-old Nate as he happily chooses Cheerios. Next, as Nate looks on intently, an orange cat puppet also chooses Cheerios. But then, still under Nate's watchful eye, along comes a gray cat puppet who chooses *graham crackers* instead.

Now, which cat puppet do you think Nate will reach for when presented with the two puppets—the one who shared his preference for Cheerios, or the one who liked something different?

Nate and nearly all the other babies his age chose the puppet who liked the snack *they* liked.

Okay, harmless enough.

But then, in the next scenario, Nate is presented with the familiar three-puppet play where the puppet in the middle is struggling to lift the lid of a box to get the toy inside. The middle puppet is now the cat who did *not* share Nate's preference for Cheerios—but liked graham crackers instead.

A dog puppet on the right comes over and helps the graham crackers–loving cat lift the lid. *Nice dog.* But then the dog puppet on the left comes over and—*bam!*—he bangs the lid shut so the cat can't get the toy. *Mean dog.* Which dog puppet will Nate now choose when both are offered—the *nice* dog who helped the graham crackers–loving cat, or the *mean* dog who slammed the lid shut on that cat?

The result was a shocker. Nate chose the *mean dog*—the one who had slammed the lid shut on the struggling puppet, the one who didn't share Nate's preference for Cheerios. An astonishing 87 percent of the babies tested reacted the same way Nate did. *They preferred the dog puppet who was mean*—who punished the cat who didn't share the babies' own snack preference.

Conclusion? There appears to be an innate tendency to create "us" and "them"—*and to want to see those who are unlike us treated badly.* This disposition to be prejudiced appears to be part of our wiring, present even before the onset of language. Contrary to what the song from *South Pacific* says, we may not have to be "taught to hate." It may come naturally.

That, in fact, is what other studies of the precursors of prejudice suggest. Preferences for "our own kind" emerge at a very early age. Three-month-olds prefer to look at faces of the race most similar to theirs. When children are segregated into different groups—even groups based on something as arbitrary as wearing different-colored T-shirts—they eagerly favor their own groups in their attitudes and behavior. Other experiments have found that it's alarmingly easy to fan children's favoritism toward their own into aggressive hostility toward those who are different.[4]

Bullying

For further evidence of children's capacity for cruelty, we need look no further than the school yard. Worldwide, one out of three students reports being bullied.[5] When I travel to other countries to do character education workshops, there are almost always stories about bullying in the news. "School Bullying a Worry in Indonesia—A Key Cause of Child Suicides" ran one headline. The article reported that a 15-year-old Indonesian girl had recently killed herself after being made fun of by classmates because she had failed several classes, and another girl had committed suicide after being teased about her father's being a street vendor.

In the US, we began to pay attention to bullying when the country was rocked by a wave of school shootings in the 1990s—fifty in that one decade—culminating in the Columbine High School killings of twelve students and a teacher. A Secret Service study of those shootings found that 71 percent of the student shooters had been bullied—ostracized, harassed, ridiculed, threatened, or otherwise persecuted by their peers.[6] The school shootings of the 1990s were followed in the next decade by a wave of student suicides that appeared to be triggered at least in part by bullying, interacting with other factors such as troubled families, peer conflicts, anxiety, and depression. In the single month of September 2009, there were nine such suicides.

But despite anti-bullying legislation in all fifty states and many bullying-prevention programs, most of the problem remains. Even after implementing the anti-bullying programs found to be most effective, two-thirds of the bullies say (on anonymous question-naires) that they continue to bully; three-quarters of the bullied kids say they continue to be victimized.[7] Says a high school girl about the junior high school bullying she did: "I made somebody bulimic. I'd say, 'You are fat. You are disgusting. How much do you weigh—four tons?'" Another girl says about her middle school bullying, "It was fun to make people cry."

A large body of research finds that bullied kids do less well academically, suffer social isolation, and are at greater risk of anx-iety, depression, and other mental health problems that can persist into adulthood and be even worse than the effects of parental abuse.[8] We should share these findings with our kids so they know the serious damage that bullying does—and so that they will help to prevent it at their school.

In view of how much suffering kids cause other kids by bully-ing, we might wonder, do kids start out with an instinct for kind-ness and then lose it? The answer is that prosocial *and* antisocial tendencies coexist from the very first year of life. Recall that Yale's infant lab found that babies, besides having altruistic tendencies, were also "little bigots." They wanted to see the puppet that didn't like the snack *they* liked punished.

We can see how that pernicious human tendency spells trouble at later ages and how it plays out on the world stage. Think of the 1994 Rwanda genocide, in which the ruling tribe, over the course of a hundred days, slaughtered up to a million members of another tribe. Think of ISIS, which terrorizes, crucifies, bombs, and beheads "the other." Think of racism or polarized politics in America. Think of bullies, who typically target the kids who look or act "different."

We need to keep in mind the fable of the two wolves—one good, one bad—warring within us. We have to take deliberate steps to strengthen our children's capacity to be kind and to curb the antisocial tendencies that, unchecked, can lead them to mistreat those who are different or vulnerable. We need to be concerned about the cultures our children inhabit—both our family culture and the culture at school. We'll look next at how we can create a family culture of kindness and respect; in chapter 14, we'll look at how good schools have done the same.

CHAPTER 4

How to Create a Positive Family Culture

6 Key Principles

I was a bully when I was younger. I stopped after my parents taught me to stand in other people's shoes. —MARCUS, 15

THE QUALITIES THAT MAKE UP good character don't grow in a vacuum. They grow in a *family culture*—one where virtues like kindness and respect are talked about, modeled, upheld, celebrated, and practiced in everyday life. Our family culture is determined by the quality of our relationships, the patterns of our daily lives, and the values we expect each other to live by. If you want to raise kind, respectful, and responsible children, you will need to create a family culture in which all members are consistently challenged to live up to a high ideal—being considerate of the needs of others and responding to those needs with a generous spirit.

Given the frailties of human nature and the stresses and strains of hectic family life, we'll often fall short of that high ideal. We'll get impatient and upset with each other. We'll yell at the kids. They'll fight with each other. They'll whine and complain when we ask them to do something. We'll get discouraged. But the test of our character as a family isn't never failing; it's never giving up. It's being humble enough to accept our failures and not let them get the best of us. It's forgiving each other and forgiving ourselves.

For many people, it's also leaning on the grace of God to keep them going.

So the real challenge is: How can we persevere in trying to be a family that loves each other and extends kindness beyond the family? Let's look at 6 key principles that can guide us in that effort.

1. Make Character a Top Priority in Your Family

Successful schools, businesses, and nonprofits typically have mission statements. Those statements identify their core values, shape their shared culture, and significantly influence the character of their members. In the same way, a family mission statement can help you identify and foster the values you want to live by as a family.

A family mission statement addresses the question, "What kind of a family do we want to be?" Creating a family mission statement is an important first step in developing an "intentional family culture." In composing a family mission statement, you want to make your core values explicit and concrete so your children really understand them at their developmental level.

Let me give you an example of one family's mission statement. When their four children were 9, 7, 6, and 4, Matt and Suzanne Davidson wrote a mission statement that they hung in the kitchen, where they could review it at the start of the week and refer to it whenever they needed to.

The Davidson Way

- We commit to being kind, honest and trustworthy, and fair.
- We don't lie, cheat, steal, or hurt someone on purpose.
- We don't whine, complain, or make excuses.

- When we make a mistake, we make up for it, learn from it, and move on.
- We work to keep our minds, bodies, and souls healthy, strong, and pure.
- We commit to learning and growing in our faith through practice and trust in God's goodness.
- We live with an attitude of gratitude and joy.

Matt comments:

We occasionally read the entire thing, but mostly we look for the parts that pertain to a challenge we're responding to at the moment. We highlight that part and discuss it. The kids are beginning to remember and use some of the language. We think the greatest benefit will be long-term. Having this in place now, before there are major issues, means we won't be starting with a blank slate when we face a problem later on.

When you develop your family's mission statement, I encourage you to ask your children what they think should be included. They'll feel more ownership and commitment if you've used some of their ideas.

One family had an embroidered sign hanging in their home: REMEMBER YOU'RE A MORFIT. It was a simple reminder, aimed at keeping kids identified with the family values. You could use something like that in combination with your mission statement.

I can't overemphasize the importance of taking deliberate steps to create and then sustain an explicit family culture through something like a family mission statement. It lays the foundation for everything else you'll do to try to raise children of character. It becomes your point of reference in family life.

If you *don't* have this foundation in place, then you won't have anything to build on when there's a behavioral problem or conflict. It can feel like you're always starting from scratch. There's no shared understanding of what it means *to be a family*, no spirit of cooperation, no commitment to working together to make a happy family. Schools that don't do deliberate character education run into the same difficulty if, for example, they haven't taught something like the Golden Rule. A conversation with a student who has been mean to someone else can't draw on a common language, a shared set of understandings.

Of course, even with the kind of explicit values framework a family mission statement provides, creating a culture of character in the family will still be a never-ending challenge. The difference is that with a family mission statement in place and integrated into family life, you won't be doing that work alone.

To show everyone's commitment to the mission statement, I recommend that you all sign it and then post it in the kitchen or some other prominent spot. Then, like the Davidson family, review it at the start of the week and refer to it when you're dealing with something that relates to it ("What part applies to what's happening right now?") You can focus on a different part of your mission statement each week and make a special effort to put that into practice. Suppose you wanted to focus on trying to have "an attitude of gratitude" (a good place to start). Gratitude is expressing thanks for what others have done for us. Frequent expressions of gratitude do a lot to create a loving family atmosphere. Being grateful is one of the most important ways of being kind. Ingratitude is a form of unkindness.

Mark Schumacker, who chairs the math department at Ankeney Middle School in Beavercreek, Ohio, gives his 7th-grade math students a weekly character challenge. One is the gratitude challenge: "Choose three very important people in your life and write them the most thorough and thoughtful expression of thanks you can imagine." The class brainstorms examples. Here is what one girl wrote to her father: "Dad, you are the person who picks me up and dusts me off after I fall. You give me hope when I have none left. You help me with my math even though I get mad easily. Thank you for everything. I love you."

Try the gratitude challenge in your family. You can take the lead by writing to the kids, then the kids can write to each parent, then to each other. Later, you can extend this beyond the family—having each family member write an appreciation note to someone (a teacher, a coach, a friend, a relative) who has done something for them, recently or even a while ago, for which they're especially thankful. Other things you can do to promote a spirit of thankfulness: create gratitude rituals such as grace before meals, start dinner conversation with a quick round of "gratefuls" ("What's something you're grateful for today?"), and make thanksgiving part of your bedtime ritual with your children. Make it a family practice to say "thank you" to each other for small things (even passing the salt) and to anyone who does you a service. Encourage your kids to thank a teacher or other school staff member at the end of a school day. Keep a gratitude journal—writing down at the day's end three things you're grateful for from that day—and share entries at the dinner table.

Gratitude will go a long way toward developing a culture of kindness in your family. (See chapter 12 for more gratitude ideas.)

2. Love Your Children

Love is the deepest human need. Dozens of studies show that a warm, caring, and responsive parent–child relationship is strongly linked to children's health, happiness, and character development.[1] When children feel loved, they feel secure. When they feel loved, they become attached to us. That attachment makes them more receptive to our values.

Children come to understand love by experiencing it. Loving our children means many things:

- taking care of them, meeting their physical and emotional needs
- showing affection and affirming them in genuine ways
- spending time with them and showing interest in their lives
- having meaningful communication
- respecting their individual interests and personalities
- challenging and helping them to become the best person they can be
- sacrificing for them

Let me elaborate on three of those ways of making parental love real and felt in our day-to-day relationships with our children.

Affirmation and Affection

In their book *Healing the Unaffirmed*, psychotherapists Conrad Baars and Anna Terruwe reported that many of their patients suffered from "emotional deprivation disorder."[2] They struggled with feelings of being unloved and unlovable. They tended to be oversensitive, insecure and afraid of life, depressed, and unable to relate easily to others and to make and keep friends. These feelings, Baars and Terruwe believed, stemmed from not receiving enough loving affirmation—and often getting far too much criticism.

Affirmation can be as simple as "Thanks for doing the dishes—the kitchen looks great!" or a note in a kid's lunch bag: "Andy, have a good day at school. I love you, Dad." Affirmation can also take the form of a treasured family tradition, such as the "Christmas love letter," as practiced by John and Kathy Colligan, parents of five. Kathy says:

Every Christmas, John and I would each write a letter to each of our five kids and put it under the tree. We'd tell them what we loved and appreciated about them, the ways we'd seen them grow during the past year, the talents and character strengths we saw emerging, all the things we cherished. It was always the last present they opened—and the one that meant the most to them.

Together Time

One study asked adults to relate their favorite childhood memories. People typically did not remember expensive toys, clothes, or trips, but the simple things they did with their parents or as a family: playing board games, taking walks, playing catch, going swimming or fishing, outings for ice cream, tenting overnight in the backyard.

I urge you to try to spend at least some one-on-one time with your children, even if you have a big family. There's a special intimacy when it's just you and one child. I once had lunch with a busy school superintendent and father of four. He opened his datebook and showed me how all the Saturday afternoons were blocked out. He said: "Each of my four kids gets one Saturday afternoon a month—just the two of us. It's sacred time. We decide together what we're going to do. I have a ton of demands on my time. If I didn't plan and protect this time with my kids, it wouldn't happen." One-on-one time strengthens the bond between parent and child. That helps to give us the inside track in a world of competing influences.

Meaningful Communication

In his autobiography, Christiaan Barnard, originator of the heart transplant, wrote about his father:

> Whenever we were ill, my father got up late at night to doctor us. When I had a cold, he would rub my chest with Vicks and cover it with a red flannel cloth. Sunday afternoons we walked together to the top of the hill by the dam. Once there, we

would sit on a rock and look down at the town below us. Then I would tell my problems to my father, and he would speak of his to me.[3]

Besides deepening the love between you and your child, this kind of emotionally intimate communication is especially important for sharing and passing on your most important values.

The Family Meal

As my colleague Kevin Ryan, founder of Boston University's Center for Character and Social Justice, puts it: "We should make a big deal of the family meal." That time is potentially an island of intimacy for sharing our thoughts, experiences, and values. To make mealtime conversation meaningful and get everyone talking, it helps to have a topic:

- What was the best part and the hardest part of your day?
- What was something you learned today—in school or just from life?
- What's a way you helped someone, or someone helped you?
- What happened today that you didn't expect or that never happened before?
- Who has a problem that the rest of the family might be able to help with?

We had a very good conversation about that last topic when our older son, Mark, was an 8th grader and he felt threatened by a big kid at school who seemed to be out for him. In another dinner discussion, when our younger son, Matthew, was in kindergarten, he asked what to do about a classmate who was supposed to be his friend but who would jump out from behind a bookcase and give Matthew a karate chop (something he had apparently picked up from a TV show). In both cases, we were able to offer advice on how they could deal with the problem. This kind of conversation teaches kids that whenever they have a problem, they can come to their family for help. (For lots more family conversation starters, see chapter 11.)

3. Exercise Authority Wisely

As parents, we must have a strong sense of our moral authority—of having the right to be respected and obeyed. In *The Moral Child*, Stanford psychologist William Damon states that how well parents teach their child to respect their authority lays the foundation for the child's future moral development.[4] In *Take Back Your Kids*, family psychologist William Doherty observes that we face "an epidemic of insecure parenting."[5] Insecure parents are skittish about exercising parental authority, are afraid to ever get angry with their kids, and often allow their kids to walk all over them. Fortunately, there's solid research showing why and how to exercise parental authority.

Berkeley psychologist Diana Baumrind observed families in their homes and identified three styles of parenting: *authoritative*, *authoritarian*, and *permissive*. Authoritarian parents used lots of commands and threats but were low on warmth and used little reasoning. Permissive parents were high on affection but low on authority. By contrast, *authoritative* parents combined confident authority with reasoning, fairness, love, and encouragement of age-appropriate self-reliance. Baumrind's research and subsequent studies have shown that at every developmental level—early childhood, childhood, and adolescence—authoritative parents have the most secure, competent, and responsible kids.[6]

In practice, authoritative parenting means at least five things.

First, we must take strong stands that are consistent with our values. Our children will benefit from this moral clarity and knowing the things we care deeply about. For example, will you prohibit TV shows, movies, and video games that contain sex, graphic violence, or foul language; music with lewd or denigrating lyrics; parties where there's drinking; prom overnights? Will you choose to limit your children's access to social media and video games? If you're churchgoing, will you expect them to attend church (temple, or mosque), even if they complain? If sports or outdoor activities are important to you, will you want the family to do one sporty or outdoor thing together on a regular basis?

Whatever your rules and expectations, you'll want to explain to your kids the reasons for them so they understand they're not arbitrary, but based on love, concern for their welfare, and the good and happiness of the family. Research finds that kids, including teens, are much more likely to accept parental rules and limits when they perceive that those limits are based on their parents' concern for their children's welfare.[7] Listen to your kids and try to find a way to factor in their perspective and interests while not compromising your core principles.

Second, we must not allow any kind of disrespectful back talk—either in tone or content. When kids cross the line into disrespect, they need immediate and sometimes stern corrective feedback, best delivered calmly but firmly ("What is your tone of voice?", "You're not allowed to speak to me in that way, even when you're upset"). We should also not tolerate disrespectful or unkind remarks ("Shut up!"; "That's stupid!") between siblings. We should make it clear that such ways of talking to each other undermine family relationships and are the opposite of the kindness and respect we're trying to practice in our family. And we should, of course, model the respect we're asking our kids to show.

Many parents today do treat their children respectfully but, unfortunately, don't require respect in return. This typically begins in the preschool years. Some parents fall into a pattern of allowing their young children to demand things instead of asking politely, bark orders at them, sass them in public, and so on. The tolerance zone for disrespect gets steadily wider as the kids get older. When we permit this to happen, we lose status and moral authority in our children's eyes. They lose respect for our rules, moral values, and wisdom about life. They are then less likely to come to us for counsel when they are teenagers. Fortunately, it's never too late to correct this pattern; see chapter 6 for "10 Ways to Give—and Get—Respect."

Third, we must take the "small stuff" seriously. A mean remark to a brother or sister, a minor lie, a failure to do an assigned chore—all these things are opportunities to hold our kids accountable to high expectations. Over time, dealing with the small stuff will have a cumulative effect on our child's conscience. If we let little things go, there won't be a foundation for dealing with bigger problems later on. If we don't correct rudeness or tantrums in a 6-year-old, we'll have trouble reigning in swearing and door slamming by a 16-year-old.

Fourth, we should discipline in a way that gets kids to take responsibility for their actions. One way to do that is to make them their own judge and jury: "What do *you* think is a fair consequence for what you did?" Whenever possible, we should require restitution: "What can you do to make up for it?" If kids say, "I don't know," give them a choice of two specific things they could do to make amends ("You can read a story to your little brother or ask him what he'd like to play.") (See chapter 7 on discipline for more restitution ideas.)

Finally, the wise exercise of parental authority requires vigilant supervision. A Child Trends research report, *Building a Better Teenager*, described "hands-on" parents as those who know where their kids are, who they're with, and what they're doing, including their online activity.[8] In the words of pediatrician Meg Meeker, author of *The 10 Habits of Happy Mothers* and *Strong Fathers, Strong Daughters*: "In today's environment, wise parents watch their children like a hawk." Vigilant parents, studies show, have teens with the lowest rates of sexual activity and the lowest rates of drug and alcohol abuse.[9]

Teach Your Kids Why They Should Obey You

If we're having trouble establishing an authoritative parenting style and getting our kids to obey, it may be partly because they've never gotten a basic idea in their heads: Kids are *supposed to* obey their parents, just as they should obey their teachers in school. Many children have little or no understanding of that obligation. In American society, there's plenty of emphasis on helping kids become "independent," much less emphasis on developing respect for authority and legitimate rules.

All people, including adults, have a moral obligation to obey institutional and societal rules and laws as long as they don't tell us to do something wrong. Without respect for rules and laws, there would be chaos. In children's moral development, respecting and obeying legitimate authority is a foundational virtue. It makes a child receptive to teaching and guidance from parents and other adults. Without that receptive attitude, children cannot be socialized. We'll have a hard time teaching them any virtues, including kindness.

If you've seen the play or film *The Miracle Worker*, the inspiring story of Helen Keller, you'll remember what Helen's teacher, 20-year-old Annie Sullivan, finds when she first arrives at the Keller household. Helen, made blind, deaf, and dumb by an illness when she was 19 months old, is now 7 years old and tyrannizes the adults around her. She smashes and destroys objects that displease her. She crams food into her mouth with both hands. If anyone tries to correct her, she flings herself on the floor and thrashes violently—and her parents give in to the tirade.

Annie Sullivan knows that if she is to have any chance of success in teaching Helen, she must get her away from the rest of the family and work with her alone. She gains the parents' permission to stay with Helen in a cottage on the grounds. There she tries to teach Helen to sew, a lesson that ends when Helen stabs her with the needle. It becomes clear to Annie that she will not be able to teach Helen anything unless Helen respects her authority and obeys her.

As this insight dawns on Annie, she writes in her journal: "Obedience is the gateway through which knowledge enters the mind of the child." Initially using food as the incentive, Annie proceeded to require and get that obedience. It was the beginning of Helen's liberation from her darkness. The rest of the story is well-known: Helen soon learned language (the manual alphabet, which enabled her to communicate by finger spelling)—and, when she was an adult, she became a world-famous advocate for the rights and needs of the handicapped.

Some years ago a learning center in Oregon attracted attention for its success in teaching previously uncontrollable children to obey their parents.[10] These children typically refused to obey even the most reasonable commands and would often terrorize other children. One boy spread his excrement all over the living room walls. His single mother had no idea how to deal with him.

The learning center taught his mother to require him to obey her requests and directions by the count of fifteen. If he didn't, he got a five-minute time-out in the bathroom (more effective than his bedroom, which these days is typically an entertainment center). If he refused to take that, a valued privilege such as watching TV was withdrawn for the rest of the day. If he still refused, further privileges were taken away. But if he did obey by the count of fifteen, he earned a point. When he had ten points, he got a small reward, such as dessert after dinner (which the mother had given him before, but now he had to earn it).

After only a few weeks of consistently following this regimen, the mother reported that her son was obeying her most of the time and no longer having tantrums. Other parents of children with extreme behavior problems experienced similar success using this disciplinary process.

We don't want children's compliance to be "blind obedience." We're right to be repulsed by the kind of Nazi-like obedience ("I was just following orders") that does whatever any authority figure, however malevolent, commands. Fortunately, even preschool children can learn to tell the difference between good and bad authority, and respond appropriately (we teach them how to do that if anyone touches them inappropriately). We want our kids to understand why obeying *legitimate* authority and rules, whether at home or at school, is helpful to the adults in charge and necessary for the harmonious functioning of the group. Here's how I recommend explaining this to children. In a calm moment—not when you or your child is upset—sit down and give . . .

The Obedience Speech

Mothers and fathers have the job of being in charge of the family. Kids have the job of *obeying* their parents—doing what we ask you to do. That makes us happy—we don't have to scold you for not doing what we ask—and that makes our home a happier place for everybody.

It's the same in school: Kids have to do what the teacher says. That helps the classroom be a place where you can learn and get things done.

So when we ask you to do something—come to dinner, pick up your toys, get ready for bed—you have to obey. You can't say no. That's not allowed. If you forget, we'll give you one reminder: *Remember our talk about obedience.* If you continue to disobey, then there will have to be a consequence, such as taking a time-out or losing a privilege.

There's one more thing: We'd like you to obey *cheerfully*, without complaining. Complaining makes everybody grumpy. Obeying cheerfully makes us happy. Okay, can you tell me what I said? (Patiently review whatever needs repeating.)

The big idea we want to teach kids is that obeying is a *virtue*. Children should be encouraged to obey, not primarily out of fear— that's a low-level motive—but *out of love*, in order to help their parents and the whole family. In this sense, obedience is an important early step in developing an orientation toward the needs of others. Even after you establish this foundational understanding, I recommend reminding kids in a matter-of-fact way when you want obedience: "Okay, this is a chance to obey (cooperate, do what I ask)—now. And I would appreciate your doing that without complaining—thank you."

A note of realism: just asking for no-complaints obedience doesn't guarantee you'll get it, especially if a child is tired or stressed. As adults, we often don't respond well either when we're in a bad mood, so in a particular situation, you may decide to cut your child some slack. But I wouldn't accept a defiant or disrespectful response; there should be a rule in place about that, with an understood consequence for disrespect (see chapter 6 on respect and fairness and chapter 7 on discipline).

4. Give Your Kids a Voice and Responsibility in the Family

Studies show that children benefit from experiences of "moral empowerment."[11] These experiences enable them to participate in decisions that affect their own lives and those of others. Over time, they help them develop confidence in their ability to have an impact on their environment, and increase their desire to make a positive difference in the world.

One authentic way to provide these experiences at home is to give children a voice in, and shared responsibility for, helping to create a happy family. Participating in writing a family mission statement and helping to apply it offer children important opportunities for voice and responsibility. Another such opportunity is the family meeting.

The family meeting—or "family chat" as my British friends like to call it—will help you put your family mission statement into practice and provide ongoing opportunities for your kids to have a voice in family life. More than anything else, the family meeting will hold all family members accountable for honoring their commitments. If you stick with it, I think you'll find it one of your most valuable tools for creating an intentional family culture of kindness and respect.

The family meeting involves sitting down together around a table to try to solve a problem, prevent one, or plan a family event. Problems that families have tackled include siblings not getting along; morning hassles; bedtime battles; screen policies; making meals more pleasant; picking up toys, clothes, etc.; and anything else that may be a source of tension and conflict. Conflicts in families—between parents, between parents and kids, and between kids—go with the territory. They can lead to yelling and screaming, poison the atmosphere of a home, and create wounds that take a long time to heal. But handled in the right way, conflicts can make a family stronger; foster mutual respect and responsibility; and develop listening and problem-solving skills that your children will be able to use in the workplace, in their own marriages, and in other relationships throughout their lives.

Unfortunately, it doesn't come naturally to most parents to sit down with their kids and ask for everybody's ideas for how best to solve a problem. One reason it doesn't come naturally is that most parents didn't have this experience when they were growing up. But all parents can learn to do this, and with a little practice it will feel as natural as having a meal together. And it can make a very big difference in the quality of your family life. Once you get good at this, you can even try it at mealtime, so long as the topic under discussion won't be too challenging to tackle while eating. (If the discussion turns out to be tension producing, you can agree to finish it at another time.)

In my work with parents, I've encouraged them to try a half-hour family meeting once a week (say, on a Sunday night). In chapter 8 I'll give you 10 tips that will help you have a successful family meeting. The most important thing is to make clear what the purpose of the family meeting is: not blaming, but cooperative problem-solving—giving everyone a chance to express their views, be understood, and find a solution together that's agreeable to all. For now, let me give just one example of a family meeting—a short one—and a family's testimony about what surprised them about the family-meeting process. Here's the short meeting:

Mom: I'd like to see if we can work out something we all think is fair regarding TV and dinnertime. I, for one, don't like the TV on while we're eating dinner.

Billy (8): But, Mom, dinner is usually ready during our favorite show. Why can't we eat earlier?

Dad: I don't get home from work until five thirty, so we really can't eat earlier. How about we just turn off the TV while we're eating?

Jenny (6): But then we'll miss our favorite show! I have an idea—we can put the TV on the table. Then we can all watch and eat without moving.

Mom: I don't want the TV on *at all* while we're eating. I'd like for us to talk to each other. Maybe I could plan dinner for right *after* your show. But then I'll be tied up later in the kitchen every night.

Dad: How about if we all help with cleanup?

Mom: Sounds good to me! I'll have dinner later if you all
    help with the dishes. Fair enough?
(All agreed.)

And here's a family with four sons, who were pleasantly surprised to find the family meeting provided a forum where they
could give their views and be listened to.

When our three older boys all became teenagers, there was
more conflict, more tension in our family. Then I learned
about family meetings, talked to my husband, and we started
to do them. It helped a lot. Later, the boys told us that at first
they thought it was going to be a lecture session. They were
surprised that it was a platform for them to present their
perspectives.

How does a family meeting foster character development? It
does so in 3 important ways.

- It teaches kids listening and perspective-taking skills that
  will be key moral competencies throughout their lives.
- It gives them an experience of human relationships based on
  mutual respect and caring, which will give them a good foundation in life for recognizing when mutual respect and caring
  are missing from a relationship.
- It involves them in helping to solve family problems and in
  sharing responsibility for creating a happier, more peaceful,
  more loving family. That job no longer falls just on parents'
  shoulders—it's everybody's responsibility.

Through the family meeting, children become cocreators of a
happy family, one that strives for peace and harmony out of love
for one another. What better way to practice kindness?

How to Handle Chores

To avoid producing entitled, self-centered kids, we should give our children meaningful responsibilities in the family, beginning in the earliest years. We want them to understand that it's a great privilege to belong to a family but that with that privilege come important responsibilities. Chores teach kids to work and help them acquire new skills, but most important, they give kids an opportunity to contribute to their family in a significant way on a regular basis. That's crucial for developing their capacity to think about others.

Catherine Musco Garcia-Prats and Joseph A. Garcia-Prats, parents of ten boys and authors of the book *Good Families Don't Just Happen*, tell how they explained to their kids the need for everybody to do their part:

> Children need to understand that their contribution is important to the whole family. We emphasize over and over again that it takes all of us working together to make the family work. . . . When each of the boys does his part, we have time to read stories or play a game instead of Mom and Dad feeling exhausted and frustrated from doing everything themselves. Our children have learned that our time is important, too, and that we like to have time to do the things that we enjoy, just as they do. That's not possible if Mom and Dad do everything.[12]

We want kids to understand and really feel that *they are needed* to make the family work. Their efforts count; their help makes a real difference. But don't pay your kids for chores: doing so robs them of the opportunity to be a contributing family member and to develop the habit of helping. An allowance can be given independent of chores—as one of the benefits, like food and shelter—of being part of a family.

An allowance is another character-building opportunity if you help kids learn to manage their money and set aside some of their allowance for spending, some for saving, and some for giving to a charity of their choice. (For more on this three-part allocation of allowance, see *The Opposite of Spoiled: Raising Kids Who Are Grounded, Generous, and Smart About Money* by Ron Lieber, financial columnist for the *New York Times*.[13])

To minimize hassles related to chores, a system is needed. You can set that up, or, better still, propose a plan at a family meeting and give your kids a chance to have input. The goal should be to establish a routine that promotes the habit of helping, ideally without complaints. You can ask kids, if they do complain, if they would like it if you complained about having to prepare meals for them, take them places, go to work to earn money to pay the family bills, and so on. Doing chores without complaining is one way of showing gratitude for the many benefits of belonging to a family. Use the family meeting to ask, "How can we pitch in and get the family work done in a generous cooperative spirit, so there's a good mood and not a sour one?"

The more everybody pitching in becomes a well-established routine, the more a this-is-the-way-we-do-things-around-here attitude should take hold. If kids slide back into complaining, refer to the relevant parts of your family mission statement and bring it up at your next family meeting. What would be fair consequences (being assigned extra jobs, for example) if people complain about doing their share of the family work?

Irene Freundorfer, a family educator, mother of six boys and four girls, and creator of the website 10kids.com, points out that even as you're working on fostering a cooperative attitude, be very clear to your kids that doing their share of family work is not an option; it's an expectation that's enforced:

In our house, Saturdays are always house-chore days. We all know 1–2 hours are needed to accomplish this mission, and it has priority before any fun stuff. Because we are consistent in enforcing it, there are few problems. Kids know: No chores? No computers, TV, video games, etc. They bite the bullet and pull their weight.

I recommend that you continue to use your family meeting to give everyone a voice and get their buy-in. You don't have to always stick with the same assignment of chores; you can change it up— and let the kids suggest ways to do that. Maybe one week Joey sets the table and Jennifer does the dishes, and the next week they switch. Whatever the plan is, post it and have the kids sign it. On her *10 Kids* website, Freundorfer explains her family's system:

In our house, the kitchen chore list rotates on a daily basis because that's what the kids liked best. However, they voted that the house chore list rotates monthly. Complaints may also mean it's time to move on to a more challenging chore. Think of something more grown-up to introduce them to. (See also Freundorfer's link to the age-appropriate list of personal and family responsibilities created by the Garcia-Pratses.[14])

Deciding as a family how to divide the chores and match chores to the ages of the kids is something each family has to do. One of my favorite examples of training kids early in the habit of helping comes from Marilyn Parker, a Chicago mother of three boys (she calls them "the Parker brothers"):

Our boys are now 2, 4, and 6. At this point, the system in our house is that you do one chore for each year of your age. We add a chore each year. Our 2-year-old pushes the button to start the dishwasher and puts the pillows in place when we make the beds. At 3, he'll help to set the table. Our 4-year-old sets the table, dust-busts the front hall and cleans the downstairs sink and tub. Our 6-year-old vacuums the stairs, makes his bed, washes the upstairs sink and toilet, scrapes the dishes, loads the dishwasher, and pours the milk at dinner. I tell them how much I appreciate their help. They're very proud of what they do.

5. Extend Compassion Beyond the Family

Besides teaching our kids to help in the family, we want them to have the experience of helping people outside the family. That's also essential for learning to care about others. One mother describes a tradition that her family has recently begun—something their 6-year-old son suggested that they do after their priest gave a moving homily on world hunger. On the first night of each week, the family has a "fasting dinner"—usually a piece of fruit for each of the kids and a cup of broth for the parents. (The kids have cereal before bed to quiet growling stomachs.) The meal begins with a prayer written by the oldest boy, age 10:

Lord, we pray for all the hungry people in the world, that they may become well and fed, and that the pain they suffer will be lifted from their hearts—and that all people will turn their hearts to generosity and compassion.

The money saved by not having a regular dinner is put into a jar and sent to a charitable organization working to relieve world hunger and poverty. Sometimes, at the meal, the mother or father reads a letter from the charity reporting progress in relieving a crisis in one part of the world or the outbreak of a new crisis somewhere else. Says the mother, "It helps us to be aware of how much suffering there is and to enter into that in a small way. We want our kids to know that God calls us to love our neighbor, wherever our neighbor is."

In *Parenting for Character*, Australian character educator Andrew Mullins describes how a friend got his 15-year-old son involved in helping the less fortunate:

> The son was badgering his father to buy him yet another pair of $200 Nikes. So the father said, "Come on, mate, let's go out for dinner." He took him into the city, and they stood together in the queue of a city soup kitchen. Now, two years later, one night each week, the son helps run the soup kitchen.[15]

Of course, not every kid exposed to a soup kitchen will be helping to run it two years later. But there are lots of stories of kids who are changed by the experience of face-to-face service. In character education, service learning has been found to increase empathy, leadership skills, and desire to contribute to the community.[16]

How do we convey to our children that people outside our own family matter to us? One of my graduate students shares a memory of something her father did:

> It was a bitter cold December day in Brooklyn. I was 10. My father and I were driving home when he noticed a man on the sidewalk, hunched over because of the cold, who had no coat, hat, or gloves. My father pulled over to the curb, got out of the car, and handed this man his coat, hat, and gloves. When he got back into the car, I asked him, "Daddy, why did you give your coat and hat and gloves to a man you don't even know?" He just smiled and said, "Because he needed them."

I was very moved by my father's act of kindness. I resolved that day to be kinder to my brother and sister and to kids at school. To this day, kindness remains a very important value to me.

Stories like this remind us that our children need to see us *doing things* that exhibit what we want them to imitate and uphold. We should also expose our children to other role models whose example of social conscience and responsibility reinforces what we're trying to teach. I've previously mentioned the Giraffe Heroes Project (www.giraffe.org) with its bank of inspiring stories. I'd also encourage you to make your children aware of groups like Doctors Without Borders, the recipient of a Nobel Peace Prize for their compassionate, incredibly courageous work, often in war zones like Syria. And as one of your child's birthday, Christmas, or other holiday presents, you could give them the opportunity to make a life-changing donation of a cow, goat, pig, or chickens to a poor family in another country through the wonderful work of Heifer International (www.heifer.org).

Our biggest challenge in developing a sense of social responsibility is to help kids see themselves as members of one human family. While we have a special responsibility for those directly in our care, we are also called to care about people everywhere.

6. Foster a Noble Vision of Life

One night, at the end of my graduate course on character education, a student stayed to talk. He said he lifted weights competitively but that it was increasingly difficult to compete because so many people in the sport were using steroids. "I don't use steroids and never will," he said, "but most people do, and they get away with it." I asked how athletes could continue to use steroids when everything you read says that steroids can make you sterile, deform your body, cause cancer, and make you depressed and even suicidal.

He said, "They know all that, but they don't care." He said the professor in one of his physical education courses had recently shown a video that reported the results of a survey of amateur weight lifters, collegiate and postcollegiate. The survey posed this question: "If you could take a drug that would guarantee you'd win every competition for the next five years, but at the end of the five years it would be certain to kill you, would you take that drug?" In this survey, a majority of the weight lifters said yes. Another survey of amateur athletes found that more than half said they would take a drug that would kill them within a year if it would guarantee their winning an Olympic gold medal.[17]

If we ask ourselves, "How is it that a significant number of young people in our society would trade their very lives for short-lived, drug-dependent success?," the answer comes back: they are spiritually adrift. They lack an ennobling vision of human dignity, human destiny, and the ultimate meaning of life. As one mother said upon hearing the results of that survey, "Those young men don't know why they're here."

Our children need to know why they're here. The annual Centers for Disease Control and Prevention's "Youth Risk Behavior Survey" finds that nearly one in five high school students say they have seriously considered suicide in the past year.[18] Many more report depression. There are lots of reasons for that, but among them is the lack of a sense of purpose that makes life worth living.

While we have our children in our care, we should help them reflect on life's largest questions. Those include questions about our origins (*Where did I come from?*); destiny (*Where am I going? Is this life all there is?*); identity (*Who am I?*); morality (*How can I decide what is right?*); values (*What matters most to me?*); and meaning (*What is the purpose of life? What significance does my life have?*).[19]

There are different ways to answer existential questions like these. We can find meaning and purpose by trying to live with integrity and compassion—doing our work well, caring for our families, helping the less fortunate, and being ethical in all our dealings with other people. For many persons, religion adds another reason for leading a good life: God expects it. We have been created for goodness and are accountable to God for what we do with our lives.

Research confirms that religious belief and practice can motivate kids to do good and stay on the straight and narrow. The Child Trends report "Religious Involvement and Children's Well-Being" found that youth who frequently attend religious services and say their faith is important to them exhibit higher levels of altruism and lower levels of drug and alcohol use.[20] Other research reviews have found similar trends for teen sexual activity, single parenthood, and delinquent behavior; youth who most often attend religious services have the lowest rates of these problems. One of the ways religion deters adolescents' involvement in self-harming or antisocial behaviors is by influencing them to choose friends who do not engage in those activities.[21]

A worldview, whether religious or nonreligious, can also provide us with a philosophy of life that enables us to love others even when they don't love us back. Here is one expression of such a philosophy, penned by the writer Kent Keith:

The Paradoxical Commandments (Anyway)

1. People are illogical, unreasonable, and self-centered. Love them anyway.
2. If you do good, people will accuse you of selfish ulterior motives. Do good anyway.
3. If you are successful, you will win false friends and true enemies. Succeed anyway.

4. The good you do today will be forgotten tomorrow. Do good anyway.
5. Honesty and frankness make you vulnerable. Be honest and frank anyway.
6. The biggest men and women with the biggest ideas can be shot down by the smallest men and women with the smallest minds. Think big anyway.
7. People favor underdogs but follow only top dogs. Fight for a few underdogs anyway.
8. What you spend years building may be destroyed overnight. Build anyway.
9. People really need help but may attack you if you do help them. Help people anyway.
10. Give the world the best you have and you'll get kicked in the teeth. Give the world the best you have anyway.[22]

It should go without saying that religion or any other worldview that places a high value on loving others and doing good, has a better chance of taking root in a child's conscience and character if it is visibly central in our own. Mary, a young mother of four, recalls her father:

Dad always closes his letters with, "Work hard and pray a lot." This never sounds phony because it's what he does. He has worked hard all his life. He built the two homes we lived in and did all the repairs. And he prays throughout the day. My most powerful image of my father is seeing him late at night, kneeling at the foot of his bed, saying his personal prayers.

Whatever our worldview, we can encourage our children to craft a life of noble purpose. A sense of purpose will give them a rudder in their quest for character. They'll need a vision that addresses the big questions about the meaning of life. They'll have to make that vision their own as they mature, but we can give them a start.

So those are 6 key principles that can guide our efforts to raise kind children: (1) make character a high priority in your family life; (2) love your children in all the ways that will help them grow in love; (3) exercise authority wisely; (4) give your kids a voice and responsibility in helping to create a happy family; (5) extend compassion and helping beyond your family; and (6) help your children develop a noble vision of life—one that includes a belief in something bigger than themselves and the desire to use their gifts to make a positive difference in the world.

CHAPTER 5

10 Essential Virtues That Help Kids Be Kind

Sow a thought and you reap an act.
Sow an act and you reap a habit.
Sow a habit and you reap a character.
Sow a character and you reap a destiny.
—OLD SAYING

WHENEVER I GIVE a talk to young people about character, I address a question that's natural for them to wonder about: "Why be good?" Why make the effort to develop a good character? Here's how I answer that question:

Look around. Who enjoys true happiness and a sense of fulfillment? Character is the key to self-respect and respect for others, a good reputation, a clear conscience, peace of mind, the development of our talents, work done well, positive relationships—in fact, to success and happiness in every area of life.

What does it mean to be "a person of character"? Put simply: *Being a person of character means being the best person you can be.* We want our kids to know that this is a lifelong challenge and responsibility. As an observation attributed to Eleanor Roosevelt puts it, "Character building begins in infancy and continues until death." If we're going to make developing good character a priority in our families, we need to challenge kids to be their best while also making it clear that we don't expect them to be perfect:

> We all make mistakes sometimes and act in ways that don't reflect our best self. Kids do; parents do. We're all a work in progress. Developing good character means trying to be your best self more of the time. When you make a mistake, admit it—and try to learn from it.

Basically, we want our kids to know that developing a good character is hard work that lasts a lifetime. But it's worth the effort; it makes for a fulfilling life. At the end of life, people don't look back and think, "I wish I didn't try so hard to be a good person." They often regret not trying hard enough.

Let's look now at the 10 essential virtues that function as a "supporting cast" for kindness. What I'm calling essential virtues have been affirmed and taught throughout human history by nearly all philosophical, cultural, and religious traditions around the world. Most of us possess these virtues at least to some degree. Our challenge is to keep getting better.

The first four virtues—wisdom, justice, fortitude, and temperance (self-control)—come from the ancient Greeks. These four character strengths are often called the "cardinal virtues," from the Latin word *cardo*, which means "hinge." To a great extent, our lives hinge on how well we practice these virtues.

1. Wisdom

Wisdom is good judgment. The Greeks considered it the "master virtue" because it tells us how to put the other virtues into practice. Wisdom means, first of all, stopping to *think*—taking the time to make a good decision by considering your choices and what's right. One 12-year-old boy said:

My friends don't really respect people, and it's like peer pressure—they try to push me into it. Usually, I would just go with it, but when we started [learning about] the virtues, I knew wisdom meant, like, right or wrong—and now I have to think, "Is this right, or is it wrong?"

Wisdom enables us to choose the best means of reaching a goal. In school, kids are often asked to set goals for academic improvement. A student in math class might say, "My goal is to get all my math homework in on time this marking period." But often, kids don't have a realistic strategy for achieving their goal, so they don't succeed. Figuring out a strategy that might really succeed requires good judgment—wisdom.

Wisdom includes moral reasoning, or the understanding of why something is right or wrong. To act virtuously means to do the right thing for the right reason. We can do a good deed such as returning a lost wallet because we want a reward, because we want to be noticed and praised, or because we want to help the person who lost his wallet. Only the last of these reasons—caring about the welfare of the other person—is a virtuous motive.

Wisdom enables us to evaluate what's most important in life (being true to ourselves, for example, is more important than being popular) and helps us decide *how* to do good. Without wisdom, we may have kind intentions but do something that is not what the recipient of our action finds helpful. We may hasten to assist someone when they'd really rather be left alone.

Finally, wisdom helps us decide how to be kind when kindness conflicts with other virtues, such as telling the honest truth. Sometimes telling the truth is hard, and it may seem kinder to evade or dissemble. But there are situations where you have to tell an uncomfortable truth, such as bad news. Kindness helps us do that with sensitivity.

2. Justice

The second cardinal virtue, justice, has two big parts: respect and responsibility. Respect says, "Don't hurt people." Responsibility says, "Do help them." Respect is the restraining side of justice; responsibility the active, contributing side.

Justice requires that we recognize and honor the inherent worth and human rights of every person, that we avoid inflicting needless suffering on animals, and that we not despoil the natural environment on which all life depends. Cruelty or abuse of any kind comes not just from a lack of kindness; it comes from a lack of respect. Recent revelations of sexual harassment by men in powerful positions gives us an opportunity as parents to teach our children that all such behavior is an intolerable violation of respect.

The Golden Rule is a principle of justice that directs us to treat others as we ourselves wish to be treated. The virtues needed for positive interpersonal relationships—such as courtesy, respect, and basic fairness—are all part of justice, all aspects of treating others as we would like to be treated. This includes considering how our actions affect others. Let me share the story of a kindergarten teacher who helped a 5-year-old boy understand the feelings of another boy, "Jonathan" (from Jamaica), whom he had been calling "tan man." This upset Jonathan so much that he didn't want to come back to school. The teacher took the offending child aside and said in a gentle but serious way:

> There are two kinds of hurts: outside hurts that you can see, like a cut or a bruise, and inside hurts that you can't see—like a hurt feeling. But even though you can't see the inside hurts, they are very real. They actually hurt more and last longer than the outside hurts. Sometimes the inside hurts last for a very long time, and sometimes they never go away. You might not realize it, but when you call Jonathan "tan man," you're

causing an inside hurt for him. In fact, it hurts so much that he doesn't want to come back to our class. I wouldn't let anyone make that kind of inside hurt for you, and I can't let anyone make that kind of inside hurt for Jonathan. Our class-room has to be a place where everyone feels safe and happy to be here. Okay, tell me what I said, in your own words. If you can't remember everything, I'll help you.

Justice includes making amends for hurts we've caused. It would be important to help the boy who called Jonathan "tan man" find a way to make things right:

You can say, "I'm sorry, Jonathan, that I hurt your feelings." You can say something nice to him when you see him in the morning. You can invite him to join a game at recess, or tell him he can draw with you at the art table if he'd like to.

Studies show that effective teachers and parents do a lot of this kind of reasoning with children. It helps them appreciate, at an intellectual and emotional level, how their behavior affects other people.[1]

Justice also includes self-respect, a proper regard for our own rights, worth, and dignity. Being kind to others doesn't mean allowing them to physically or emotionally abuse us. This is something we need especially to stress with our daughters when it comes to their relationships with boys and men.

Responsibility is the second big part of justice. It requires us to help those in need, starting with our families and extending to those outside our families. It requires us to do our work well, so that it benefits others. Justice requires us to keep our promises, honor our commitments, and fulfill our obligations as citizens. It includes the capacity for moral indignation in the face of injustice. We want our children to be concerned, and even distressed, when they see anyone being treated unjustly. We want them to grow up to be the kind of person who has a social conscience that is aroused by injustice and the violation of human rights wherever it occurs. Martin Luther King Jr., one of America's champions of justice, urged all of us, whatever our calling in life, to be part of humanity's ongoing struggle for human rights:

Whatever career you may choose for yourself—doctor, lawyer, teacher—let me propose an avocation to be pursued along with it. Become a dedicated fighter for civil rights. Make it a central part of your life. It will make you a better doctor, a better lawyer, a better teacher. It will enrich your spirit as nothing else possibly can. It will give you that rare sense of nobility that can only spring from selflessly helping your fellow man. Make a career of humanity. Commit yourself to the noble struggle for human rights. You will make a greater person of yourself, a greater nation of your country, and a finer world to live in.[2]

Our children can start with something small, like befriending or sticking up for kids who are excluded or mistreated in the neighborhood or at school.

3. Fortitude

The opening sentence of M. Scott Peck's bestselling book *The Road Less Traveled* states a basic truth: "Life is difficult." "If life isn't difficult for you," one mother said to her children, "you're probably making it difficult for someone else."

We need fortitude to cope with the inevitable difficulties of life. Fortitude is the inner toughness, the mental and emotional strength, to deal with disappointment, handle hardship, overcome obstacles, and endure suffering. It's the guts to follow our conscience in the face of pressure or temptation when it would be easier to give up or give in.

Fortitude is made up of virtues such as courage, determination, grit, endurance, and resilience. We won't develop these character strengths unless we face up to life's challenges. One of the biggest mistakes we can make as parents is to try to protect our kids from the hard tests of life—from having to deal with disappointment, frustration, and failure. Without such tests, our character remains soft.

Many parents find it difficult to say no to their child, even when they think they should, because they don't want their child to experience the pain of disappointment. I remember a poignant conversation with a mother who went against her better judgment and let her 10-year-old daughter go to a classmate's sleepover party where the planned entertainment was a movie about three teenage girls competing to see who could lose her virginity first. "I knew how much she wanted to go and how terribly disappointed she would be if she couldn't," this mother said, "but my conscience has bothered me ever since."

In our center's character education work, we've recommended to parents and teachers the book *Uncommon Champions: Fifteen Athletes Who Battled Back* by Marty Kaminsky, a 4th-grade teacher in upstate New York who has also written for *Sports Illustrated*. It's a great read-aloud. Each chapter tells the story of a male or female athlete whose promising career was threatened by a tragic accident, debilitating illness, struggle with addiction, or some other major adversity.

In each case, the athlete was able to overcome the adversity through fortitude (along with support from family, friends, and often their faith in God). In every case, they were stronger, better people for having faced and risen above the challenge they confronted. Marty says he wrote this book because increasingly he found that his students whined and complained in the face of even small difficulties and frustrations. He wanted them to believe that they, too, could develop the fortitude—the hope, courage, and inner toughness—to meet whatever challenges life brought their way.

We should teach our children that if they don't give in to feeling sorry for themselves, they will grow more from their setbacks than their successes. We should share the sufferings we've faced in life and how they've helped us grow stronger and wiser.

Courage is a key part of fortitude. Winston Churchill said, "Courage is rightly esteemed the first of human qualities because . . . it is the quality which guarantees all others." C. S. Lewis said that courage is "the form of every virtue at the testing point." If we don't have courage, we may fail to put other virtues into practice. "It takes courage to stick up for your friend," says one 9-year-old boy. It takes courage to even talk to a kid at school who has no friends and who the popular crowd tells you to ignore.

4. Self-Control

Self-control is the ability to govern ourselves. It enables us to control our temper, regulate our appetites and passions, and pursue even legitimate pleasures in moderation. An old saying recognizes the importance of self-control in the life of character: "Either we rule our desires, or our desires rule us."

In their bestselling book *Willpower: Rediscovering the Greatest Human Strength*, psychologist Roy Baumeister and science writer John Tierney observe that many major problems, personal and societal, are to a considerable extent failures of self-control. Compulsive spending and borrowing, impulsive violence, underachievement in school, procrastination at work, alcohol and drug abuse, unhealthy diet, and explosive anger—all reflect shortcomings in self-control. In a recent survey of more than a million people around the world, self-control was the character strength people were least likely to see in themselves. When they were asked to name their failings, a lack of self-control topped the list.[3]

If we're going to be kind and do right by others, we have to be in control of ourselves. Bullying, binge drinking, sexual assault, and other reckless, cruel, or criminal behaviors flourish in the absence of self-control.

5. Love

The ancient Greeks covered a lot of the character territory but by no means all of it. A fifth essential virtue is love. Love means wanting and doing what is best for another person. A whole cluster of important virtues—kindness, empathy, compassion, generosity, sacrifice, service, loyalty, and forgiveness—make up the great virtue of love. Love gives more than what fairness requires. If we ask our kids to do something (say, read a story to a younger sibling before dinner) and they protest (for whatever reason), saying "It's not fair!," that's a chance to teach them the difference between fairness and love. We can say:

> It's not a matter of fairness; it's a matter of love. Sometimes we do something because it's the fair thing to do, but other times we do it because it's the kind and loving thing to do. In a family, we do many things for each other because we love each other. That's what makes a family a family. I do things for you every day because I love you. I'm asking you to do this for me out of love.

Among the virtues that make up love, forgiveness is often the most difficult to practice, especially in family life. Humility helps us remember that we all need forgiveness. We have all done things that hurt others.

We want to teach our children that the surest way to be happy in life is to do things to make other people happy. In seeking the happiness of others, love is willing to sacrifice. It puts the need of the other person ahead of our own. In the parable of the Good Samaritan, the first two people passed by the man who had been beaten by robbers and left by the roadside. Those passersby were worried about themselves: "If I stop to help this man, what will happen to me?" The Good Samaritan, however, reversed the question: "If I do not stop to help this man, what will happen to him?" Love motivates us to do good for others regardless of inconvenience or risk to ourselves and regardless of whether we are recognized, rewarded, or even thanked.

6. A Positive Attitude

We should share with our kids what researchers have found: people with a positive attitude live longer, are healthier, enjoy life more, deal more effectively with hardship, are more adventurous, have more friends, and are more successful in their careers.[4] We should also teach them that their attitude is always a choice, no matter what their circumstances. A great book for teaching that life lesson is Viktor Frankl's 1946 classic, *Man's Search for Meaning*. Frankl, a Jewish psychiatrist, survived two years in the Nazi concentration camp at Auschwitz. In his book he wrote:

> We must never forget that we may find meaning in life even when confronted with a hopeless situation, when facing a fate that cannot be changed. For what matters then is to bear witness to the uniquely human potential to transform a tragedy into a triumph. When we are no longer able to change a situation—just think of an incurable disease such as an inoperable cancer—we are challenged to change ourselves.[5]

Frankl's belief helped him retain his humanity and hope despite the horrors of the death camp.

In her bestselling book *The Happiness Project*, Gretchen

Rubin—a writer, lawyer, and busy mom—describes, month by month, how she deliberately went about trying to be a generally happier person. Before she started this project, she had often found herself slipping into sadness, even though she had meaningful work, a happy marriage, two kids she loved, and much else to be grateful for. She knew that ancient wisdom and modern research tell us that if we want to be happy, we should be good. But she discovered that the wisdom of the ages and current science tell us the reverse is also true: *If we want to be good, we should try to be happy.* She writes:

> [R]esearch shows that happy people are more altruistic, more productive, more helpful, more likable, more creative, more resilient, more interested in others, friendlier, and healthier. . . . [I]t was certainly easier for me to be good when I was happy. I was more patient, more forgiving, more energetic, more lighthearted, and more generous.[6]

In our efforts to develop good character in our kids and ourselves, we should all work on cultivating the art of happiness.

7. Hard Work

A seventh indispensable virtue is plain old hard work. Hard work and the virtues that make it up—such as best effort, initiative, diligence, resourcefulness, perseverance, and striving to improve—constitute our "performance character." We need performance character in order to do the hard work of developing our talents so we can use them to contribute to the lives of others. Moral character inspires us to want to do good; performance character enables us to do good *well*. People who make a positive difference in the world have both.

One of the most widely admired figures in the history of sports is the late John Wooden, the legendary basketball coach of UCLA.

In twelve seasons, from 1964 to 1975, Wooden's basketball teams won *ten* national championships—a feat no other collegiate men's team has ever come close to. And yet Coach Wooden never talked to his players about winning; he talked about character.

In his memoir *Wooden: A Lifetime of Observations and Reflections On and Off the Court*, he gives much of the credit for that emphasis to Mr. Lawrence Schidler, his 10th-grade math teacher at Martinsville High School in Indiana. One day, Mr. Schidler asked his students to write a paper defining "success."[7] Wooden says that assignment got him thinking hard about the meaning of success for the next several decades. When he was coaching in football, tennis, basketball, and baseball, he didn't want winning to be the final measure of his athletes' achievement or success. He says, "It seemed to me that it was possible to win and be outscored, or to lose even when you outscored an opponent." Here is the definition of success he finally arrived at:

> The goal in life is just the same as in basketball: make the effort to do the best you are capable of doing—in marriage, at your job, in the community, for your country. Make the effort to contribute in whatever way you can. You may do it materially or with time, ideas, or work. Making the effort to contribute is what counts. The *effort* is what counts in everything.[8]

In his memoir, Wooden says, "Don't measure yourself by what you've accomplished, but rather by what you should have accomplished with your abilities."

Being kind often involves hard work. Especially in ongoing relationships, kindness requires sustained effort, working out conflicts, forgiving hurts, and sacrifice. It's been said that human maturity consists of the capacity to love and the capacity to work. Loving other people is often the hardest work we do.

8. Integrity

Integrity means sticking to and standing up for our moral principles, following our conscience, and being honest with ourselves and others. A decade ago, David Callahan's *The Cheating Culture: Why More Americans Are Doing Wrong to Get Ahead* documented the accelerating erosion of integrity at every level of American society, from the boardroom to the bedroom.[9] Cheating destroys trust and spawns unethical practices. After the 2008 economic crash, it was revealed that some of the lawyers and auditors—whose job was supposed to be keeping the banks and Wall Street honest—had been looking the other way as they collected ever-bigger fees from their clients.

Surveys of high school students find that between three-fifths and two-thirds of students admit to cheating on a major test or assignment in the past year.[10] One high school student interviewed about cheating said, "Businessmen cheat. Politicians cheat. Athletes cheat. Why shouldn't students?" A friend who teaches 6th grade asked her students to write down (without signing their name) if they had ever cheated in school—and if they would do so again. Two-thirds said they had cheated, and most of those said they'd do it again.

Many students point to parents as a big part of the problem. In a focus group I did with high school students on why students cheat, one boy said: "Parents compare you with other kids: 'Why aren't you getting the grades so-and-so is getting?'" Another responded: "My parents have encouraged me to do well—but to do it without cheating."

Cheating is one side of dishonesty; stealing is another. A turn-of-the-century article in *U.S. News & World Report* cited a survey finding that one-third of college students said they would steal from an employer, compared to only 6 percent of those over forty-five who said they would do so.

The connection between integrity and kindness becomes clear if we consider how we'd feel if we were the victims of somebody's cheating in a business transaction or in an intimate relationship. If we want kids to become kind adults in every sphere of their lives, we need to teach them to have integrity.

9. Gratitude

Gratitude is the virtue of being thankful for benefits received. It's been called "the secret of a happy life." The psychologist Robert Emmons, who has studied gratitude for more than a decade, reports that grateful people are more alert, sleep better, have more positive relationships, and are more aware of situations where they can be helpful. When people report feeling grateful, they also feel more loving, forgiving, and joyful.[11]

In their book, *Making Grateful Kids*, psychologists Jeffrey Froh and Giacomo Bono report their research with thousands of children and teens in the US and four other countries showing that gratitude improves young people's mental health, life satisfaction, and sense of purpose. It also motivates them to want to help others and use their gifts to contribute to society.[12] In classrooms where children have kept gratitude journals, parents and teachers have observed an increase in children's expressions of appreciation.

If we want to raise kind kids, we'll foster an attitude of gratitude. The previous chapter described how to do that in family life; chapter 12 gives ten more ways.

10. Humility

The virtue of humility drives the whole quest for character. It makes us aware of our imperfections. It motivates us to try to become better people. Pride, the opposite of humility, has been called the worst vice, because it blinds us to our faults. C. S. Lewis said that pride is a "spiritual cancer," causing us to want to feel superior to others.[13] Half of the harm done in the world, T. S. Eliot said, is due to people who want to feel important.

Humility enables us to see and take responsibility for our faults and failings and make amends. A humble spirit is necessary even in a small child. It takes humility to say "I'm sorry"—and really mean it—when you've hurt a playmate or sibling. It also takes humility for adults to apologize, which is why many seldom do. If we want to raise children who are kind to others at home and school and grow into kind adults, we'll teach them the importance of being humble—and set an example by admitting when we're wrong, apologizing for our lapses, and then striving to do better.

Finally, humility enables us to recognize the most fundamental fact about the moral life: it's hard. It's easier to give in to temptation than to resist it. It's easier to focus on our own feelings than to take the perspective of another. It's easier to lose our temper than control it. It's easier to be selfish than generous, especially if generosity requires sacrifice. It's easier to become part of uncharitable gossip than to refrain from it or, harder still, to say something good about the person being put in a bad light. It's easier to look the other way than to confront an injustice. It's easier to defend our mistakes than acknowledge them. It's easier to nurse a resentment and hold a grudge than to forgive.

If we really want to help our children make progress on the road to character, we'll have to be traveling that road ourselves. We can't teach character if we don't have it. We can't get kids to work on their character if they don't see us working on ours. Sincerely striving to become a better person—kinder, more patient, more honest with ourselves and others, more self-disciplined, more courageous, more grateful, more forgiving, more humble—will require a greater commitment to introspection than may come naturally to most of us.

But if we do that as parents, we'll be helping our children aspire to what we are all called to: becoming the best persons we can be, and making our time on Earth count for good.

CHAPTER 6

Respect and Fairness

A FEW YEARS AGO I gave a talk entitled "Raising Children of Character" to an auditorium full of middle school parents at a school that was starting the second year of its character education initiative. After the talk, the PTA asked parents to fill out, on the spot, a one-page questionnaire listing a dozen character traits and to rank "the three you think the school should be emphasizing more." They collected the questionnaires, quickly went through them, and reported the results to the audience. An overwhelming majority of parents ranked "respect" as the number one character quality they wanted the school to stress more.

I then asked, "Would anyone who ranked respect as your top priority be willing to explain your reason?"

Hands went up all over the room. People said they felt kids had less and less respect for their parents, for adults in general, and for one another—and they thought this reflected a significant decline of respect in our whole society. Often, when individual parents come up to me after a talk to speak privately, they say, "I'd like to get more respect from my children."

Why is respect so important?

We can't teach our children to be kind if we haven't first taught them respect—starting with respect for us as their parents. If that's not in place, we're going to have trouble teaching them anything. We won't be able to hold them accountable to standards of behavior. We won't be able to exercise the moral leadership in our family that is needed to create a culture of kindness.

In his book *Character Building*, the educator David Isaacs, points out that there are 3 major kinds of respect that parents and teachers should seek to instill in young people:[1]

1. *The "special respect" we owe people because of the role or position they occupy.* Parents, teachers, and public officials deserve this special respect because of their authority and responsibility. If we disagree, even very strongly, with someone who holds a position of legitimate authority and responsibility in society, "respect for the office" requires that we express our views respectfully. As mothers and fathers, we should have a strong sense of the special respect we deserve as parents. A mother who had this sense put it well: "I remind my kids that 'Honor your father and mother' is high up there in the Ten Commandments—ahead of 'Thou shalt not kill.'"

2. *The "general respect" that we owe every human being, without exception.* This respect is not "earned" in the way that admiration or esteem is earned (as in, "I really respect that person for how hard he works"; "I don't respect that teacher because she's unfair"). All people deserve this "general respect" simply because they are human beings. By this standard, all people, without exception, have equal moral worth regardless of their age, status, or value to society. The Third Reich notoriously had a category of "life not worthy of life" that, in their view, justified killing Jews, gays, Gypsies, deformed or retarded people, and citizens of Nazi-occupied countries. US law recognizes that even prisoners who have committed terrible crimes must be treated with respect; they still have human rights (for example, they can't be tortured or deprived of food or shelter). International law recognizes that prisoners of war must be treated with respect too. Despite these areas of moral consensus, conflict continues concerning abortion, although here, too, common ground may be emerging; in a 2015 poll by the Marist Institute for Public Opinion, 84

percent of Americans agreed with the statement that "laws can exist which protect both the health and well-being of a woman and the rights of the unborn."

3. ***Respect as an inner attitude, not just external behavior.*** We are not being truly respectful toward other people if we're inwardly contemptuous of them. Respecting others means trying to see the good in them, just as we want them to see the good in us. You're not really respecting somebody if you act nicely while thinking to yourself, "You jerk"—and your children are not being respectful if they resentfully do what you ask while looking at you with contempt or muttering under their breath that you are so annoying.

People can and should treat one another with respect even if they disagree about important values, beliefs, or behaviors. Respect enables us to "agree to disagree" in a civil, nonaggressive, and even gracious manner. This kind of respect makes authentic tolerance possible. We should encourage our children not to be offended or indignant if someone disagrees with them.

10 Ways to Give—and Get—Respect

How can we get respect from our children? In *Take Back Your Kids*, family psychologist William Doherty offers helpful guidelines that are consistent with the character-based approach to discipline I will outline in greater detail in chapter 7. See the "Expecting Respect" chapter of his book for a fuller discussion of his guidelines; here is my summary:

1. ***Respect your child.*** Show a genuine interest in how your children thinks and feels. Draw them out. Encourage them to express their own opinions, tastes, and feelings. When they do, listen in a way that shows sincere interest. Especially when

they're expressing a viewpoint that is different from yours, use "active listening" (paraphrasing) to show you've heard and understood what they're saying ("Okay, so you feel that . . .").

2. *Expect respect.* Respect should be a clear expectation in the family. Without it, little else will go well. Use words like "respectful," "disrespectful," "polite," and "rude" to develop a common language of respect in the family. Give a couple of examples of what it sounds like to express feelings in a respectful way and what it sounds like when a person speaks disrespectfully.

3. *Explain your policy on respect to your children.* If you've let your kids get away with disrespect before, they may not even realize that they are being disrespectful. Meet with them at a quiet time to explain your new policy of requiring respect in all family communication.

4. *Tune your ears to the sound of respect and disrespect.* Insist on respect in both the *content* of what kids say and the *tone* of how they say it. A raised voice ("Mom, you're not being fair!") isn't necessarily disrespectful. But a sarcastic tone of voice is.

5. *Nip disrespectful behavior in the bud.* Respond immediately by saying sharply: "That was disrespectful," "What is your tone of voice?," or "Please say that again—and be careful to do so *respectfully.*"

6. *Use a stern tone of voice in response to any form of disrespect.* Your reaction should send a clear message: "You're in dangerous territory—back off immediately."

7. *Use time-out or another appropriate consequence if your child does not stop the disrespectful behavior.* Tell your kids that if they speak disrespectfully, you'll give them one reminder ("What will happen if you continue to speak disrespectfully?"). If they don't stop, there has to be an appropriate consequence (for example, "Go to your room and come back

when you can discuss this in a respectful way"). With a teen, you may want to walk away from the conversation rather than try to enforce a time-out against physical opposition. The key is to pronounce the behavior as disrespectful and end the conversation rather than let it escalate.

8. *Be firm but keep your cool.* Confident parenting is almost always calm, clear, focused, and assertive in times of conflict (although non-abusive, appropriate parental indignation is sometimes needed and justified, as we will discuss in chapter 7).

9. *Challenge every disrespectful behavior—without exception.* That's the only way your child will understand your expectations and the meaning of the behavior you want to extinguish. Don't expect an immediate cessation of rudeness so much as a steady decrease.

10. *If the problem is chronic and these strategies don't work, consider family therapy.* If both parents don't agree on how to handle disrespect, consider getting professional help to develop an agreed-upon approach. It is also important that you treat each other respectfully too, even—or especially—in times of conflict or disagreement. If your children see you treating each other disrespectfully, they are likely to take it as a cue to do the same.

Let me underscore the importance of modeling respect in *all* of your family interactions. When I interview parents, I always ask them: "What did your parents do to help you develop good values and good character?" People speak of many things, such as their parents' love, high standards, strict discipline, and wisdom about how to live. But far and away, the most common answer is simply, "They set a good example."

One mother remembered her parents' respect for each other, their kindness toward others in the community, and their genuine interest in people and the world around them:

My parents weren't perfect, but they were respectful of one another and supported each other in their child-rearing decisions. No one in our family cursed. My mother was always helping out others in the community. My father showed tremendous kindness toward people and animals. Both of my parents were really interested in how people lived in past generations and in different cultures. They would also frequently voice their opinions about societal issues.

Another woman recalled, "My mother was the only person who refused to sign a petition to block an African-American family from getting housing in our neighborhood. And when the family finally did move in, she baked them a cake to welcome them."

Our modeling of respect should include how we talk to—and about—people inside and outside the family:

- Do we treat our spouse with kindness and respect, even when we disagree?
- Do we forgive and reconcile soon after a fight—or hold on to anger and resentment and perhaps refuse to speak? Healthy families, research shows, have "reconciliation rituals" that enable them to make up quickly.
- Do we avoid saying disrespectful and unkind things about relatives, friends, neighbors, and teachers?

These are all important ways we can model respect. We'll look more at how to teach respect in the family and deal with disrespect in chapter 7, on discipline.

How to Teach Fairness in the Family

Just as it will be much easier to encourage our kids to be kind if we've taught them respect, it will be easier to teach kindness if

we've addressed issues of fairness in the family. Kids don't naturally, in day-to-day family life, talk about what's kind and what's
not ("Hey, that's not kind!"). But they *do* talk about what's fair and
unfair—all the time! What parents haven't heard the complaint
"It's not fair!" more times than they want to remember? If we *don't*
deal with kids' concerns about fairness, we'll have a hard time
getting them to care about kindness. So let's take a look at how you
can acknowledge the priority they attach to fairness, build on that,
help them understand what "fair" *doesn't* mean, and develop their
understanding of fairness into something more flexible and open
to a spirit of kindness.

By the time they're 4—sometimes even sooner—children are
using the language of fairness. While 2-year-olds say, "I want it!,"
4-year-olds think, "I want it—and so it's not *fair* if I don't get it!"
That may not seem like developmental progress, but it is—in the
sense that they're now seeing and talking about their desires from
a moral viewpoint. It's a very egocentric viewpoint, to be sure, but
it's part of the long developmental process of learning to think
morally—to reason about questions of fairness and unfairness,
right and wrong. (In my book *Raising Good Children*, I describe
the six stages of moral reasoning and how you can reason with
your child at each stage in ways that promote progress to the
next one.)

By elementary school, kids' sense of fairness has typically developed into a tit-for-tat morality: "You do something for me, and
I'll do something for you." The flip side of this is a belief in an-eye-
for-an-eye revenge; every push, every name called, and even every
dirty look has to be paid back. This new sense of fairness also
typically includes the belief that it's not fair for adults to "boss kids
around"—kids and adults should have equal rights! When 7-year-
old Jason's mom said he couldn't go out and play because it was
too close to dinnertime, he protested, "I should have my rights,
just like you have yours!"

To kids at this age, fair treatment means equal treatment—*exactly* equal treatment. Comparisons are constant. "David's got more than I do!" "How come Ernie gets to have a friend sleep over this weekend, and I can't?" "Why are you asking *me* to clear the table—what's Jackie doing?" The irony in all of this is that kids have a supersensitive unfairness detector when it comes to all the ways they think others are being unfair to them, but they often have a big blind spot when it comes to all the ways they may be acting unfairly.

How can we connect with our kids' preoccupation with fairness to help them see things from another person's point of view, realize that constant comparisons make everybody unhappy, learn to solve conflicts in ways that are truly fair, and understand why families don't work very well unless, in addition to fairness, there's a lot of loving kindness?

My first recommendation is to appeal to the concept of reciprocity. Reciprocity is the rule of equal exchange: "I did that for you, so you should do this for me." You can hear elementary school kids using this principle in their peer interactions: "Okay, I played what you wanted before, so you should play what I want now."

Parents can plug into their children's understanding of reciprocity. For example, when his father asked him for help with the yard work, 6-year-old Michael protested that he didn't want to. "Hey," his father said, "when you asked me to take you over to Jed's yesterday, what did I do?" "You took me," Michael said. "So now that I'm asking you to do something for me, what's the fair thing for you to do?" Michael got the point.

Appeals to reciprocity can also be used in a forward-looking way. Suppose your 9-year-old daughter resists when you ask her help with something around the house. You can say, calmly, "When you ask me for something today or later this week, like drive you to your friend Nellie's house for a playdate, what would you like me to say? You'd like me to say yes, right? So what should you say now, when I'm asking for your help?" These appeals to reciprocal fairness might not defuse all resistance, and you might have to simply assert, "If you expect to be able to [whatever nice thing they're looking forward to], then I need you to [whatever you're asking], *right now*—and no complaining, please. Thank you." Even if you have to lay down the law, you will have made the point about reciprocity.

Give Kids a Fair Hearing

In chapter 4 we talked about the research on the desirability of an *authoritative* parenting style, which combines authority, love, mutual respect, and reasoning. At all developmental levels, authoritative parenting is more effective in developing confident, respectful, and responsible kids than *authoritarian* parenting (all top-down in authority and weak in love and reasoning) or *permissive* parenting (kids rule the roost). Authoritative parents set clear rules and don't give in to whining or tantrums. But they also give their children a fair hearing and sometimes change their minds when a child or teen makes a reasonable appeal in a respectful way.

Because kids by elementary school age really believe they have a right to hold and argue their point of view, they need to be able to go back and forth with you to try to get what they think is a fair shake. But that doesn't mean a fifty-fifty compromise where you end up caving in on an important value or principle. An example: when our first son, Mark, was 13, his friends were going to see a lot of movies that we weren't permitting him to see because of their moral content. We explained that just as we didn't want him putting bad stuff into his body, we didn't want him putting bad stuff into his mind, heart, and soul. "But I won't be influenced by it!" he would insist.

Our argument that we're all influenced, whether we realize it or not, by what we take in didn't stop him from pressing to join his pals at the latest cool R-rated flick in town. Finally, I said, "Look, as your father, I have to be able to answer to my conscience— and to God. But I don't want you to miss out on seeing movies with your friends. You can rent a good movie—something that we're okay with—from the video store and have everybody over here. [This was before Netflix.] We'll provide the popcorn, pizza, and soda. Fair enough?" Happily, that combination carried the day.

One 15-year-old girl captured the spirit of authoritative parenting when she described her parents as being "firm—but democratic." The trick is to keep kids from becoming what one mom called "Philadelphia lawyers," giving you an argument about everything. So it's wise to say: "Look, sometimes I'm willing to go back and forth about what's fair and to try to work something out. But there are other times when I don't have the energy or time to do that—in which case I need you to take no for an answer. Do you understand that?"

If a child continues to feel strongly that a particular parental decision isn't fair and that they haven't had a fair hearing, it can be discussed at a later time that's better suited to back-and-forth dialogue.

Teach That "Fair" Doesn't Mean "Same"

We also need to teach our kids that "fair" doesn't mean "same." Fair doesn't mean a parent gives the same amount of time or help to every child in the family. One child may have learning or behavioral challenges and need more support. It's the same in a classroom. One student needs more help with reading, another with math; another may do fine with little help in any subject. A teacher is fair by treating her students differently, according to their needs.

Fair also doesn't mean having the same chores as your brothers or sisters, as chores vary with age and ability. Fair doesn't mean that a 6-year-old gets to stay up as late as his 10-year-old brother, have a sleepover, or go to all the same places. "You can't go on this bike trip with your brother; he couldn't go that far either when he was your age," is a perfectly fine thing to say. More privileges and responsibilities come with age and maturity. Older kids get a bigger allowance, because they need it. You don't get to drive a car when you're 12; you do when you're older and get your license.

I recommend putting "FAIR" DOESN'T MEAN "SAME" on the refrigerator or on the wall in your kitchen. It is a crucial thing for kids to internalize and understand.

We should also help our kids understand that constant comparisons in the family cause tension and unhappiness. In our family, we eventually adopted a "no comparisons" policy. We explained, "Making comparisons—'How come he gets to do that and I can't?' and so on—guarantees that you'll almost always be dissatisfied because you can find some way that somebody else has more or has it better. That's true for kids, and it's true for grown-ups. Comparisons do not make us happy; they make us unhappy. You'll be a lot happier in life if you're thankful for what you do have, not resentful of what you don't have. Try it and see." *No comparisons* became a rule in our house and, over time, with patient reminders, part of the family culture.

Once we've taught kids that "fair" doesn't mean "same," that making comparisons is not what we do in our family, and once we've pointed out the many ways we do try to be fair to them and everyone else in the family, we should avoid being drawn into endless justifications. You have to decide, of course, when a particular issue does require more back-and-forth. But you also need to tell them that the family will not be a happy place if there is an argument about everything.

Use a Fairness Approach to Settle Conflicts

Sometimes a quick appeal to fairness can work wonders in solving a conflict. "Can you guys solve this problem fairly—or do you need to go to separate rooms?" "Can you settle the argument about the video game, or do you need to put it away?"

Sometimes kids will need our help in figuring out a fair solution. For example, Owen and Richard were good friends. But when they got together, they often couldn't agree on what to play, and ended up frustrated and cross with each other and wasting most of their playtime. Owen's mother suggested that at the start of their time together, they sit down and each make a list of what they'd like to do. Then they'd agree on a fair plan that included one or two things (depending on how much time they had) from each of their lists. When they did this, things went much more smoothly.

When our son Mark was 13, he'd sometimes have four or five friends over after school to play Dungeons and Dragons in the family room. Matthew was just a 3rd grader at the time, and didn't get to be a player, but he hovered around the table, taking an intense interest in the game and reacting to people's moves. He and Mark did a lot of things together, despite their five-year age difference, so he expected a piece of the D-and-D action. But 13-year-olds want to do their own thing without somebody's little brother looking over their shoulder, so Mark's friends asked him if Matthew was going to do this at every game. Mark then asked Matthew to do something else when he had his friends over for Dungeons and Dragons, and that didn't go down well with Matthew.

Before the next D-and-D game, I mediated a fairness meeting between the two of them. In less than fifteen minutes, we had a solution that they both thought was fair:

Matthew can be in the room while the game is going on but has to sit in the big chair at the other end of the family room [close enough for him to still hear the conversation]—and not say *anything*. If he does, he has to leave the room.

Problem solved. Matthew never had to leave the room, but he eventually lost interest and did other things.

With time and practice, kids can learn to use a fairness approach to solving conflicts without our mediation. I suggest having a "talk-it-out space" in the house where your kids can go to sit down and work out a fair solution to a conflict. In some classrooms, the teacher provides a small "peace table," where kids go to solve their disputes; they sit on opposite sides of a table and put both hands, palms down, on the table—which keeps either person from pointing an accusing finger. Other classrooms have a "solutions circle" marked out with red electrical tape on the floor. You can adapt any of these strategies to the home; the important thing is to have a dedicated space for conflict resolution.

In a family meeting, describe the "talk-it-out" approach to solving sibling conflicts and say you'd like to try it out in your family. I suggest printing steps like the following ones on a big sheet of poster board and hanging it in your designated talk-it-out space:

Talk It Out

1. Calm down (take three deep breaths, or count slowly to ten).
2. Take turns saying what you think the problem is.
3. Show understanding by "active listening" (say back what the other person said).
4. Take turns saying what you think is fair.
5. Agree on what you think is a fair solution.

In the beginning, you'll need to coach your kids through these steps, helping them understand and do each one (being sure not to skip showing understanding). They'll get better with practice. Then observe from a distance and see how they do on their own. In elementary schools where, at every grade level, every classroom has a "talk-it-out space," children master these skills of speaking, listening, and finding solutions—often without adult help—that meet both person's needs. That's a huge accomplishment and a human relations asset that will help them throughout their lives.

Teach the Difference Between Fairness and Kindness

Fairness is an aspect of justice (giving people what they have a right to receive). Kindness goes beyond justice; it gives more than fairness requires. Kindness doesn't think, "What's in this for me? How can I get a fair deal?" It thinks, "What can I do to make this person happy? What do they need?"

So while we want to acknowledge and respect our children's strong sense of fairness, we also need to teach them that in a family, as in life, fairness isn't nearly enough. Families run on love. Sometimes in a family you do something because it's only fair, but more often you do it because it's the kind and loving thing to do.

The essence of that love is the willingness to sacrifice for the sake of others. When parents get up in the night to take care of a sick child, they don't think, "What have you done for me lately?" Love doesn't keep score. As children's moral reasoning develops, it will be easier for them to see the difference between fairness and kindness—and to understand why both are needed in all human relationships and most especially in family life.

Still, fairness is fundamental. It's the heart of the Golden Rule. When we foster our children's sense of fairness and help them apply it to concrete situations, we're nurturing an important part of their character development. We're teaching them not only that they should be fair but also *how* to be fair. I think fewer marriages would end in divorce if more people had learned, as children, to solve conflicts fairly.

Teaching fairness in the family will equip our children to deal fairly and effectively with the conflicts they will inevitably encounter as they make their way through their widening social and moral world. And if we do a good job of teaching them fairness, they'll be more receptive to our efforts to teach them kindness.

CHAPTER 7

Discipline

What's in Your Toolbox?

WHEN TEENAGERS ARE ASKED about discipline, they often say they wish their parents and teachers had been stricter and demanded more of them. Many say they don't like it when teachers or parents let them get away with bad behavior. Kids need and want the structure and security that firm, fair, and reasoned discipline gives them; they thrive on it. Unfortunately, in a great many families, discipline is where character formation breaks down.

A character-based approach to parenting says that discipline must teach character. It must develop the character skills and habits, like good judgment, empathy, kindness, and self-control, that underpin respectful and responsible behavior. Discipline must also teach appropriate behavior in the moment. If your kids are fighting, you have to stop the fighting. If they're being disrespectful or disobedient, you have to deal with that. Discipline's first job is to hold kids accountable to the behavioral expectations we've established.

But mere conformity to rules in the presence of an authority figure does not equal good character. We want moral rules to be *on the inside*, part of their conscience. If discipline is going to develop our children's character, it has to impact their attitude—the way they think and feel. It has to lead them to *want* to behave better and to believe that they can.

If that sounds like a lot to aim for, it is. What's hard about aiming high is that it can set us up for disappointment and frustration when our child's behavior is cranky, disrespectful, or self-centered despite our best efforts. The way to avoid getting discouraged is to realize that in any given situation on any given day, we may get just external compliance, not the cooperative inner attitude we're hoping for. But even in those situations, keep working toward the higher goal ("Elizabeth, I'm going to ask you again to please do this without complaining; it makes things much more pleasant for everybody.").

Remember, you're a character coach. Like a good coach, you're trying to bring out the best in your kids and help them develop their full potential. Doing that will require all the things good coaches do, including "demandingness" and tough love. Good coaches bench players when that's what's needed; effective discipline in a family uses consequences in character-developing ways.

Let's look at 15 different tools and strategies that put a character-based approach to discipline into practice.

1. Keep Building an Intentional Family Culture

Getting obedience and cooperation will be easier—not easy, but *easier*—if you have been working on creating a loving family culture based on mutual respect, fairness, cooperation, and kindness through your family mission statement and family meetings. It will be easier if everybody is pitching in on the family work, enjoying shared family activities and traditions, worshipping and praying together if that's part of your family culture, and making space for the emotionally intimate one-on-one time that's vital for knowing your children as individuals and deepening your relationship with each of them.

All of that contributes to family cohesion; it's the "glue" that holds the family together. It's what makes you a family, not just a collection of individuals living under the same roof. It's what makes you a home, not just a hotel where the roomers lead their own separate lives—which is what families can easily drift toward when there aren't the kinds of conversations and shared activity that keep the family culture strong and growing.

Without a strong family culture, discipline will be harder. A family culture gives you "something in the bank" to draw on in a discipline situation, whether it's using your family mission statement as a point of reference, holding kids accountable to what you agreed on in the last family meeting, or drawing on the leverage that comes from maintaining a strong emotional connection with each child. In our own family, bedtime reading with each of the boys was an important ritual that helped keep our bond with each of them strong. In our son Mark's family, gathering every night at 9 p.m. for family prayer and singing "Salve Regina" has been a sustaining ritual. The authority we need when we're holding kids accountable to behavioral standards builds on the love and cohesion we're nurturing the rest of the time.

The power of "connective rituals" has been demonstrated by research on alcoholic families.[1] In some alcoholic families, the children do not grow up to have the classic problems of "adult children of alcoholics." These "healthier" alcoholic families did things like make a big deal of birthdays and holidays, go regularly to church or temple together, have meals together, and read or tell stories at bedtime. Make sure connective rituals are part of your family culture.

2. Make Your Expectations Clear—and Set Them High

If we don't expect much from our children, that's what we'll get. If we expect more, we'll get more. First, we have to be clear and specific about the behaviors we expect:

"Say 'please' when you'd like something and 'thank you' whenever someone does something for you."

"Don't interrupt."

"Look at the person who's talking to you."

"When someone greets you by name, use their name when you greet them back."

"Pick up your toys, and put your dirty clothes in the hamper."

"Cover your nose when you sneeze, and your mouth when you cough."

"Don't leave cups, glasses, dishes, food, or trash around the house—clean up after yourself."

"Turn out the lights when you leave a room."

"Come when you're called—and say 'Coming' so I know you've heard me."

"When you want something that your brother or sister has, *ask nicely* for it, don't grab."

"When someone asks you a question or says something to you, respond."

"Don't call your mother or father from another room and expect them to come to you; go to where they are."

"When you answer the family phone, identify yourself: 'This is Sarah Smith, who would you like to speak to?'"

Literally hundreds of teachings like these communicate to children, "This is what we do," "This is how we live."

What if kids forget some or many of these things, as they will invariably do much of the time? Remind them. Patiently. And then remind them some more. Judith Martin, the humorous but wise "Miss Manners" advice columnist who wrote *Miss Manners' Guide to Rearing Perfect Children*, consoles parents, "There is no quick and easy way to rear a child. It takes eighteen years of constant teaching." She added: "And perhaps another ten of review."[2]

3. Ask a Question or Request a Redo

An alternative to simply repeating yourself is the "ask-don't-tell" approach. Ask a question that gets kids to *think*—a question that makes *them* responsible for remembering and applying the rule they're not following. This can be as simple as "What are you forgetting?" ("To say please." "To clear my dishes." "To respond." "To put down my phone and look up when you're speaking to me.")

Or ask them, "What's the rule about . . . ?" "What's the rule about video games?" ("Ask permission first.") "Calling me from another room?" ("Come to where you are.") "Dirty clothes?" ("Put them in the hamper.")

If your child's behavior has been inappropriate, you can also ask for a redo. Suppose your 10-year-old makes a disrespectful response (say, an impatient "*Okay!*" to a request you make). A redo could be: "John, could you please say that again, more respectfully?" Or suppose your 12-year-old son asks his 7-year-old sister for something in a snappish manner. You might say, "How about a redo on that. . . . What would be a kinder way to ask her?"

It's important to set this up in advance, so your child isn't surprised when you ask for a redo. You want your kids to understand that you're giving them a second chance—which will be better for them, better for you, and better for happiness in the house than your getting upset with them about their first response. Asking for a redo conveys your confidence that they know better.

If a child responds to a request for a redo with a resentful and sarcastic mouthing of "respect," it's time for a sit-down discussion of why that behavior is *totally* unacceptable—and whether a written plan is needed to avoid it in the future. It may be. Many kids have heard their friends speak sarcastically to their parents and may have come to think it's no big deal. But it is. If there's been a pattern of disrespectful responses from a child, I'd take a long walk with them to get across how offensive that is, how you don't talk to them that way, how you don't want anyone in the family speaking to any other family member disrespectfully, and how children owe a special respect to their mothers and fathers. If there's still resistance, it's time to ask them, "What consequences would help to motivate you to speak respectfully?" and then build those into a behavior contract. I'd also use the family meeting to strengthen the norm of mutual respect in the family. A shared commitment to respect should certainly be part of your family mission statement.

We'll get as much respect as we require and as much disrespect as we allow.

4. Be Mindful and Flexible

Mindful parenting means being sensitive to the particular situation and really trying to enter into what your child might be experiencing at the moment that could be causing him or her to act or react in a particular way. Ask yourself, "What's going on that might be affecting my child's behavior? Is she tired? Irritable from too much screen time (and what might I try to do about that)? Angry? Not feeling well? Coming off a hard day? Upset with a friend or sibling?" Mindfulness means not being so rigid about your high expectations that they get in the way of a loving and supportive relationship with your child—and end up keeping you from modeling and teaching the kindness and respect you hope they'll learn and practice.

Mindfulness can influence your timing in responding to problem behavior. In the following story, note the mother's sensitivity to timing in how she handled a lapse in respect on the part of her 20-year-old son:

I called Jim to say I'd be a little late picking him up after work. He could see on his phone that it was me calling. He answered with a curt "*What?*" Not, "Hi, Mom," or "What's up?" I was taken aback by that, but I know his summer job has been very stressful—he's dealing with young kids all day, most of them from troubled homes—and I'm sure he was wiped out on this day and irritable. So I ignored his answering my call with "What?" and just said I was running late but would be there soon.

On the way home, we chatted about other stuff, but after we got home and he was getting something from the fridge, I said, "I know you're really worn to a frazzle by the end of the day, but still, I was surprised by how abruptly you answered my call. Even if you're really tired, I'd still like to hear, "Hi, Mom." He said, "You're right, Mom. That was rude of me. I was tired, but that's no excuse. I apologize."

If Jim didn't offer an apology, his mother could have requested one: "I'd appreciate it if you said, 'I'm sorry.'" One reason Jim did apologize without having to be asked is that his parents had worked hard, over many years, to make respect part of their family culture. He knew that his "What?" when he answered his mother's call was out of line.

5. Be Proactive, Make a Plan

Being mindful about discipline also means being proactive—in other words, planning ahead. It's not human nature to always be thinking, "What problems might I encounter in this upcoming situation—and how can I head them off?" But you'll be able to avoid a lot of behavior problems—or at least keep them from being so bad as they might otherwise be—if you get better at being proactive. For example:

- You are about to get in the car with your kids—to go to school, church, vacation, wherever. In the past, the kids usually start bickering about who's going to sit where. To be proactive, before they get in the car, or before you even leave the house, you could ask: "How can we avoid an argument about who's going to sit where? I'd really appreciate that."
- You're about to grocery shop with your 3-year-old, who in the past gets upset when you won't get the sugary cereals. Before you enter the supermarket, you could say, "Remember, no sugary cereals but you can help choose something from the fresh fruits or the snack aisle. So be thinking about what you'd like."
- You're about to take your 5-year-old to the park. In the past, when it's time to leave, he protests and wants to stay longer. When you insist on leaving, it often ends up in a teary tug-of-war. To be proactive, before going to the park, make a plan:

> "I know you like going to the park, and I like taking you if we don't have trouble when it's time to leave. So when I say, 'It's time to leave,' I'd like you to say, 'Okay, Mom.' I'll bring the timer and give you a ten-minute warning and then a five-minute warning, so you can see how much time is left. Fair enough? But you have to stick to the plan—or I won't be able to take you to the park the next time you ask. Okay, tell me what the plan is."

6. Avoid Power Struggles by Giving Kids a Choice

Especially with young children, when you anticipate a conflict about a rule or request, offering a "choice within limits" can avoid a battle of wills. In our house, we found that toys at the table invariably caused some kind of a problem between our boys. So if my wife or I saw Mark or Matthew bringing one of their Star Wars action figures to the dinner table, we'd say, "You guys know the rule about 'no toys at the table'—would you like me to put Luke Skywalker over here, high up on the refrigerator, or over here on the counter? You pick." That worked; they were satisfied to have Luke looking on.

Other examples of offering choices: "You have to hold my hand when we're crossing the street. Which hand would you like to take?" Or, "Would you like me to carry you or take your hand?"

To a young child starting to go into a tantrum at the table: "Can you calm down and stay with us at the table, or do you want to sit on the stairs until you can calm down and then come back to the table?"

For a child who resists taking a bath: "Tonight is bath night. Would you like to take it right now, or should I set the timer for five minutes?"

By giving your kids a choice, you're acknowledging their wishes and respecting them as individuals; that helps build mutual respect. By setting the limits within which your child gets to make a choice, you're exercising your parental authority and teaching your child to respect that.

7. Engage Your Kids' Upper Brain—and Don't Underestimate Their Brain Power

Being "brain smart" is another important tool in your discipline toolbox. When your child is having a meltdown—or you're having a bit of a meltdown yourself (it happens to all of us!)—the lower brain is in the driver's seat. The lower brain is where desires, impulses, strong emotions like anger and frustration, fight-or-flight reactions, and other knee-jerk responses come from. By contrast, when you're having what feels like a rational exchange with your child, the upper brain, the cerebral cortex, is in the driver's seat. Our upper brain has the job of information processing, two-way communication, weighing alternatives and considering consequences, adapting to new challenges, creative and critical thinking, self-reflection, and doing the right thing for the right reason.

External circumstances—how tired or stressed or hungry we are, whether we've developed self-control strategies that can serve us well under stressful conditions, whether the people around us provide the support that helps us calm down and think clearly—all these factors greatly influence, in adults as well as children, the balance of upper and lower brain activity and how well we cope in the face of any challenge. So in any parenting situation, you want as much as possible to engage your child's upper brain—and avoid scenarios that invite the lower brain to take over. That's why it's often not effective to do a lot of reasoning with your child when they're crying, defiant, or otherwise upset—or when you yourself are really upset. You'll have a better chance of getting through to their upper brain when they—and you—are calm.

Let me offer a cautionary note about how the new brain science is sometimes misapplied. Some "brain-based" parenting advice can lead you to seriously underestimate what children are capable of. You could take away the message "Don't expect too much self-control from your 4-year-old or even your 14-year-old; their brains are still developing!"

A few years ago, a popular book, *The Primal Teen: What the New Discoveries About the Teenage Brain Tell Us About Our Kids*, was, in my judgment, a perfect example of the misapplication of recent brain research. It said that adolescents have strong passions but "may not get good brakes [the prefrontal cortex that inhibits impulses] until they are twenty-five." Young people can't control their passions until they're 25? If that's really true, society faces a bigger character education challenge than anybody thought. Driver's licenses probably shouldn't be offered until people turn 25.

Unfortunately, bad brain science like this gained a good deal of uncritical acceptance. Around this time I was asked to speak at a conference on helping young people make wiser sexual decisions, to avoid the physical and emotional dangers of premature sexual involvement, and develop a "future orientation" that would help them fulfill their hopes and dreams of finding true love. During the Q and A after my talk, a physician in the audience stood up and said, "All these logical arguments for not having sex as a teenager are well and good, but how effective are they with a teenage brain that isn't going to be fully developed for another ten years?"

I responded: "Well, suppose we brought one hundred randomly selected fifteen-year-olds into this room. We could line them up on a continuum—from those who have never had sex or engaged in any high-risk behavior to those who are having sex several times a week and engaging in drugs, drinking, and other high-risk activities. Their brains would all be fifteen years old, all ten years away from being 'fully developed.' Why, then, the great variability in adolescent behaviors that require the regulation of impulses? One answer: Teens differ greatly in their maturity of character and in the educational and family support they receive for exercising self-discipline, including sexual self-discipline."

Statistics comparing teens and adults do not support the stereotype of the impulse-driven teenager. American adults between the ages of 35 and 54 are actually much more likely to engage in risky behaviors than teens.[3] Middle-aged adults are much more likely to have fatal car accidents, binge-drink, commit suicide, or require hospital treatment for overdosing on drugs.[4]

Robert Epstein, former editor in chief of *Psychology Today* and a contributing editor for *Scientific American*, argues that studies of other cultures around the world do *not* present a picture of immature adolescent behavior stemming from an "immature teenage brain." On the contrary, he says:

> [T]eenagers are as competent as adults across a wide range of adult abilities, and other research has shown that they are actually *superior* to adults on tests of memory, intelligence, and perception. The assertion that teenagers have an "immature" brain that necessarily causes turmoil is completely invalidated when we look at anthropological research from around the world. Anthropologists have identified more than 100 contemporary societies in which teenage turmoil is completely absent; most of these societies don't even have terms for adolescence. . . .[L]ong-term anthropological studies . . . show that teenage turmoil begins to appear in societies within a few years after those societies adopt Western schooling practices and are exposed to Western media. Finally, a wealth of data shows that when young people are given meaningful responsibility and meaningful contact with adults, they quickly rise to the challenge, and their "inner adult" appears.[5]

This global anthropological evidence is aligned with what we've already seen in chapter 2 about the effects of cultural expectations on how much self-control and responsibility young children display in family life.

We can also find examples of self-discipline in American children. If we think back to the early days of our republic, it was not uncommon for children to have a host of important responsibilities on the farm. We can also find evidence of impressive self-control on the part of young American children as recently as the 1970s. In a series of experiments popularly known as the "marshmallow study," psychologist Walter Mischel observed how 653 4-year-olds in the Bing School at Stanford University responded to this offer: If they could hold off from eating a marshmallow placed before them—while the experimenter ran an errand—they would get not one but *two* marshmallows. The majority of the 4-year-olds surrendered to temptation well before the experimenter returned. But impressively, about a third of them managed to wait and earned that second marshmallow.

How did the gratification delayers do it? A hidden camera captured their self-control strategies. Some covered their eyes; some put their heads down and tried to go to sleep; some turned their back on the marshmallow; others played games with their hands; still others talked or sang to themselves about the second marshmallow that they would get if they waited just a little bit longer. These 4-year-olds were able to wait—to control their desire for the marshmallow in front of them in order to double their reward—by using resourceful ways of tapping into the regulatory power of their upper brain.

What would the marshmallow-experiment subjects—those who could wait and those who couldn't—be like as teenagers? Mischel found that those who had delayed gratification at 4 were, as teens, better able to make plans and follow through on them; more likely to persevere in the face of difficulty; more self-reliant and dependable; better able to concentrate on a task; and significantly more academically accomplished (including a 200-plus point superiority on their combined SAT scores). Mischel concluded that the capacity to regulate an impulse in the pursuit of a goal is a "meta-ability," determining how well or how poorly we use other psychological capacities.[6]

Mischel also found that when the experimenter taught the marshmallow grabbers strategies for resisting temptation such as looking away, their ability to wait improved. Similarly, as part of their character education initiatives, a number of schools have successfully taught children the STAR system for controlling impulsive behavior and making good choices:

Stop (whenever you have to make a decision).

Think. ("What are my choices in this situation? Do I have to call somebody a name because they called me one?")

Act. (Do what you think is the best choice.)

Review. ("What were the consequences of that choice? Should I make the same choice or a different one in the future?")

With daily coaching and practice, kids who had been highly impulsive prior to STAR training made observable progress toward greater self-control. So even if you're an impulsive marshmallow grabber at age 4, there's still hope for you.

8. Protect Talk Time for Yourselves as Parents

If we set high expectations, explain our reasons, and stay the course, those expectations will come to seem natural to our kids—just "the way it is" in our family. One mother says, "We have a very important rule in our house that once you asked to be excused from the dinner table, there's no hovering around or interrupting after that. It's time for Mom and Dad to talk." A second couple did something similar, starting when their youngest was only 3 years old. They'd send the kids off to play, and then spend 15 minutes over a cup of coffee catching up with each other. The father explains:

When kids forgot the rule and did interrupt, we gently but firmly told them—unless it was something very important—to wait because we were having our coffee. Before long, they left us in peace for a ritual that became a cornerstone of our marriage. When my wife and I would describe this ritual to friends, you would have thought we were from another planet. Leave the parents alone for fifteen minutes? Most children won't leave their parents alone for thirty seconds! Years later, our children told us it gave them a secure feeling to know that we were talking with each other in this way.[7]

Note that both couples who established a post-dinner talk time for Mom and Dad put a high value on this—and created a ritual to protect it. In many American families, parents are often so focused on their kids that they forget about the marriage. These days, when I talk to parents about raising children of character, I begin by urging them to make their relationship their first priority. (I urge single parents to find a buddy parent and talk once a week if possible.) When there are problems in the marriage, there are often problems in the parenting. The stress from marital conflicts often spills over into parent–child relations, and parents who aren't getting along often undermine each other by having different behavioral expectations and inconsistent responses to their kids' misbehavior.

I encourage couples to think of their relationship as a work in progress. My wife and I have been married fifty-one years, and we still joke about "working on the marriage." Part of what keeps a marriage strong and growing is regular—daily, if possible—time to talk and reconnect. Some of that couple talk will naturally be about the kids—sharing things you've noticed in recent days, some good news the other parent might not know about, a scheduling thing that needs to be worked out, how to handle a particular behavioral issue, and so on. We did a lot of that sort of talking when our kids were growing up—usually after they were in bed—and it helped us to keep on top of what was happening and be on the same page in our parenting. Check out William Doherty's *Take Back Your Marriage* for other communication tips and relationship-building rituals.

9. Work *with* Your Kids to Solve a Problem

If you tried to establish an after-dinner parent-talk time in your family, would the kids leave you alone? Suppose they didn't; how could you work *with them* to help them do what you're asking them to do? You could have a quick family meeting and say something like, "Look, you guys know how important it is for your mother and me to have this quiet time to talk—but we keep having to remind you not to interrupt, which makes things unpleasant. Let's think about how we can solve this. What would help you remember not to interrupt during our after-dinner talk time?" Remembering is a cognitive skill; kids need our patient help in developing it.

Putting your heads together to solve a problem or conflict is especially important for avoiding power struggles with strong-willed children. In her book *You Can't Make Me (But I Can Be Persuaded)*, Cynthia Ulrich Tobias tells the following story as an example of how to solve conflicts constructively:

Eleven-year-old Kelsey announced calmly at the Sunday morning breakfast table: "I'm not going to go to church anymore."

Her mother shot back: "What? You most certainly are going, young lady! Your father is the pastor, for heaven's sake!"

Kelsey's father looked at her thoughtfully before speaking. "Kelsey, why don't you want to go to church?"

She shrugged. "I don't know. There's nothing to do. It's boring, and I'm tired of it."

"Sometimes I feel that way too," her father said, to Kelsey's surprise. "We all get a bit tired of the routine sometimes. But the whole point of going to church is to learn more about God and to spend time with others who want to do the same. Tell me, what do you think would motivate you to want to go to church again?"

"I don't know," Kelsey said. Her dad scooted his chair closer to hers. "Kelsey, what about going to church today, and instead of just listening, write notes about what you think might make things more interesting. There are probably other kids who feel like you do, and you may be able to come up with some great ideas for making church better for everyone."

Kelsey was intrigued in spite of herself. "Well," she said, "I think I know some things that would make Sunday more fun."

"Good," her dad said. "I think you'll be a great source of ideas for us."[8]

The strategy here is to avoid an unproductive battle of wills, draw out your child's thoughts and feelings, listen with interest and respect, share your own perspective and expectations as a parent (notice that Kelsey's father still expected her to attend church with the family), reach a mutual understanding, and then work out a solution that takes everyone's viewpoint into account.

Even young children are capable of this kind of collaborative problem solving. Fabiana Santos, a Washington, DC–based journalist and mother of two, shares a story about her 5-year-old daughter, who had recently started kindergarten and was anxious about "keeping up."[9] This anxiety seemed to be spilling over at home in the form of increasingly frequent meltdowns over small things (the doll's arm coming off, bedtime, chores). A child psychologist offered advice that is very much in the spirit of a character-based approach to parenting: he urged her to make her child feel respected by acknowledging what she was feeling and having her participate in solving the problem. He suggested that when a meltdown began, the mother ask, in a calm voice: "Is this a big problem, a medium problem, or a small problem?"

Santos reports: "For my daughter, those moments of sincerely thinking about what is going on have become magical. Every time I ask the question, we find a way to solve the problem, starting from her perception of where to look for the solution." One morning, when her daughter was choosing clothes for school, the pants she wanted to wear were in the wash, and she started to melt down. Santos recounts:

> I asked, "Alice, is this a big, medium, or small problem?"
> She looked at me sheepishly and said quietly, "Small." And
> I reminded her that we already knew that small problems
> are easy to solve. I asked for her suggestions on how we
> could solve that small problem, and she said, "Choosing
> other pants." I added, "And you have more than one pair of
> pants to choose from." She smiled and went to get another
> pair of pants. I congratulated her on having solved the problem herself.

Work with your child to solve whatever problem you're confronting. You might need more than one discussion, but it's worth the effort. This process makes you allies in a common cause: finding a solution.

If, despite your best efforts at cooperative problem solving, you're *still* having ongoing conflicts with your child—if there's a negative pattern where you make a request and your child seems constantly to push back—you may need a longer, deeper conversation. At a time when neither you or your child is upset, try to explain patiently and lovingly the kind of cooperative, let's-work-together relationship you'd like to have. Here's one way to do that: Find someplace comfortable like the sofa, bring a pencil and a sheet of paper, and have something to munch on that helps create a positive, relaxing mood. Then say something like this:

> Look, in all relationships, people have problems. Moms and dads do, parents and kids do. But in any relationship, if people love each other, they can solve their problems by working together. I'd like us to do that. Here's *you* [draw a circle]. Here's *me* [draw another circle, right next to the first one.] And here's our problem *over here* [draw a third, significantly smaller circle that's a little farther removed, with the parent and kid circles side by side, facing the problem circle together].
>
> Our relationship is a lot bigger than this problem, but the problem is causing unhappiness for both of us. I'm confident we can solve it if we put our heads and hearts together. So let's try to figure out why we've been having this trouble and what we can do to make things better, OK? I'd like to start by listening to your feelings about it. [Then active-listen your child's feelings, as you would in a family meeting, and ask her to do the same for yours.]

Note that the circles put the parent and child *on the same side* in an effort to solve the problem that is detracting from the happiness of the relationship. Also note the repeated use of "we" in this explanation and appeal. It's not *parent vs. kid*. It's *"We're in this together. We can make this better."* If you and your child have already experienced the power of "we" through successful collaborative problem solving in family meetings, then "we can do this" will have a credibility that comes directly from your shared experience of doing exactly this sort of thing.

Does this "we" approach reduce your authority as a parent? On the contrary. You actually *gain* authority and influence when you bring your child into a collaborative role. With strong-willed and defiant kids, parents lose authority and influence if they get pulled into a power struggle with their child. In a collaborative approach, you are still very much the parent, still exercising authoritative leadership. You're expecting your child to be part of the solution instead of part of the problem.

A child's will can be strong as iron. We want to get their will and ours on the same side, working together to make things better. Not simple, not easy, not without its own frustrations—but it beats the alternative of power struggles every time.

10. Make Allowances for Your Child's Temperament

Discipline that respects your child as an individual requires taking into account his or her particular temperament. Some kids are temperamentally easy, others more difficult. "Difficult" children typically have more than one challenging temperament trait. The groundbreaking research on the role of temperament in child development and behavior was carried out by doctors Alexander Thomas, Stella Chess, and Herbert Birch of New York University and reported in their landmark book *Temperament and Behavior Disorders in Children*. They followed 133 children, beginning in infancy, and found that a child's temperament was evident by 18 months, if not sooner. The table below describes 10 temperament traits, nine identified by the New York Longitudinal Study and one (self-control) added by Stanley Turecki, a child and family psychiatrist and author of *The Difficult Child*.

Trait	How It Is Manifested in a "Difficult" Child
1. Activity Level	"hyperactive"
2. Self-Control	poor, impulsive
3. Concentration	poor, distractible
4. Intensity	high, loud, forceful
5. Regularity	irregular, erratic
6. Negative Persistence	high, stubborn, won't give up
7. Sensory Threshold	low, physically sensitive
8. Initial Response	withdrawal, holds back
9. Adaptability	poor, rigid
10. Predominant Mood	negative, serious, cranky[10]

A conservative estimate is that 15 percent of children are temperamentally difficult. If you have a child with a difficult temperament, I recommend reading Dr. Turecki's *The Difficult Child*. In the chapter on "managing temperament" he recommends describing to your child—in a specific, supportive, and unemotional way—how one of your child's temperament traits may be manifesting itself in the situation at hand. For example:

Temperament	How to Describe What Is Happening
High activity level	"I know it's very hard for you to sit still."

Impulsivity	"It's hard not to interrupt."
Distractibility	"I know it's hard for you to pay attention."
Negative persistence	"I know it's hard for you to give up when you want something."
Initial withdrawal	"I know it takes you time to make new friends."

Describing the situation in this way, Turecki points out, shows kids that you understand them and will help them better understand their temperament traits and deal with related challenges ("I'm not used to it yet—give me a little more time"). This sympathetic understanding of your child is a very meaningful way of treating him or her with respect for the unique individual he or she is. In the process, you're modeling the kind of respect and patience you want them to have toward others—in the family (perhaps toward a sibling who has some difficult traits) and in any social environment.

Parenting a child with challenging temperament traits can help you, as an adult, become more aware of your own temperament challenges. What at first may seem like a behavioral problem on your child's part may actually be a clash between one of your temperament traits and your child's opposite (or highly similar!) quality. Being aware of when family frictions stem from temperament can help to deal with them more thoughtfully and patiently.

11. Don't Be Afraid to Deliver a Stern Correction When Needed

When our son Mark was one year old, we visited friends whose 1½-year-old daughter, Tiffany, in the course of the weekend, bit

Mark twice on the arm, causing him to cry, and finally pushed him over backward in the kitchen in the presence of her parents and us, causing him to bang his head hard on the floor and again burst into tears. Each time, Tiffany's college-educated parents gave her a mild scolding along the lines of, "That's not nice, Tiffany—look, you made Mark cry." This made no impression whatsoever on Tiffany.

What would cause otherwise intelligent people to fail to discipline their daughter more effectively in a situation like this? Many parents think that "unconditional love" for their child precludes doing anything—such as scolding them sternly or making them take a time-out in a chair—that might upset their child and cause them to feel "unloved." These parents confuse unconditional *love* with unconditional *approval*. Our children do need our unconditional love—we will always be there for them, like the father in the prodigal son parable. But they *don't* need our unconditional approval; on the contrary, when they misbehave in a way that is deliberate, as it was in Tiffany's case, they need our very clear, strong disapproval. Tiffany wasn't getting that.

In a situation like this, appropriate emotion on our part ("No biting!") is needed to arouse appropriate emotion on our child's part. Character education trains the heart as well as the mind; we want a child not just to *know* that something is wrong, but also to *feel* that it is wrong. Most adults and even most kids *know* what's right and wrong, but many often do something they know to be wrong anyway and feel little remorse for having done so. Bland parental responses to hurtful behavior won't produce an active conscience in a child.

Wise parents take their children's transgressions seriously, and that affects how their children will respond when they see someone hurting. One study of early conscience development observed how children between the ages of 1½ and 2½ responded to another toddler who was crying on the playground.[11] Some showed concern and offered comfort or help. Others were simply curious or walked away. Some were irritated by the crying toddler and even scolded him for crying.

The researchers then compared the mothers of these children. The children who were compassionate responders on the playground had mothers who were warm and nurturing. But they did something else as well; in the past, these mothers had reacted strongly when their child had done something that had hurt another child. A 2-year-old girl who responded compassionately to the crying toddler on the playground had once pulled another little girl's hair. When she did that, her mother had responded:

"You *hurt* Amy!" *(pointing out the consequence of her child's behavior)*

"Pulling hair hurts!" *(an instructive generalization about the hurtful behavior)*

"*Never* pull hair!" *(a small moral absolute)*

This mother wasn't screaming at her child or telling her she's a rotten kid. She was providing *moral clarity* and expressing *emotional concern*. Her daughter learned how her hairpulling had hurt the other child—*and* she learned, "Mom gets really upset when I hurt somebody." As a result, this child was subsequently disposed to take it seriously and respond compassionately when she saw another child hurt and crying on the playground.

By contrast, the children who didn't respond compassionately when they saw the crying toddler had mothers who, in the past, had reacted more casually when their child had done something hurtful: "Now, that's not nice, don't do that." The mother's response was bloodless (like that of Tiffany's parents), and made little impression on her child. The takeaway for us as parents: provide clear correction—pointing out how our child's actions have affected another—and do so with appropriate feeling.

Very similar findings come from a study of teenagers.[12] Researchers divided teens into two groups, based on the maturity of their answers to questions such as, "Why is it wrong to lie, cheat, or steal?" "Why is it wrong to pick on another kid?" Teens who scored relatively high on this test of their moral reasoning understood that these actions are wrong because they betray trust, hurt other people, and so on. Less-mature teens focused on avoiding getting into trouble as the main reason for not doing these things. The study then asked both groups of teens how their parents would respond to various hypothetical situations, such as:

- They find out that you and your friends broke into a vending machine.
- They hear that you participated in making fun of a neighborhood child.

Those teens who were more mature in their moral reasoning were much more likely than teens whose moral reasoning focused on avoiding punishment to say that their parents would:

- express disappointment in them
- show indignation
- point out the unfairness of their actions
- appeal to their sense of responsibility
- demand apologies and reparation

In the eyes of the morally mature teenagers, their parents would react to their wrongdoing in a way that included both moral explanation and moral passion. This is the same combination of parenting practices—clear teaching and deep feeling—that produced compassionate behavior in the playground study of toddlers.

The message such parents convey: Morality matters. Hurting people is a big deal.

Our children will remember how we responded to the times when they were less than their best selves. Catherine, now 29, says:

> My dad was a strict but tender father. In tenth grade, I had adopted the ungracious habit of referring to certain classmates as "losers." My father took me aside and pointed out that it wasn't right to dismiss anyone like that—as if they weren't persons, as if they didn't have a soul. That habit ended that day.

12. Involve Kids in Setting Fair Consequences

Sometimes a disciplinary consequence is needed to get kids to take a parental rule or directive seriously and to motivate them to do better the next time. But in imposing consequences, many parents come down too hard in a moment of anger ("You're grounded for a week!"), only later to feel like a "meanie"—especially when kids play the suffering victim—and end up going back on what they said and reducing the consequence, which undercuts their authority.

A better approach is to ask a child, "What do *you* think is a fair consequence for what you did?" That makes them their own judge and jury. Most of the time, kids won't let themselves off easily. And if *they* come up with a consequence, they're much more likely to see it as a fair result of their misbehavior than something we have unfairly imposed. As an 8-year-old boy put it, "A punishment is something an adult does to you. A consequence is something you do to yourself."

An example: Sam got a ten-speed bike when he graduated from

6th grade. He agreed to lock it whenever he left it anywhere; his father had shown him articles in the paper about bikes being stolen in their community. But on his first trip to the playground, in his hurry to warm up the pitcher for a ball game, Sam left the bike leaning against the bleachers, unlocked. His father saw this when he arrived at the game and pointed it out to Sam, who apologized and promised to do better the next time. But the next time, the same thing happened.

This time his father said, "Look, Sam, we had an agreement. This is the second time you haven't kept it. I'm sure you feel bad about that, and so do I. You're lucky it hasn't been stolen. I think we need a consequence that will help you take seriously your promise to lock your bike. I'd like you to come up with a consequence you think will motivate you to do that. What do you think is a fair consequence?"

"That I should lose my bike for three days," Sam said. "Fair enough," his father said. That was hard for Sam, but he didn't complain about it—he had proposed it. If the father had imposed a similar consequence ("Okay, that's it—you're losing your bike for the rest of the week"), what would the outcome have been? Sam would have been more likely to feel sorry for himself than for not keeping his promise. When kids come up with a consequence they think is fair, they are disciplining themselves. That in itself is an important step toward taking responsibility for their actions.

13. Require Restitution

Another kind of consequence with character-building potential is restitution. Negative behavior usually creates some kind of damage—to things, feelings, relationships, or the peace and harmony of the group. If we've created damage of any kind, we have an obligation to try to fix it.

Restitution is greatly underused by both families and schools. One day, when our younger son, Matthew, was in 1st grade, he got into an argument on the playground with Eddy (not his real name) that ended with Eddy's stomping on Matthew's Spider-Man lunch box. It looked like a pancake when he brought it home.

"What happened after Eddy stomped on it?" we asked.

"I told the teacher," Matthew said.

"What did she do?" we asked.

"She made Eddy say he was sorry."

"That's all?"

"Well, we had a class meeting. The class decided that in the future, nobody should take their lunch box out on the playground because something could happen to it."

Restitution would have required Eddy to replace the lunch box (it was beyond repair). Apologizing is only the *first* thing our kids should do when they've done something wrong. The second thing is to ask, "What can I do to make up for it?" Restitution is an apology of action.

If our kids forget to ask, "What can I do to make up for it?," we can remind them: "Don't forget to ask, 'What can I do to make up for it?'" After that, we can suggest an appropriate restitution. For example:

- You can make up for not being nice to your brother by reading him a story while I'm getting the dinner ready.
- I need some help in the yard today. You can make up for being in such a sour mood by doing the yard work without complaining.
- Please write me a sincere letter saying why you're sorry and how you're going to remember not to do this in the future.

Once our kids have had some practice making restitution, we can shift more of the responsibility to them by asking, "What do *you* think you can do to make up for it?" Whenever possible, restitution should include teaching empathy. For example: "You hurt your sister's feelings—what can you do to make her feel better?"

One family institutionalized restitution with a jobs jar. It contained strips of colored paper, each of which described a job that needed doing in the house or yard. When you broke a family rule or did something else to disturb the family peace, the family policy was that you were to make amends by pulling three strips from the jar, choosing one to do, and then putting the other two back in the jar.

A mother of 4- and 8-year-old sons recently asked me, "My two boys are at each other *constantly*. Should I try to adjudicate and figure out who was at fault?" I don't recommend trying to determine who bears what degree of responsibility for the conflict; that often just intensifies the argument. Restitution in this case could take the form of asking the boys to go to your dedicated space for solving sibling conflicts—and staying there until they have a solution to report to you. Have a family policy requiring them to do that as soon as a conflict starts rather than after it escalates (this is a good topic for a family meeting). Have them practice doing so under your supervision in order to get it in their wiring.

14. Affirm Positive Behavior

An important part of discipline is recognizing and affirming kids when they do what's right. But how should we do that? Some "incentives" for good behavior can backfire and inadvertently undermine the development of good character. Here are my recommendations for recognition and affirmation practices that support rather than subvert character development.

Teach kids to do the right thing for the right reason.

Do a simple exercise with your children. On a sheet of paper, write the following:

Reasons for Doing the Right Thing

1. You'll get punished if you don't.
2. You'll get rewarded if you do.
3. It's the right thing to do.

Then ask them: "Which of these three options is the most important reason for doing the right thing? Why?" We want our children to understand that reason number three is the most important: they should do the right thing because it's the right thing to do.

Two character quotations can be used to teach that point:

Character is what you do when nobody's looking.

Character is what you do when other people are looking.

The first quote is true because if you have good character, you won't lie, cheat, steal, and so on—even if you can get away with it. The second is true because if you have good character, you'll do the right thing even if it isn't "cool" in the eyes of your peers. You'll stand up for your beliefs, befriend an unpopular kid, decline to take part in drinking games at a party, turn away from pornography, and so on, regardless of what other people think of you for doing so.

Do what's right—in private and public—because it's the right thing to do. That's the big idea we want to get across.

Don't use extrinsic rewards to motivate doing what's right.

Many parents and many schools, in keeping with the behaviorist psychology of B. F. Skinner, make regular use of extrinsic rewards—money, candy, toys, screen time, special privileges, and the like—to motivate children to follow rules, do ordinary household chores, and so on. But, in general, you should avoid giving kids external rewards for appropriate behavior—except when they are temporarily needed to "jump-start" behavioral improvement with very difficult or highly antisocial children (see Turecki's *The Difficult Child*). Studies show that these external rewards may produce a temporary increase in the desired behavior, *but they weaken intrinsic motivation—the motivation to do the right thing when there is no reward.* Children given material rewards for doing kind acts are *less* likely to continue doing kind acts when the rewards stop.[13] A 2008 study in *Developmental Psychology* found that 20-month-old toddlers who were given a reward for helping an adult were *less likely to help again* than toddlers who had not received a reward.[14]

We want kids to know that the reward for doing good occurs naturally through the good feeling that comes from helping. Even just observing someone do a kind act can create a warm, uplifting feeling.[15] Besides the good feeling that comes directly from helping others, there's the good feeling that comes when someone thanks us or otherwise appreciates our efforts. From a character standpoint, it's a good and natural thing when family members thank each other for helpful actions. It strengthens relationships, expresses gratitude for the good that others do, and helps to build a family culture based on kindness and helpfulness.

15. Guide the Development of Their Moral Reasoning

Because discipline's ultimate goal is character development, your aim should be to help your kids learn to reason morally—to be able to see the right course of action even when circumstances might at first cloud their judgment.

One night when I was putting our younger son, Matthew, to bed, he shared something he was very troubled about. Jack (not his real name), a boy in his 6th-grade class, had asked him to draw a picture for him (Matthew was a good artist) that Jack would then submit to the art teacher as his own. Matthew said okay, he would do it. He was now very worried that he would not have the time to get it done—and, to my surprise, apparently *not* worried about whether it was right in the first place to participate in this deception.

I asked him, "Do you think it's right for Jack to submit a drawing to the teacher that's not really his—and for you to help him do that?"

"Well, no, not really," Matthew said.

To help him imagine how this planned deception might play out, I continued: "Would the teacher believe it was Jack's drawing if he hadn't ever done artwork like that before? And what would Jack say if she asked him if it was really his work? What would *you* say to the teacher if Jack confessed that it wasn't his work, and then she wanted your explanation of why you did this?"

"But I *told* him I would do it—I'm committed!" Matthew protested with great distress.

"I can understand the pressure you're feeling about that," I said. "But suppose somebody asked you to give them money to buy food for their family, and you said you'd do that, and then you found out they intended to use it to buy illegal drugs—would you feel you had to honor your commitment to give them the money?"

"Well, no," he said. "But what am I going to tell Jack when I see him in the morning?"

"Why don't you call him right now?" I suggested.

He jumped out of bed and dashed to the phone. When he came back, he said, "Whew, that's a load off my mind! Now I'll be able to go to sleep!"

What struck me about this whole incident is that Matthew had been coming home from religious education classes complaining that the moral dilemmas they were discussing there were "so obvious, so simple." And yet he wasn't thinking at all clearly about the real moral problem in the Jack-and-the-drawing dilemma—dishonesty on Jack's part, dishonesty on his, and how both acts of dishonesty would violate the trust of their teacher in a way that would prove painful for all concerned.

Why wasn't that obvious to him? What made this real-life dilemma harder to think clearly about than the hypothetical ones in religious ed? For one thing, he obviously didn't want to refuse a friend's request. Then, having said yes to that, he didn't want to go back on what he had said and face his friend's unhappiness. That peer pressure—in this case from just one peer!—was powerful and kept him from using the moral reasoning capabilities that he had been bringing to bear on hypothetical dilemmas in religious education class.

I was glad I was able to help Matthew solve this moral problem—and I came away with a deeper appreciation of how emotions and friendship can keep kids from using their best moral reasoning. I also had a renewed conviction that as parents, we need to try to stay in the loop of the real-life social and moral dilemmas our kids may be wrestling with. They need our guidance in order to come out on the right side of those problems and to develop more mature moral reasoning that they will be able to call on in future situations when we might not be there to help them.

~

So those are some character-based tools and strategies to consider for your discipline toolbox: (1) keep building an intentional family culture; (2) make your expectations clear and set them high; (3) ask your child what rule applies to the situation at hand, or request a redo when behavior is inappropriate; (4) be mindful—and flexible; (5) be proactive, make a plan; (6) avoid power struggles by giving kids a choice; (7) engage kids' upper brain—and don't underestimate their brainpower; (8) protect talk time for yourselves as parents; (9) work *with* kids to solve problems; (10) make allowances for your child's temperament; (11) don't be afraid to give a stern correction when needed; (12) involve kids in setting fair consequences; (13) require restitution; (14) affirm positive behavior; and (15) guide the development of their moral reasoning.

Try a few of these tools at a time, be glad for incremental progress, be patient with your child and yourself, and don't let discouragement keep you from staying the course. Keep your eye on the goal: becoming a better character coach and doing all you can to help your child on the road to character.

CHAPTER 8

Family Meetings

Working Together to Create a Happier Family

IN CHAPTER 4, I described family meetings as one of the most important things you can do to enable your kids to share responsibility for creating a happy family. Here I'd like to spell out some of the steps that will help you have harmonious and productive family meetings. I'll give you several examples of actual family meetings that show what they can accomplish and will also point out some things *not* to do. And I'll share a story that shows the potential of these family discussions to go beyond nuts-and-bolts problem-solving to draw out your kids' thinking about a range of issues and give you a chance to communicate a value or perspective you may not have adequately addressed before.

The family meeting, I believe, is one of your most important tools for building a positive family culture on a continuing basis. It draws on the positive power of the group, something that's often greatly underused.

As Americans, we tend to be influenced by the emphasis our culture puts on the individual. That can affect, consciously or unconsciously, how we approach parenting. We may think of character development in terms of the individual child, and our parenting mainly or even exclusively in terms of our separate interactions with our individual children. Those interactions are certainly crucial for bonding, correcting, and capitalizing on "teachable moments."

But if those individual interactions are our only focus, if we don't also bring to bear the positive influence of the family *as a group*, then we're failing to use a resource that's right under our nose. The norms of a group—how group members expect others in the group to behave—are a significant influence on each individual member's behavior. To maximize our influence as parents, we need to tap into the collective power of the family: to define shared values, set expectations that hold all family members accountable to those values, and foster a shared sense of family identity—of "who we are." Says a mother who stressed honesty as a core value: "We have a saying in our family: Liebermans don't lie." A strong sense of family identity is a sign of a strong family culture.

When we sit down together as a family unit—all too rare given our packed schedules and screen-dominated lives—we can be fully present. Of course, that should also happen at family meals as we share our day, and at other times when we participate in an important family tradition. But the family meeting is special: It's the time when you are the most explicit about the kind of family you want to be. It's where you can regroup and shore up each other. If it's been a really rough week, you can start by acknowledging that—"I'm glad this week is over!"—and then talk about how you can make the next week a better one.

Whatever challenges you're facing, if the family meeting is part of your home culture, you won't be facing them alone. For parents exhausted by the combined pressures of work and family, a process that functions as a support system and problem-solving vehicle can make all the difference in keeping the morale up and staying on track with your goals and core values.

Once you've had experience with family meetings, I think you'll find it's a vehicle you can turn to any time needs arise. For example, a five- to ten-minute "mini-meeting" can be used to focus on what's right in front of you: "How can we get everybody off to school this morning without anybody getting upset?" "How can we have a happy bedtime tonight?" "How can we get the Saturday chores done by noon so we all have the afternoon free for other things?"

In our very first family meeting, our older son, Mark, was 7 and our second, Matthew, was only 2. We sat on the living room floor. Matthew played with a puzzle. Judith, Mark, and I each had a 3 x 5-inch index card with two sentence-starters that we thought would be good ones for our first family meeting: "One thing I like about our family is . . ." and "I would be happier in our family if . . ."

I can no longer find those cards, but I remember that Mark wrote, in response to the first sentence starter: ". . . that everybody in our family loves each other." That was nice to hear. My wife wrote that she would be happier "if Tom would spend more time with the boys." I completely understood her feeling about that; despite my best intentions, unfinished work from the week was creeping more and more into the weekends and creating a background tension that never really went away. We spent part of the rest of the meeting talking about how I could protect more time to play with the kids, and that did improve.

On my index card, I wrote that I'd be happier if we could get Mark off to school—he walked—without a problem getting him up. He proposed the solution: "When you wake me up, remind me of something that's going to happen that day that I'm really looking forward to—like one of my favorite TV shows—and that will help me be in a better mood about getting up." So, we made a list of something for every day that we'd remind him of, and that really did help.

10 Tips for a Good Family Meeting

In teaching parents to do family meetings, I've encouraged them to start with a half-hour meeting once a week (say, on a Sunday night) and to stick to that weekly commitment for a while in order to get better at the process and to experience its benefits for building a family culture. As time goes on, you might do them less often—or *more* often in an especially challenging week when it seems like things are falling apart. Here are 10 tips that will help you have a good family meeting:

1. Choose a practical problem, such as kids being unkind to one another, morning hassles, bedtime battles, TV, phones, or iPad/computer policy, making meals more pleasant, or chores— or perhaps a problem that was a source of tension and trouble during the previous week.

2. In the days before your first family meeting, lay the groundwork that will help it be a success. Talk individually with each family member: How do they feel about the problem? Explain that the family meeting will give them a chance to express their feelings and that the goal is for everyone to understand each other's feelings—and then find a solution that's *fair to everyone*. Set an agreed-upon time to meet, and if the scheduled meeting time arrives and the family atmosphere isn't good, find another agreed-upon time.

3. Have popcorn or some such snack to help make the meeting something to look forward to. We used to start with a prayer: "Dear Lord, help us to love each other and to show our love by working together to make the next week a good one." To create a flow of positive feelings, do a quick round of "appreciation time": "What's something that someone in the family did for you lately that you appreciated?" (You can say more than one thing.)

4. As parents you can propose the rules for discussion, but I recommend also asking for kids' input: "What rules will help us have good talking and good listening?" Make a list and post it. Helpful ones to include:

- One person speaks at a time.
- Look at and listen to the person who's talking.
- No interrupting, put-downs, or blaming.
- Say things in a nice way. (For example, instead of saying, "Jordan is always taking my stuff without asking!," say nicely, "I would appreciate it if Jordan would ask me if it's okay to use or borrow something.")

5. Emphasize that the purpose of a family meeting is *cooperative problem-solving*, not blaming. Ask for everybody's commitment to that goal: "Let's have a *positive* discussion where everybody helps to solve the problem, okay?"

6. Go around the table, giving everyone a chance to share their thoughts and feelings about the problem at hand. After each person speaks, summarize what that person said, using his or her own words. ("Okay, so you feel that . . .")

   Paraphrasing might seem a little unnatural at first if you're not used to it, so explain why you're doing this:

   "I want to make sure everyone feels heard and understood. This is called 'active listening.' If you do it sincerely, it's an act of respect and love. It can be very helpful, even essential, in achieving mutual understanding and solving conflicts."

7. Go around a second time, asking everyone for suggested solutions.

8. Discuss the proposed solutions and combine them into an agreed-upon plan.

9. Sign and post your family agreement—including when you'll meet again to discuss how it's working and what changes, if any, are needed to make it work better.

10. Be sure to hold a follow-up meeting, because that's what makes everybody accountable to the agreement.

After a few meetings, have everybody write something in response to: "Something I like about our family meetings is . . ." and "One improvement I would make is . . ." Make it clear that the family meeting belongs to everyone in the family—to shape in whatever ways help to meet family needs. And don't worry if kids don't love family meetings; that's okay. We had been doing family meetings for a couple of years when Mark, then 10, said, "The family meeting is like taking a shower. I never think I'm going to like it before I get into it, but after I do, it's really fine."

A Productive Family Meeting

Let me share a mother's account of her first family meeting—with her two children, James (7) and Elizabeth (5). (Dad got involved later on.) Her description nicely illustrates the three big parts of the family meeting process: (1) achieving mutual understanding; (2) coming up with a solution everybody feels is fair; and (3) following through—by having at least one follow-up discussion (more might be needed): "How is our plan working? What's been better? Any improvements we need to make?"

Here's the problem this mom wanted to tackle: "James and Elizabeth are constantly fighting. I end up yelling at them, and that upsets the whole house." See the following box for the mother's step-by-step account; notice how important the listening is for creating the mutual understanding needed for finding a fair solution; and note how each step throughout the process builds on the one before.

Achieve Mutual Understanding

Step 1: State the goal of fairness.

Mother: James and Elizabeth, we're having a problem with you two getting along. I'd like to talk with you about it and see if we can come up with a fair solution.

Step 2: State the goal of understanding.

Mother: First, I want you to understand how I feel about this situation, and then I want to find out how you each feel.

Step 3: State your feelings as a parent.

Mother: Kids, I get so irritated when I see the two of you fighting. Then I start to yell at you, and everyone becomes upset. I'd like to see the two of you try harder to get along.

Step 4: Ask your kids to say how they feel about the problem.

Mother: I've told you how I feel. Tell me your feelings.

James: Elizabeth always wants to do everything I do. She wants to sit in the same seat that I do, and she wants to play with the same toys. Sometimes she hits me.

Elizabeth: James punches me. He makes me cry. He won't play with me. And I don't like it when you yell, Mommy.

Step 5: "Active listen" (paraphrase) your kids' feelings.

Mother: James, you feel Elizabeth always wants to sit with you and play with you. Also, you don't like it when she hits you. Elizabeth, you say that James makes you cry when he hits you and won't play with you. And you don't like it when I yell.

Step 6: Ask your kids to active listen to your feelings.

Mother: Can you remember what *I* said about the situation?

James: You want us to try not to fight because it upsets everybody.

Mother: That's right, James. Elizabeth?

Elizabeth: What James said, Mommy.

For most parents, just getting to mutual understanding is a major achievement. The mom and the kids have each shared their feelings about the problem and, even more important, have *shown*, through active listening, that they understand each other's feelings. This mutual understanding is *essential* if you're going to find a solution that all agree is fair. Mom, James, and Elizabeth were now ready to try to solve their problem fairly.

Solve the Problem Fairly

Step 7: Brainstorm fair solutions.

Mother: How can we make this situation better? Let's make a list of things we can do that are fair to everyone.

[They then came up with these possible solutions:]

- Don't hit.
- James should try to teach Elizabeth some of his games.
- Mommy shouldn't yell.
- Elizabeth should try to find things to do by herself sometimes.
- Everyone should say and do nice things.

Step 8: Make a fair plan and sign it.

The mother says, "We agreed on the following plan:

- No hitting or yelling by anyone—Mommy, James, or Elizabeth.
- James should play with Elizabeth at least once a day.
- Elizabeth should try to play by herself sometimes.
- Everyone should try to say and do nice things.

"We all signed our agreement."

Step 9: Plan a follow-up meeting.

"We posted our solutions on the fridge. Next to that was a list for nice things said and done during the next two days. James agreed to record Elizabeth's additions. We agreed to tell Dad about our plan and meet again in two days to see how we were doing."

Follow Through

Step 10: Hold a follow-up meeting.

The mother said, "We read the list of nice things people had said and done. We decided that everyone had indeed tried to be kinder."

Mother: James, I'm so pleased that you've included Elizabeth in your playing. I've had to speak to you only twice in two days. And, Elizabeth, you are certainly trying to be nicer to everyone.

James: I'm glad you're not yelling, Mommy. And Elizabeth hasn't hit me.

Elizabeth: James played with me, and he let me sit in the beanbag with him.

The mother concluded: "Our home is happier now. We keep adding to the list of nice things we say and do for each other. Dad has also gotten involved. We'll use this fairness approach to discuss other kid problems and even issues between my husband and me."

My advice on the follow-up meeting: It can be short, as it was in this example. Sooner is better than later if you want to assess and affirm progress on a problem that's causing continual family stress, as the constant fighting between James and Elizabeth was. In this example, the mother's follow-up was just two days later. With problems not so pressing, follow-up can happen as part of your next weekly family meeting.

A Family Meeting That Didn't Go So Well

Let me describe a family meeting that didn't go well so you can see mistakes to avoid. This family meeting ran into trouble because it didn't have enough structure. The family jumped into debating things about which family members had strong feelings—and did so in a way that only made things worse. The mother describes the tension in the air before the family meeting started:

> Our 15-year-old daughter, Carolyn, had just had another altercation with her 12-year-old brother, Gary. Gary was calling me unfair for my handling of the situation. Dad had just come home from work and was upset to hear Carolyn and Gary going at it again.

Not only was this the wrong kind of atmosphere for attempting a first family meeting, but the parents hadn't done anything to lay the groundwork. They hadn't talked to Carolyn and Gary individually ahead of time to explain the purpose of a family meeting—not blaming anyone, but working together to solve a problem—and to get them on board with that positive goal. They began the meeting without an absolutely essential step: establishing agreed-upon rules for respectful talking and listening. And they began without doing anything to create good feelings, such as "appreciation time": "What's something someone in the family did for you recently that you appreciated?" (If you think your kids will roll their eyes if you propose that, you could say, "This may seem sappy at first, but let's give it a try, okay?," or together you could come up with another appreciation/affirmation ritual that fits your family. In our family, we really enjoyed doing the round of appreciations.)

The mother opened the meeting by asking a very general question, "How can we try to make things a little happier around here?" That unfocused question didn't get family members working together to solve a concrete family problem but instead opened the door to complaints and accusations.

> *Gary* (12): I'd be happier if everybody around here would try to be a little bit nicer.
>
> *Carolyn* (15): I'm always getting dumped on! I'd be happier if Mom didn't *baby* Gary and didn't yell at *me* about school stuff and my friends. When you don't trust me, that gets me mad. I also don't like it when you complain about my clothes and room.
>
> *Mom:* Well, *I'd* be happier if I didn't have to be a nagging mother.
>
> *Dad* (to Carolyn): I think it's only reasonable for us to expect you to care about how your room looks.
>
> *Carolyn:* Every kid gets their room dirty!
>
> *Dad: I'd* be happier in this family if there was a more positive atmosphere.

The mother says, "We ended the meeting in a funk, with no progress on anything."

Before trying another family meeting, this mom and/or dad should have individual conversations with Carolyn and Gary to ask them to agree to contribute in a positive way at the next meeting, in order to help solve an identified family problem. They should also propose a problem that is truly a *family* issue, not just a problem between Carolyn and her parents, as the conflict about her room apparently was.

Conflicts involving only one child should be addressed in a separate problem-solving conversation with just that child. The messy room problem would have been appropriate for a family meeting only if that problem had involved *both* Carolyn and her brother and the goal was to establish an agreed-upon *family policy* regarding reasonable expectations regarding their rooms.

Getting Kids to Solve Their Conflicts Without Your Help

I recently spoke with a father who told me that he and his wife have been doing family meetings for just over a year. They have four kids: a 15-year-old boy, a 14-year-old girl, a 13-year-old boy, and a 10-year-old girl. He said:

> After the kids learned in our family meetings how to solve conflicts by talking things out, they began doing this on their own with other conflicts. For us, this was a surprise—and one of the big benefits of doing family meetings.

Other families have had similar experiences. A mother says:

> In our first family meeting, my 13-year-old daughter and her 11-year-old brother solved a long-standing conflict about what should happen when *either* has a friend over and wants to be left alone. They agreed they must communicate this in a *nice* way, and the other must say okay and leave. Several days later, I heard them working out an agreed-upon solution to an entirely different conflict they often have. I was delighted.

Of course, not all kids will, on their own, transfer the conflict-resolution skills learned in family meetings to other situations. And those kids who do make this transfer, won't necessarily do it consistently. Most will need some reminding and some coaching. In chapter 6, on fairness, I explained a five-step conflict-resolution process you can teach your kids so they learn to solve problems on their own without turning to you as a referee. I encourage you to make that an important family goal.

Use the Family Meeting to Address a Range of Issues

Don't feel that you need to limit family meetings to just talking about last week's family problems and how to avoid them next week. Discuss whatever family members are interested in. Talk about what's in the news or what's going on at school. Let kids bring things up. Let discussion go where it wants to go as long as people are talking in a mutually respectful way. Have a family meeting jar with slips of paper on which anyone can write whatever they'd like to talk about at the next family meeting. That's another way to give kids more voice and ownership.

As with good dinner conversation, things may come up and come out that you'll be glad you got a chance to discuss. Listen again to the father of 10-, 13-, 14-, and 15-year-olds:

In one family meeting, we got to talking about school. Our 13-year-old son, Frank, said his teachers were giving way too much homework, in his opinion. He said he didn't really see why *any* homework was needed—your time after school should be your own, to do with as you want. "I want a life!" he said.

I was taken aback by that and said, "Don't you think school is part of life?"

"Well, yeah," he said, "but it shouldn't take so much time that you can't do what you really enjoy doing."

"Like what?" his mother asked.

"Well, like gaming. My friends and I really enjoy that."

"Okay," I said. "I understand that." Actually, his mother and I had been concerned about how much time he was spending gaming. We think his grades this year don't reflect what he's capable of.

I continued:

"I'd like to come back to what you said about school and life. What about your *future* life and what you might want to do for work or career? Have you thought about that? How might what you do in school now affect that?"

The father commented to me: "What was most significant to us was that Frank hadn't thought about school as a preparation for the next stage of his life—and how not doing well in school now could have very real consequences for that. We brought the other kids into the discussion—what did they think about the connection between school and life?" The father went on to tell me that, in fact, education had always been a very high value for him and his wife. "But our son's comments made us realize we hadn't communicated that as well as we needed to."

A really valuable thing about this family meeting was that it gave us a chance to say to *all* of the kids just how important we think education is. How it's worth the sacrifices involved in studying now and doing your best in order to reap the rewards later. The family meeting can be an effective way to teach an important concept or value like this—everyone is part of the same conversation at the same time. We might not have had this conversation about education and life with all four of the children—at least not in this way—had it not been for the opening this family meeting gave us.

Studies have found that over time, family meetings make for kinder, more respectful, more cooperative kids—and happier, less stressful households.[1] But it turns out there are other positives too. These discussions give you a vehicle for important conversations that can impact your children's value system and future life at the same time that they shape and enrich your family culture. I hope you'll make them part of yours.

CHAPTER 9

Getting Control of Screens

ARGUABLY THE MOST PERVASIVE cultural challenge we face as we try to cultivate kindness in our families is the omnipresence of screens. Let's step back and look at how screens—smartphones, computers, TVs, video games, Xboxes, PlayStations, iPads, iPods, etc.—have lulled us into profoundly altered ways of living and relating to each other and consider what we can do to mitigate their impact.

Let me make it clear that I depend on and benefit from communication technologies nearly every day of my life. Email keeps me swapping messages and photos with our grandchildren. It also keeps me in touch with colleagues around the world. I'm able to collaborate on international projects in ways once impossible. The Web puts a vast fund of knowledge at my fingertips so that research that once took days can now be done in hours or even minutes. I never cease to be astonished by how many useful and entertaining videos are available on YouTube on every conceivable thing you might be interested in (I finally learned, in my seventh decade, how to set a mousetrap by watching a YouTube video).

But all of these blessings have come at a cost. A visitor from another planet would be struck by the universal and apparently irresistible power of screens to attract and mesmerize humans of all ages. Recently, my wife and I traveled to Ontario to hear a talk on parenting and character by my Australian friend Andrew Mullins. He opened with a brief video clip intended to depict the digital world in which we must now raise our children. In the clip, an adorable and alert baby, about 9 months old and still crawling, is on all fours on a carpeted floor, looking at his mother about ten feet away. She is holding a very cute stuffed animal, making it bounce and dance merrily, and saying "Come on, come on!" as she tries in every way possible to entice the baby to crawl to her and get the stuffed animal. No luck. The baby stares with mild interest, and doesn't move an inch.

Then the mother puts away the stuffed animal and replaces it with a smartphone, saying nothing. The baby's eyes light up; he springs forward and scurries over to get it as fast as his little legs can crawl. Although the audience watching this video had probably already witnessed smartphones' magnetic attraction for young children, they gasped.

Children's use of electronic media, at ever younger ages, increases every year. In 1970, kids began to regularly watch TV at 4 years old. Today, they begin interacting with digital media at 4 *months* old, according to the latest report of the American Academy of Pediatrics.[1] Common Sense Media, in its first national survey of children's use of mobile devices, found that in 2011 only one out of ten children under 2 had used a digital device. Just two years later, that figure had jumped to four out of ten.[2] By 2015, *most* 2-year-olds were using mobile devices on a *daily* basis.[3]

Beyond that, four out of five families now own a home device for video games. The *average* age for first use of a video console game has dropped to 3 years, 11 months. Millions of children start sooner. Many develop an addiction-like involvement with video games.

What about older kids? Common Sense Media recently reported on media use by tweens and teens[4] (not counting school use or homework):

- Tweens (8- to 12-year-olds) now spend six hours a day engaged with all forms of media (including listening to music and reading on a device). Most of that (four and a half hours) is screen time.

- Teens (13- to 18-year-olds) now spend nearly nine hours a day interacting with media. Most of that (six hours and forty-five minutes) is screen time. That's forty-seven hours of screen time a week—more than a standard full-time job.

Teens send, on average, one hundred texts a day.[5] Half of American teens describe themselves as "addicted" to their phones, and 60 percent of parents say their teens are addicted to their phones.[6] Among social networking sites, Facebook remains the most popular, but the majority of teens today maintain a "social media portfolio" of multiple sites that include Instagram (52 percent), Snapchat (41 percent), Twitter (33 percent), Google+ (33 percent), Vine (24 percent), and Tumblr (14 percent).[7]

Six out of ten American children who are 8 or under watch television every day. Among kids 8 to 18, nearly three-quarters watch TV for an average of two and a half hours a day. An estimated one-third of children ages 2 to 7 have their own TVs. So do half of all tweens and 60 percent of teenagers.[8]

How We Influence Our Kids' Use of Screens

What part do parents play in these trends? In November 2016, the American College of Pediatricians published a comprehensive research review entitled "The Impact of Media Use and Screen Time on Children, Adolescents, and Families."[9] Some of its findings:

- Most children and teens live in homes where there are no parental rules about screen time. In one study, more than 70 percent of 8- to 18-year-olds said they had no household rules regarding television. Two-thirds said TV was left on during meals, and nearly half said the TV was left on most of the time.

- The amount of time a parent watches television is a stronger predictor of kids' viewing time than house rules about TV time or even whether the child had a TV in the bedroom.
- An online survey of six thousand children found that 54 percent said their parents checked their smartphones too often. More than half of the parents agreed that they "probably checked their smartphones too frequently."
- A Boston Medical Center study of parent–child interactions at fast-food restaurants found that most caregivers used a cell phone during the meal, and nearly a third used it throughout the entire meal.

We can draw two conclusions from these surveys and other associated studies:

1. We don't rule screens; screens rule us. They dominate family life. Our children spend vastly more time interacting with them than with us. Most parents don't regulate the screen content their kids consume. If such patterns are the norm in our family, who's really raising our children?
2. In the digital age, many parents complain that they must constantly compete with screens for their children's attention. But the research reveals that the problem goes both ways; kids say they have to compete for our attention too.

Values are transmitted and character formed to a large degree through human interactions, especially face-to-face conversations. We bond through these interactions. We give and receive love. We learn to listen and to consider the perspectives of others. We discover the different ways people think and feel. Stories are passed down, lives shared. We grow from other people's knowledge, experience, wisdom, and advice.

One-on-one conversations are especially important. Says a mother of five, three of whom are now teens:

> These days, after I go to bed, there's usually a knock on the door from one of the kids who wants to talk about something—a problem that happened that day, something the next day that they're worried about, or just something that's on their mind that we haven't had a chance to talk about. They sit on the edge of the bed, and we talk. These conversations are precious to me.

Whatever infringes on these crucial conversations depletes the moral soil in which character grows. Late-night conversations are increasingly rare. Kids go to sleep with their phones. Says a grandfather, "When I pick up my 14-year-old grandson after soccer practice, I'm looking forward to a conversation—but as soon as he gets in the car, out comes the phone." A father bemoans the fact that when he gets home from work, he often finds his kids listless and sprawled out on the floor or couch, having spent an hour or more on their phones or iPads. Their facial expressions are blank. "Attempts to engage them," he says, "are met with only vague recognition that a conversation is taking place."[10]

Screens, especially video games, can create tension and conflict in the home. "*Pokémon Go* divided our family," a mother of three confides. "It was incredibly addictive. It started fights between our kids. My husband and I argued about how much to let them play it."

The family meal is potentially an island of intimacy in our busy lives—a time when we can reconnect, talk about our day, and share thoughts and experiences. Even before smartphones, the family meal was becoming an endangered species of American family life. But now, when families do have a meal together, phones often distract and disrupt. Most families have a rule about not bringing phones to the table, but kids say it's frequently broken. Parents will often take calls during dinner.

Phones have also increased the intrusion of work into family life. Many parents now say that because of phones, they're never really away from work. It's always there, on your phone. "When you're home, you're not really home" is a common lament.

How Screens Affect Children's Sleep, Attention, and Social Behavior

Drawing on dozens of studies, the 2016 American College of Pediatricians' research review reported the following negative effects—on children's sleep, attention, and social behavior—of (1) too much screen time, and (2) problematic screen content such as violence and sex:

- Higher levels of screen time and nighttime use of electronic devices are associated with shortened sleep duration and poor sleep quality. Sleep deprivation in children is linked to obesity, diabetes, learning problems, and hyperactivity.
- The more hours children watch TV from ages 1 to 3, the more likely they are to have attention problems at 7 years of age. The more time middle and high school youth spend playing video games and watching TV, the more likely they are to have attention problems.
- More than two thousand studies find that high levels of viewing media violence increase the risk of aggressive behavior in certain children and adolescents and desensitize them to violence. Said one 11-year-old boy, "You see so much violence that it's meaningless. If I saw someone really getting killed, it wouldn't be a big deal."

- Nine out of ten video games marketed to children 10 and older have violent content, and the top-selling video games are the most violent. Ninety percent of youth say their parents never check the ratings of video games prior to purchase and don't limit their playing time.
- Children and teens who play violent video games exhibit lower levels of empathy and prosocial behavior, interpret others' behaviors more negatively, and are more aggressive.
- The more teens watch television featuring sexual content, the more likely they are to engage in premature sexual activity. A longitudinal study of more than six thousand 10- to 14-year-olds found that early exposure to sexual content in popular movies was predictive of earlier sexual activity.[11]

Electronic Screen Syndrome

How do screens affect your child's brain? In 2013, the long-awaited fifth edition of psychiatry's *Diagnostic and Statistical Manual of Mental Disorders* announced a new dysfunction: "disruptive mood dysregulation disorder." This new category was created because mental health practitioners were seeing more and more children with chronic irritability, poor focus, rages, meltdowns, and disruptive "oppositional-defiant" behavior. There was concern that such children were being misdiagnosed with ADHD or bipolar disorder and put on medications they didn't need, that didn't help, and often had undesirable side effects.

Then Dr. Victoria Dunckley, a Los Angeles–based "integrative child psychiatrist" who does expert appearances for *NBC Nightly News* and other media outlets, asked a question that changed the conversation: What if this new psychiatric "disorder" is not a biologically based mental health problem but something that is *environmentally* caused? In a 2012 blog for *Psychology Today*, Dunckley coined a new term, "electronic screen syndrome" (ESS), to name what she believes is a widespread but largely unrecognized disorder.[12] She challenges us to confront "an inconvenient truth": the electronic screens that we have welcomed into our homes are overstimulating our children's brains, stressing their immature nervous systems, and having observable negative effects on their mood, cognition, and behavior.

In her family psychiatric practice, Dunckley was seeing increasing numbers of parents who said things like, "My son is revved up all the time," "He can't focus and is totally defiant," or "My daughter is exhausted and has meltdowns even when she's slept enough." In response, she created an online parents' course on reducing kids' screen time called "Save Your Child's Brain." She says she got dozens of emails from mothers around the world saying they intuitively thought that too much screen time might be the cause of their child's symptoms but their concerns had been dismissed by their child's doctor or therapist. For them, support for curtailing screen time was a salvation.

In 2015, Dunckley published *Reset Your Child's Brain*, describing the results of the screen-time remedy she recommends: a strict, four-week "electronic fast"—involving the removal of all electronic screens from a child's home life for that length of time. At that point in her practice, she had used the four-week electronic fast over the course of ten years with more than five hundred children, teens, and young adults. The following are some of the changes she reports seeing in children during and after the fast:

> Within days, the child's initial negative reaction to the plan—tearfulness, anger, arguing, and so on—subsides. The child's mood, attitude, and compliance begin to improve. The child begins to sleep better, and may go to bed earlier. . . .
> Within weeks, meltdowns become less frequent or less severe, or both. . . . The child's attention improves, sometimes

dramatically, and the child stays on task more easily. . . . [H]omework becomes less "tortuous." The child exhibits better sportsmanship and better manners in general. . . . conversations are longer.

Within months, . . . signs of social improvements become more apparent, such as enhanced empathy . . . [and the] child continues to develop self-awareness.[13]

Once the brain is rested and rejuvenated by the electronic fast, it can "reset." After the four-week break from all screens, parents can gradually restore some level of screen time, in small doses, carefully observing their child's response. Adequate limits will vary. Some kids show an immediate regression to previous screen-induced symptoms—such as hyperactivity, poor impulse control, and aggression—the very first time they go back to playing a video game with a friend.

What's the link between all these effects of screens and our efforts to nurture virtues such as kindness, respect, and self-control? If our kids are excessively dependent on screens, then we're swimming upstream in our efforts to develop their character. If we're allowing screens to overstimulate their young brains, we're our own worst enemy. Children's capacity for empathy and kindness; for cooperation and conversation; for respect, manners, and self-regulation; and for focusing on a task are all affected by how well that complex, delicate mechanism called a brain is working. We should do everything we can to help our kids take good care of it.

Dan Siegel, a pioneer in the study of neurobiology and healthy brain functioning, maintains that the healthy, "integrated brain" has five characteristics: It is "flexible, adaptive, curious, energetic, and stable."[14] Building on Siegel's framework, Dunckley urges us to provide five key conditions that support our child's "optimal brain integration":

First, the brain cannot become healthy if it's under constant stress. . . . Second, the brain requires adequate downtime—to rest, to recuperate from daily stress, and to process information and emotions. Third, the brain requires nurturing, in the form of parent–child interactions, which include eye contact, talking and sharing of feelings, touch, being held or hugged, having basic needs met, and being understood. Fourth, the brain needs a variety of stimulation, but in appropriate amounts at appropriate times; this is most easily achieved by the child interacting with and learning from the natural environment, along with periods of low stimulation. Lastly, the brain needs the body to move and feel, to obtain both gentle and rigorous exercise . . .[15]

Screens and Teens: The Epidemic of Anxiety and Depression

Recent research from various countries points to a link between screen time and adolescent depression. A Denmark study found that greater screen time during the teenage years was associated with greater likelihood of depression in young adulthood. A study of Australian 12- to 14-year-olds found that greater leisure-time screen use was associated with increased risk of depression.[16]

If you read *Time* magazine's November 7, 2016, cover story by Susanna Schrobsdorff—"Teen Depression and Anxiety: Why the Kids Are Not Alright"—the opening paragraph likely stayed with you:

The first time Faith-Ann Bishop cut herself, she was in eighth grade. It was 2 in the morning, . . . she sliced into the soft skin near her ribs. There was blood—and a sense of deep relief. "It makes the world very quiet for a few seconds," says Faith-Ann. "For a while I didn't want to stop, because it was my only coping mechanism.[17]

On many days, according to *Time*, her anxiety caused her to throw up before school. She was anxious about everything—grades, relationships, her future. She could not explain or justify her sadness. She had a good life. She loved her parents and felt loved by them. She knew they would support her if she told them about her sadness and the cutting, but she couldn't bring herself to do so.

Faith-Ann's cutting was a symptom of the anxiety and depression that now plague millions of American teens. Girls are more likely to engage in cutting, but it's now estimated that 30 to 40 percent of those who do so are male.[18] Today's adolescents appear to be more stressed, more overwhelmed, and less resilient than their parents' generation. Anxiety and depression among US high schoolers had been stable for several years, but both have been rising since 2012, afflicting all demographic groups—suburban, urban, and rural—and especially girls. The numbers:

- In 2015, the most recent year for which federal data are available, about three million 12- to 17-year-olds had at least one "major depressive episode."
- More than two million report experiencing depression that impairs daily functioning.
- About 30 percent of girls and 20 percent of boys have or have had an anxiety disorder.

Why so much adolescent anxiety and depression?

Today's teens arrived at puberty at a time when technology and social media were transforming society. Janis Whitlock, director of Cornell University's Research Program on Self-Injury and Recovery, says that because of social media, today's teens "are in a cauldron of stimulus they can't get away from, or don't want to get away from, or don't know how to get away from." Maintaining a social-media identity can be exhausting. "Every fight or slight is documented online for hours or days after the incident," Whitlock says.[19]

Though teens may be in the same room as their parents, *Time* points out, they might, thanks to their phones, be immersed in a painful emotional tangle with dozens of their classmates. "Or they're looking at other people's lives on Instagram and feeling self-loathing. Or they're caught up in a discussion of suicide with a bunch of people on the other side of the country they've never even met."[20] According to the latest Centers for Disease Control and Prevention report, the suicide rate for teenage girls has reached a forty-year high.[21]

Because so much of teens' lives is spent online, they are "hyperconnected" and at risk of being "overexposed."[22] Cindy Eckard is a Maryland mother who is spearheading legislation in her state to create medically sound safety guidelines for the use of digital devices in public schools. In a 2017 guest blog for *Psychology Today*, "Growing Up in a False Reality," she pointed out what many parents have seen: social media's growing power over their children's emotions and increasingly fragile sense of identity:

> Our children's self-esteem is now hinging on uncontrollable virtual approval and invisible, shifting, unpredictable digital feedback. . . . Whatever approval kids may receive from one another is fleeting, fickle, and unreliable. . . . What used to happen and be forgotten in a week when we were kids, now lingers and taunts. A cell phone snapshot can persist online forever. . . . Who's in and who's out and who said what and what picture was posted, and what replies were sent becomes an obsession. . . . [It] motivates kids to check their virtual experience nonstop, or be left out of everything.[23]

Our children, Eckard says, "are losing the ability to converse or to cope with emotions, their own, or anyone else's." They require constant stimulation from their phones, or they quickly become bored and, increasingly, anxious, depressed, and sometimes even suicidal.[24]

Healthy character development is a process of growing beyond the self, of becoming more secure, not less so. To the extent that screens make our children more fragile and anxious, more dependent on the unpredictable validation of social media, and more susceptible to depression, it retards their progress toward a stable, healthy identity and social maturity.

You should talk to your teenage children about all of this. Share some of these stories and statistics; ask for their thoughts. As with other important topics, this isn't one conversation but many. Over time, your goal should be to encourage them to seek the greater measure of freedom, self-assurance, and peace that will come from living much more in the real world and less in the artificial, stressful, and destabilizing world of phones. Doing that may be tough for teens at first, as it is for kids in the first stage of a four-week electronic fast. But we can support them in taking small steps in this direction—and help them notice the positive effects on their lives.

Given the transformative power of face-to-face helping relationships, we would also be wise to explore with our teenage children opportunities to contribute to their community in ways that make a tangible difference in the lives of others. Ask your child's school, your faith community, or a youth organization like 4-H, Scouts, or Boys and Girls Clubs about such opportunities near you. Also google the possibilities. After getting involved in meaningful service, young people typically speak of benefits such as gaining greater empathy and compassion for others, a stronger sense of their own capabilities, and a deeper sense of personal purpose.

Establish Family Guidelines for Screens

How as a parent can you get control of screens so they don't damage your child's mind and heart, swallow up family life, and replace you as your child's primary moral educator? How you approach this challenge will depend on the age of your kids and your assessment of your family's situation. Before you sit down with your kids to discuss your family screen policy, talk to your spouse and to other parents about what you think is truly best for your family and your kids. Discuss the research and recommendations in this chapter, check out Dr. Dunckley's website (www.resetyourchildsbrain.com), and browse Common Sense Media (www.commonsensemedia.org) and the resources and recommendations there. Take a look at websites such as screenit.com and kidsinmind.com that will give you the lowdown on the latest movies. Take enough time to get on the same page and try to watch (with your older kids) psychology professor Adam Alter's provocative April 2017 TED talk, "Why Our Screens Make Us Less Happy."[25]

If you compare the screen use recommendations of different organizations, you'll find differences on some points. For years the American Academy of Pediatrics warned that exposing kids under 2 to any kind of digital platform could lead to stunted language development and poorer reading skills. Then, in October 2016, the academy relaxed that guideline (without any new research to warrant a change) and it now recommends that children 18 months and younger be kept away from screens. I would encourage you to go by the older "no screens before 2" rule as the safer bet, given what we can observe for ourselves concerning the addictive nature of digital devices. The American College of Pediatricians has stayed with the stricter recommendations. Here are the guidelines I recommend to families, following those of the American College of Pediatricians:

1. Don't permit TV viewing or other screens (including on smartphones and iPads) for children under the age of 2.
2. Discourage the use of electronic toys for younger children and encourage games that foster thinking and creativity, such as blocks, puzzles, Legos, and drawing materials.

3. Limit all media exposure for entertainment purposes (television, movies, computer/video games, and music) to *one hour or less per day* for children under 10, and avoid developmentally inappropriate content all together.

   • Turn off the TV during mealtimes.
   • Do not allow your child or teen to have a TV, computer, phone, electronic game board, iPad, or Internet access in the bedroom.
   • Determine appropriate time limits for teens' use of social media and limit younger adolescents' access to social media and monitor their social media sites.

4. Encourage alternate forms of entertainment, especially those involving physical activity, with the participation of all family members.

5. Screen and monitor the media viewing of your children and adolescents:

   • Watch television with your children so you know what programs they are drawn to and what lessons they are receiving. Every TV program and video game will teach your children something; choose programs and games that support your family's values.
   • Ask questions while watching the program. Do your kids understand what is happening? Do they think what is happening is real?
   • Explain commercials to your children. Commercials are made to encourage us to spend money. Children can understand that we do not need a certain product to really be happy.

6. Know the rating of the games your children play; remove inappropriate ones from their devices. Video games often become more violent and more sexual at higher levels, and

pornography is often embedded in and accessed through a variety of games aimed at youth.

- Check the levels of the games. Set limits, just as with television.
- Disallow the playing of video games on the Internet with unknown players.

7. Be good role models:

- Limit your own use of media—turn off the television, smartphones, and computers during mealtimes.
- Don't text or talk on cell phones while driving.
- Think of other ways to entertain your child while traveling, such as listening to or singing songs together, making up stories, and bringing books for your child to read.
- Consider using Internet or router filters such as Covenant Eyes or Router Limits, or Internet provider services such as Integrity Online to decrease the likelihood of inappropriate access to obscenity or high-risk online activities.
- Be aware of what your kids are reading in school, and keep an eye out for the increasing use of sexually explicit material in high school literature classes.

It may be hard to claw back privileges if your kids are used to playing video games in their room, to unmonitored use of social media, or to watching a lot of TV. Here is how I recommend framing a family meeting to discuss the screen policies you want to prevail in your home:

The use of the media in the family is a privilege, not a right. That means parents have the final say, just as we do in other areas of family life. But just as with chores and the other things we've discussed in family meetings, we want to consider your ideas too. Let's come up with a family media plan that works for our family.

Expect resistance, because kids will see the writing on the wall: they are about to lose some—maybe most—of the freedom they've gotten used to. I suggest you address that head-on by saying something like this: "Parents who care about their kids set limits on these things. We want to do this because we love you."

When our sons, Mark and Matthew, were 9 and 4, respectively— long before the proliferation of screens families now have to deal with—we got to the point where we felt the television was running, and ruining, our lives, even though we steered clear of shows with objectionable moral content. Evening shows were crowding out bedtime reading; there was always a "down" feeling after they were over and an increase in uncooperative behavior by the boys. They were like zombies on Saturday mornings after watching two to three hours of cartoons; my wife and I were wasting hours watching meaningless shows, and so on.

I called a family meeting.

I opened with this: "I've come to really hate the TV. It's the cause of constant problems. Frankly, I'd like to get rid of it. I'd like to put it in the attic or the cellar."

That caused instant panic in the kids. My wife remembers thinking, "A total ban will never work." She proposed a compromise: a "specials only" policy. No one would turn on the TV unless there was a special program we judged worth watching as a family. We all agreed to try this. Mark and Matthew thought it wasn't such a bad deal because it was the Christmas season, and there would be a special of some sort practically every night: *Frosty the Snowman*, *A Charlie Brown Christmas*, *How the Grinch Stole Christmas!* and so on.

But after Christmas, blessedly, the specials stopped. The TV was hardly ever on. Amazingly, no one seemed to miss it. We went from watching more than twenty hours a week to about two. In the months and years that followed, the television became a mostly silent member of the family.

When Judith told a friend we were watching almost no television anymore, the friend said in a shocked tone, "Really? What do the kids *do*? Don't they fight a lot more?" Judith responded, "On the contrary, they fight a lot *less* because they're in a better mood. And I don't have to keep hassling them to turn the set off. Plus there's not the constant background noise of the television. I can't believe the peace!"

Consider the experience of a mom of three boys, ages 7, 3, and 1. The 3-year-old and 7-year-old had each had his own iPad and had often played many hours a day. The mother says, "I had suspected for some time that the iPad was particularly disruptive to my 3-year-old, but I truly didn't think I could 'survive' without the quiet that the tablets provided. How would I get anything done? What would the kids *do* with all that time?" After googling "Is the iPad bad for kids?" she found Dunckley's website and book, learned about the four-week electronic fast, and decided to give it a try. She says:

> My 3-year-old went from three to five meltdowns a day to one or less; from struggling with transitions between activities to no more struggles of that sort; from aggression towards his 1-year-old brother to playing gently and enthusiastically with him; from general instability in his personality to being much more even-keeled. Small things no longer set him off.

Her 7-year-old used to "routinely complain how *bored* he was—after he had watched every video he was remotely interested in on YouTube." His mother would say, "You have a room full of toys you never play with, go find something," and he would respond with "how boring *all* of his toys were." But after the electronic fast, "he now plays enthusiastically with his toys, pretending with everything, from Star Wars to building with blocks and drawing.

"At first," the mother says, "this was more work." She had to jump-start their involvement in nonscreen activities. "But four weeks in," she says, "they now find their own activities to keep them busy and entertained. We also now have a stash of board games to play in the evenings rather than stare at screens, and I've found that I absolutely *treasure* the extra time I spend with them."

So in this area of family life, as in all areas, I encourage you to aim high. If you make only small changes, you won't feel much difference. You and your children deserve a family life that's healthier, more balanced, and just plain happier than one that's dominated by the digital devices we've allowed to reshape our lives. You won't regret having strict limits in this area, and you'll have more success in teaching kindness and its allied virtues if you do. Go for it. Take back your family.

CHAPTER 10

How to Help Your Kids Develop Good Habits (and Break Bad Ones)

*We are our own potters; for our habits make us, and we make
our habits.* —FREDERICK LANGBRIDGE

HABITS ARE PATTERNS of thinking and behavior learned
through repetition. The good side of our character consists
of our virtues, our good habits; the bad side of our character consists
of our bad habits. In a very real sense, we *become* our habits. They
affect every aspect of our lives: our relationships, the quality of our
family life, our reputation, our work, our health, and our happiness.

In his book *Nicomachean Ethics*, Aristotle gave us the first
theory of how virtue develops. He said that moral virtues are
acquired largely through "habituation": "Just as we become build-
ers by building and harp players by playing the harp, we become
just by doing just actions, temperate by doing temperate actions,
brave by doing brave actions."[1] If we take Aristotle to heart, we'll
help kids perform virtuous actions repeatedly, until it becomes
relatively easy to do so and relatively unnatural to do the opposite.

What would that look like in a school? At St. Rocco School
(K–8), a Blue Ribbon School in Providence, Rhode Island, students
start the school day by taking out their Good Deeds Journal. They
write in their journal a good deed they did the day before—at
school, in their neighborhood, or at home with the family—or a
good deed they intend to do in the day ahead. With these daily

opportunities for practice, kindness gradually becomes more habitual, a disposition to act in caring and compassionate ways. Parents at this school have commented on the positive effects of the good deeds initiative. One mother wrote to the principal:

> Doing good deeds daily has helped our sons become more conscious of others' needs in the family, community, and world. When we're grocery shopping, they now remind me to purchase canned goods for the needy. They readily shovel snow for an elderly neighbor without expecting or accepting money in return. They are also now more sensitive about social issues when watching TV.

We don't need to wait for the school to have our kids keep a good deeds journal. We can do something similar at home.

Helping a Son Break a Bad Habit: One Mom's Story

Building a better character involves two kinds of work: forming good habits and breaking bad ones. It may be harder for us to help kids break bad habits, but it's an act of love to do so. They deserve our kind but honest feedback about how they can be their best self more of the time.

Schools struggle with verbal cruelty, the most common form of bullying. Many times put-downs are practiced at home. Says a mother of a 14-year-old: "When Jennifer isn't snapping at her younger sister and brother, she's making catty remarks about girls in her class." Many parents may throw up their hands in the face of such behavior, but the mother of 15-year-old Blair had higher expectations. She wanted to encourage him to rein in his habit of shooting zingers at his friends and 8-year-old brother, Michael. So she presented this challenge:

Blair, you have a gift with words. But you know your sarcastic humor always gets Michael upset. And even though your friends act like it doesn't bother them, have you ever wondered whether they really wish you'd lay off a little? How about going for a week without *any* put-downs and seeing what difference it makes?

Blair agreed to try the experiment. Three days later, a surprised Blair said to his mother:

Fred King actually thanked me today for not needling him. Tim also seems more relaxed around me now. Michael asked me if I could keep this up—at least more like this than before. I can see how sarcasm puts people off. I'd rather have people feel comfortable around me than uncomfortable.

In helping Blair break his put-down habit, his mom did 3 wise things: (1) she began positively, by affirming his gift with words; (2) she challenged him to consider how others felt about being on the receiving end of his cutting wit; and (3) she persuaded him to find out for himself how people would respond if he refrained from sarcasm for a week. Because of his mother's efforts, Blair learned an invaluable life lesson: he could break a bad habit if he wanted to.

There's another lesson from Blair's story: our habits of speech matter. The words we say impact others and also shape our own character. If we can control our tongue, we'll be better able to control everything else—including how we treat other people. To underscore the point that words are powerful, I recommend sharing with your kids the following wisdom (and perhaps posting it on the fridge):

Language matters. It impacts others. It can affirm and inspire, or disturb and denigrate. It can set a good example or a bad one. It influences how others think of us. It can strengthen our self-control or weaken it. It can elevate our character or coarsen it. We are at our best when we use our best language.

The family is where kids should learn to use the power of words to create happiness, not hurt.

Break a Bad Habit by Strengthening the Opposing Virtue

The story about Blair illustrates the direct approach to breaking a bad habit: Make a frontal assault. Help your children become aware of the undesirable behavior and its effects on others, encourage them to curb it, and affirm their progress.

But there's also an indirect approach to breaking a bad habit that can be just as effective or even more so. This indirect approach is expressed by an old psychological principle: *If you want to weaken a negative behavior or attitude, strengthen its psychological opposite.* Combat the negative by promoting the positive.

If you want to break a bad habit such as being very critical of other people, replace it with a good one—such as paying them compliments. If you want to be less annoyed by the faults of others, make a sincere effort to focus on their virtues. If you have a habit of complaining, count your blessings by keeping a daily gratitude journal. If you want to forgive people who have hurt you, do kind and generous things for them. If you want to be less self-centered, do something every day to make someone else happy.

Let me give a character education example of this principle of promoting the positive in order to inhibit the negative. At an inner-city school, vandalism was a big problem. Students were destroying the high-rise projects and other property on the way to school. When a new principal came on board, she established a character education program that included having every student do weekly community service. The vandalism sharply declined. The principal commented: "You're less likely to tear something down if you're building it up." The bad habit of vandalizing the community had been replaced by the good habit of community service.

Helping kids break a bad habit often requires teaching and practicing a very specific behavior to take the place of the bad habit. When one of our granddaughters was an exuberant 3-year-old, she would interrupt an adult conversation when she came into a room by saying, "Excuse me!" If that didn't gain her the floor, she'd repeat in rising volume, "Excuse me! *Excuse* me! *EXCUSE* ME!" Her parents would remind her not to interrupt, but it would happen again the next time. It had become a habit.

The solution was to teach her a specific alternative behavior: to silently touch the arm of the person speaking, as a signal that she wished to speak. The person speaking would then glance at her and nod to acknowledge her. The speaker would continue talking for just a short time (usually no more than a couple of sentences), then smile and say, "Thanks for waiting, honey—what would you like to say?," and she would take her turn. This, of course, took patient reminders and practice, as establishing new behaviors almost always does. This approach to interruptions became a family tradition that's been used with all our grandchildren.

Both teachers and parents have used the replacement strategy to help teens curb bad language, a growing problem because they hear so much bad language all around them. Here's how it works: Ask your child to come up with a replacement word ("duka" was the word one high school class chose) for whatever swear words they may have been using, and then practice saying that in situations where swearing has become a habit. Because this may be a hard habit to break, I recommend using the "counting and charting" method described later in this chapter. You may also want to couple that with an incentive. Some families have established a fines jar for offenses against appropriate language—with agreed-upon amounts for both parents and kids.

Identity-Based Habits That Define Who We Are

Each of us has a self-image—a sense of identity, of the kind of person we are. As parents, we want our children to develop a positive self-image, a sense of identity that has being a good person at its core. We can help our children develop that kind of self-image through the habits we help them form.

This was demonstrated by an educational experiment, carried out by Paul Vitz and Phil Scala, that had junior high school kids from tough New York City neighborhoods perform an altruistic act of their choosing every day for seven weeks—and record those acts as they did them.[2] Here are some of the acts they entered in their journals:

I did the dishes for my brother (it was his turn).

I gave an old lady my seat on the bus.

I helped a friend study for a test.

I shoveled the snow on my neighbor's sidewalk.

I straightened out the entire house when no one was home.

I tutored a sixth grader in math.

I picked up litter in the school yard.

I gave some of my old clothes to the poor.

At the end of the experiment, the researchers asked these students to write a short reflection about how this experience had affected them as a person. More than two-thirds said things that pertained to their self-image, or sense of identity. For example, one boy wrote: "I know I'm a good person because I do good things." The experience of performing altruistic deeds day after day, for nearly two months—actions for which they received no external reward—changed their sense of who they were.

Research finds that a strong sense of moral identity is a reliable motivator to do what's right.[3] Repeatedly doing good things for the right reason (to help others, not to get a reward) will dispose our children to think of themselves as good people. That positive sense of identity will, in turn, incline them to do more good. When we affirm our kids for doing something good, we can compliment them *on the kind of person they are being*. For example, instead of saying, "Thanks for sharing some of your candy with your sister," we can say, "Thank you for being a generous person," or "Thanks for being the kind of person who shares with others."

"Be a First-Class Citizen"

A good habit can be something as simple as picking up a piece of litter. An elementary school principal describes something he says to students during the opening school assembly:

> We're starting the school year with a clean building and a clean campus. If we all do our part, we can keep it that way. There are three kinds of citizens when it comes to littering. A third-class citizen litters. A second-class citizen never litters. A first-class citizen never litters . . . *and* picks up litter whenever he or she sees it. So be a first-class citizen. At next week's assembly, I'm going to mention some examples I saw during the week of people being first-class citizens in our school.

At the following week's assembly, he announced what he called his "anonymous thank-yous." "This past week, I saw two first graders being first-class citizens in the cafeteria, three third graders being first-class citizens in the hallway, and two fifth graders being first-class citizens on the playground." And so on. Because he didn't name names, any students who had been first-class citizens in the ways the principal described could think he was talking about them.

When I've taken our grandchildren for a walk or to the park, I've explained the three kinds of citizens and challenged them to be "first-class citizens." Needless to say, I do the same. They have taken pride in picking up a discarded bottle, can, or candy wrapper. It's become a family tradition and, for them, what I hope will be an enduring habit.

Focus on One Habit for a Month

Help your child choose one very specific behavior to work on for a whole month. Explain that habits develop through repetition, and so it takes time to develop a new habit or break a bad one. Better still, make this a family project where parents and kids each work on forming one good habit or breaking a bad one. Sample behaviors family members might focus on, and the reason why each is a good habit:

- Say, "May I please have . . ."—not "I *want* . . ."—when you're asking for something. *(It's good manners, and will be appreciated.)*
- Look at a person when he or she is speaking to you—or, as one dad says, "Listen with your eyes." *(It's respectful, and the person who's speaking to you feels you're really listening.)*
- Return a greeting when somebody greets you, and use his or her name ("Good morning, Mom."). *(It's the friendly and*

polite thing to do, and it makes people feel good when you say their names.)

- Pick up your things when you leave a room. *(If everybody leaves their stuff all around, pretty soon the house is a mess.)*
- Do your chores without being reminded. *(Parents don't like to nag.)*
- If your brother or sister asks for a turn, don't make them wait or have to ask again. *(It's kind and avoids an argument.)*
- When you've done something you shouldn't have done (like hitting or hurting someone's feelings), don't deny it—just admit it right away and say you're sorry. *(It's the right thing to do, you'll feel better, and it will restore peace.)*
- Don't say bad things about other people behind their backs. *(It's not kind or respectful—you wouldn't want them to say bad things about you.)*

If parents and kids are each working on a particular habit, each family member can have an "accountability buddy" who asks how you're doing on your goal and congratulates you on progress.

Keep Track of Your Progress by Counting and Charting

How will you know if you're making progress in forming a good habit or breaking a bad one? One way to assess progress is to keep a daily count and make a chart. The days of the week go along the chart's horizontal axis at the bottom of the page. The vertical axis (on the left) gets numbered 1, 2, 3, 4, 5, etc., with equal intervals between the numbers. (I make the intervals between the numbers fairly big so that a change of even 1 in the recorded frequency of a behavior looks like progress to feel good about.)

At the end of each day, if it's a good habit you're trying to form, you mark how often you did the desired behavior you're trying to increase. Each day, connect the points you've plotted, giving you a graph line that shows your day-to-day progress for the week (or month). Or, if you're trying to break a bad habit, you plot the frequency of the behavior you're trying to reduce or eliminate, and look for the graph line to go down.

I first learned about "counting and charting" from the behavioral psychologist Ogden Lindsley.[4] He reported success in teaching this method to classroom teachers as a way to help misbehaving students curb disruptive or aggressive behaviors. Lindsley found that helping such students chart their behavior—so they could clearly see its exact, day-to-day frequency—was, for many children and a variety of behavior problems, an effective motivator and means of improvement.

If you try counting and charting to help your child break a bad habit, have the chart be a secret between the two of you. Let them decide if and when they want to share the results with others in the family. You can, if you like, offer to have some kind of family celebration if the bad habit is conquered or significantly reduced.

The first parent I taught counting and charting to was trying, without success, to find a way to help her 7½-year-old daughter stop sucking her thumb. Molly, a second grader, was self-conscious about still sucking her thumb, got upset when classmates teased her about it, and said she wanted to stop—but couldn't because it relaxed her and she had been doing it for so long. The dentist said her teeth were crooked but couldn't be straightened out until she stopped sucking. But nothing he said or her parents did—not encouraging, scolding, or offering a reward—had helped her stop.

After her mom explained counting and charting to Molly, she agreed to try it. She was to keep count of the number of times she sucked her thumb each day; her mother promised not to say anything to remind her. At the end of the week, her mother said, they would have a "celebration" if there was an improvement. The mother reports what happened:

Each night, Molly was eager to fill in her chart. I never questioned her as to whether she had recorded the correct number. I saw her suck her thumb only once during the week, and that evening she marked down 1. She always sucks her thumb while she watches television, but this past week she did not. Each night she became more excited about the plan and also more confident that she could succeed. By Saturday, she announced triumphantly to the whole family that she had stopped sucking her thumb. We all went out to McDonald's to celebrate.

When you keep count of a behavior you're trying to increase or decrease, don't be discouraged if there are bad days. "Don't sweat the slipups," says habit-formation expert Richard O'Connor in his book *Rewire*. "The good news is that all the brain research shows that every time you practice a good behavior, you're building up a little network of neurons that make it easier to do the same thing next time."[5]

Goals Make a Difference

The effort to develop a good habit—or break a bad one—typically begins by setting a goal. A longitudinal study, published as *Talented Teenagers*, tracked two hundred teens who were extraordinarily gifted in areas such as music, art, science, mathematics, and athletics. It found that teens who developed their talent to high levels were those who set goals and managed their time effectively to pursue them. They were also more likely than underachievers to come from supportive families, have teachers who encouraged them, associate with friends who were also goal-oriented, and have conservative sexual attitudes.[6]

Parents can play an important role in helping kids acquire a goal-oriented mind-set and in thinking of ways to achieve their goals. A father of seven whose children were known to be likable, courteous, and hardworking was asked what he had done as a parent. He said:

> Well, there is one thing I remember doing since my kids were young. At the start of the month, I'd ask each child, "What goal do you have for yourself this month?" At first, I'd have to help them think of something—whether it was taking out the trash without being reminded, going a week without getting in a fight with their brothers or sisters, or getting better at some skill in a sport they played. We'd talk for a few minutes about how they could accomplish their goal. Then every few days I'd check in with them and ask, "How are you doing with your goal? Need any help?" As they got older, they started to come to me and tell me what their goal for the month was. It had become a habit—and I think it helped them become self-directed.[7]

Read a Good Book About Habits—with Your Child

Stephen Covey's *The 7 Habits of Highly Effective People*, one of the bestselling books of all time, helped to usher in the present era of renewed attention to the importance of habits. Books on habits continue to roll off the presses: Phil Stutz and Barry Michels's *The Tools*,[8] Hal Urban's *Life's Greatest Lessons*,[9] Charles Duhigg's *The Power of Habit*[10], and Richard O'Connor's *Rewire*.

Parents and teens can benefit from reading any of these books, but for teens I recommend starting with *The 6 Most Important Decisions You'll Ever Make*[11] by Sean Covey, a son of Stephen Covey and a father himself. Using entertaining cartoon art and lots of true stories from the lives of teens, it's full of solid advice on making wise choices about friends, school, building a positive relationship with parents, sex and love, gaining self-confidence, and steering clear of drugs, pornography, and other addictions. Your teen will get the most out of the book if you also read it. Create an enjoyable context—such as going out for dinner or a pizza or taking a walk—for discussing what you each found interesting or valuable about a particular chapter ("What did you take away that you think you might actually use?").

~

Our character consists of our habits. Habits are *dispositions*—tendencies to think and act in certain ways. If we want our kids to develop essential virtues like kindness, respect, and honesty, we'll have to help them develop good habits. That takes patience on our part and effort and practice on theirs. But if we and they make that investment, doing the right thing—the kind thing, the courteous thing, the honest thing—can become second nature.

CHAPTER 11

How to Talk About Things That Matter

WHEN OUR OLDER SON, Mark, was 13, our conversations were characterized by a pattern familiar to most parents. I asked the questions, and he usually gave one-word answers. "How was school?" "Fine." "How'd the game go?" "Great." If you've asked "What did you do at school today?" of your elementary schooler, you may have gotten the response: "Nothing." (When I asked an audience of parents in Mexico how their children responded to that question, they responded in unison, "¡Nada!")

I decided to try a different approach with Mark. One day I said, "You know, I ask all the questions. I'd appreciate it if you'd ask *me* a question for a change and we had an actual conversation." He smiled and said, "Okay, Dad, how are your courses going?"

When he asked that, I realized I had never said one word about my college teaching to either one of our sons, even though, as a college professor, teaching was a big part of my life. How was it that I had never shared anything about this crucial part of my life with my children? I told Mark about the courses I was teaching that semester and how three were going well and one was definitely not—and why. Then I asked him how his courses were going in junior high. It felt like a real conversation.

After that, whether we were cleaning up the kitchen or just had five to ten minutes in the car, we'd do back-and-forth questions—"What's been the best part of your day?" "What happened today that you didn't expect?" "What's on your mind these days?"—usually for at least a couple of rounds. If he wasn't sure what to ask me, I'd say, "You can ask me the same question I just asked you." Soon he was coming up with his own questions.

Back-and-forth questions became a family tradition. I was always struck by the thoughts, feelings, experiences, and information it elicited, even in a short period of time. My wife and I soon began doing back-and-forth questions with each other ("What have you been thinking about this week that we haven't had a chance to talk about?" "What's a project you have in mind for this summer?"), whether we were out for dinner or weeding the brick path in the backyard. No matter how much communicating we had done during the week, back-and-forth questions made conversation more interesting and brought out things we hadn't yet had a chance to share.

Now we do questions with the grandchildren. Ben, who is 9, had developed the habit of heading straight for my wife's iPad when he and the other grandchildren came to the house. So my wife proposed, "Ben, before you play on the iPad, let's have a conversation. I'll set the timer, and we can do back-and-forth questions for five minutes." They sat down at the kitchen table, and Ben got the hang of it quickly. He's the one who wants to be a chef, so he liked asking Judith questions related to her cooking ("What's your favorite tool to use in the kitchen?" and "What's your most favorite dessert you've ever made?"). The third time they sat down to do this, he said with a grin, "How about we set the timer for *ten* minutes?" Needless to say, his grandmother was very pleased.

Whenever I speak to groups of parents, I say, "If you do only one thing differently after tonight, I hope you'll try back-and-forth questions. It will enrich your family relationships and teach your children the art of conversation—a gift that will last a lifetime." I share a story about teaching this conversation format to Singapore parents, who say that most parent–child communication in Asian families tends to be one-way, parent to child. I had the Singapore parents practice back-and-forth questions with each other, and then for homework asked them to try it that night with at least one of their children. The next day, a father stood up and proudly described to the group how he and his 5-year-old daughter had pulled up two chairs and—with his wife and the other two children looking on in amazement—had enjoyed doing back-and-forth questions for an entire hour!

Not all kids will take to back-and-forth questions so enthusiastically as that little girl. It's wise to anticipate some resistance and to give this rationale:

> In a good conversation, one person doesn't do all the talking. Both people are involved. It's more enjoyable that way. Asking questions in a conversation shows you're interested in the other person. You want to know what they think, what's going on in their life. If you do all the talking and don't ask about the other person, you'll come across as self-centered. In a book on conversation, two Harvard professors say that the distinguishing mark of a good conversationalist is curiosity about the other person. Curiosity is what leads a person to ask questions.

A father who tried back-and-forth questions with his 15-year-old son said to me recently, "Now, when I pick up my son after school, he says, 'How was your day, Dad?'" I was happy to hear that. But even better than asking "How was your day?" (which can be answered with a simple "Great") would be a question like, "How was your day, and what made it that way?" The best questions are open-ended and can't be answered with just a word or phrase. "What's something good in your life that's happened since we last saw each other?" is a better question than "How's it going?" (which typically evokes something like "Pretty good") or "What's new?" ("Not much").

Most of the open-ended questions on the following pages can

be used in one-on-one conversation. Other questions or topics such as, "What do you wish we did more often as a family?" or "Who has a problem that the rest of the family might be able to help with?" are more appropriate for family meals or a family meeting.

40 Conversation Starters

1. What was the best part of your day and why?

2. What was the best and the worst part of your day?

3. What's something nice you did for someone today?

4. What's something nice someone did for you?

5. What is an act of kindness you saw someone perform this week?

6. What is an act of kindness we could each do tomorrow?

7. What is something you learned today in school or from life?

8. What happened today that you didn't expect?

9. What was an interesting conversation you had today?

10. What's something you accomplished this week that you feel good about?

11. What's something you're looking forward to?

12. What are you grateful for today?

13. What's something you're worried about?

14. What's some good news that you haven't shared yet?

15. What's the hardest thing about being your age? The best thing?

16. What are two goals you have this week? (This month? This semester? This year?)

17. What is something that someone in the family did for you recently that you appreciated?

18. Who has a problem or challenge that the rest of the family might be able to help with?

19. If you could be granted three wishes, what would they be?

20. What are two things other people can do to make you happy?

21. How can somebody help you get out of a bad mood?

22. What does "success" mean to you?

23. What does "being in love" mean?

24. How do you know if someone is the right person to marry?

25. What is something you did during the past year that took courage?

26. How do you know if somebody is a true friend?

27. Who is someone you really admire?

28. If you had $100 to give to a charity, what charity would you give it to and why?

29. If you could talk with anyone from history, who would it be? What would you ask them?

30. If the house were on fire, what would you try to grab on the way out?

31. If you were President, what are two things you'd try to change?

32. What do you wish we did more often as a family?

33. What is a way you've changed in the past two years?

34. If you could change one thing about yourself, what would it be?

35. What do you wish you were better at, or would like to learn how to do?

36. Moral dilemma discussions: Read a letter to an advice columnist but not the answer—until everyone has had a chance to say what advice they would give.

37. Bouncing question: One person asks another a question (such as any on this list), then that person asks someone else a question, and so on until everyone has been asked a question. (If you don't wish to answer a particular question, you can request another.)

38. One-word topics: Choose any topic (school, teachers, sports, TV, news, movies, books, friends, heroes, God, prayer, decisions, music, politics, etc.). Anyone can say anything about the topic that comes to mind.

39. What was good about your trip? When someone comes back from an experience (a trip, summer camp,

etc.), each family member asks the person a question about it. ("What were two highlights?" "How was it different from what you expected?" "How did it affect you as a person?")

40. Are you more like a rose or a daisy? In what way? More like a dog or a cat? The city or the country? A lake or a brook? (Choose one pair and invite everyone to answer.)

Mealtime Conversation

The family meal—whatever time of day you have it, and however many family members can be there—is an important opportunity for meaningful conversation, deepening relationships, and passing on your most important values. All too often in our fast-paced lives, family members eat and run. Because of overcrowded schedules, an increasing number of families just "graze"—grabbing something from the refrigerator when they're hungry instead of sitting down together and sharing a meal. Many families, if they do sit down together, eat with the TV on or with electronic devices on the table. Often kids will bicker, bolt down their food, and leave the table as soon as they can. Yet approached thoughtfully, the family meal can be one of your most effective ways of shaping and strengthening your family culture.

A father of two boys, ages 9 and 12, made a point of preserving the family meal despite his kids' busy schedules: "When the kids have soccer practice, we just eat early. Dinner is one of the times we're certain to be together. Part of the kids' identities comes from what we do as a family. There's a value system I want to be part of their lives. Dinners with the family give them a support base."[1]

And here's a mother of five grown children speaking of the importance the family meal came to have in their lives:

When the kids were teens, we had to vary dinnertime between 4:30 and 8:30 p.m. depending on the season, sports,
and so on. We asked our children to make this commitment.
We put away all phones. The TV was off. We made a rule that
only positive conversation would be allowed—no criticism,
carping, or tattling. We began by saying grace, asking God
to help us love and appreciate each other. We pointed out the
specialness of each person—which got us looking at the goodness in each other. At first, the kids complained fiercely. Now
they are all parents themselves, and we've asked each of them,
independently, "What is one thing we did as a family that
you want to do with your children?" All of them have said,
"The family meal."

For some families, a family breakfast may be easier to do than
a family dinner (though I'd encourage you to try to gather everybody for dinner at least once or twice a week). The last time I was
in England, one of the newspapers carried a feature article on
Dutch families, whose children, according to a recent survey, have
been found to be happier—less prone to anxiety and depression—
than kids in other European countries. According to the article,
one tradition that sets Dutch families apart is that they regularly
eat breakfast together. This contributes to family connectedness
and helps everyone feel loved and supported as they begin a new
day. At the time, I happened to be staying at the home of a British
colleague whose family—the father, mother, and three kids (ages
17, 15, and 11)—have made a family breakfast, including Scripture
reading and praying for the graces they'll each need for the day
ahead, an important ritual in their lives. I got to see first-hand how
much this meant to the family.

How can you make your family meal an important, culture-
shaping family ritual, something you look forward to, and a vehicle for teaching what you value most? Here are some ways.

Explain why you want to make a shared meal a priority in your family life.

You might just say that life is so crazy that you want to find more ways to be together and stay close as a family. You could point out that as life gets more and more hectic, other families are doing the same thing. For nearly a decade, Harvard's Family Dinner Project has championed the family dinner "as an opportunity for family members to connect with each other through food, fun, and conversation about things that matter." Created by Harvard fellow Shelly London, the Family Dinner Project has spread across the country. It points to research showing that regular family meals are associated with healthier eating habits, lower rates of depression and anxiety in kids, stronger resilience and self-esteem, reduction of teen problems like drug use and pregnancy, higher grade-point averages, and better vocabularies. The Family Dinner Project invites families to sign up for its free online dinner program, *Food, Fun and Conversation: 4 Weeks to Better Family Dinners*, which includes healthy recipes, dinner activities, and conversation starters.[2] It also encourages marking on the calendar every time you have a family dinner.

Establish "manners for talking" as well as table manners.

Invite family members to suggest manners that will help you have good conversation. After you establish agreed-upon conversation manners, review them as needed at the start of the meal until they're habits. Civilized, respectful conversation doesn't just happen; it has to be taught, practiced, and insisted upon. Three conversation manners to be sure to include: (1) don't interrupt; (2) look at and listen to the person who is speaking; and (3) no put-downs. In our family, we also find it helpful to silently signal when you'd like an item passed so you don't have to interrupt the person speaking to ask for the butter or salt and pepper. We also have asked the kids to wait to be excused until everyone had shared something in response to the topic of conversation. We want the family to see mealtime as a sharing of thoughts as well as food, and to value both.

Have a topic that all family members are invited to respond to.

You might start the meal with unstructured, free-flowing conversation and then propose a focused topic, or you could begin with a topic. Sometimes our family will have spontaneous conversation for the whole meal, but usually we have a topic for at least part of it. Have family members take turns proposing one. The benefits of having a topic are that you talk about things that matter and nobody dominates the conversation.

Having a topic for discussion may not feel natural at first, but it will soon become so. For us, having a topic has become part of the family culture; if the adults don't think of something, one of the grandchildren may say, "Can we have a topic?," and then suggest one. See this chapter's "40 Conversation Starters" for possibilities, and, of course, you can come up with your own. The Family Dinner Project has dozens more you can draw from. Here's a sampling from their website[3] (for other conversation resources see the blog *Balancing Beauty & Bedlam*[4]):

- What are 3 things that are fun for you to do?
- What do you like most about school this year?
- What do you worry about at school?
- If you were a teacher and could teach your students anything, what would you teach them?
- If you were free to do anything you wanted all day long, what would you do?
- What makes you feel loved?
- Have you ever been teased? How did it make you feel?

- Have you ever done or said something when you saw someone being bullied or left out? If not, what might you do?
- Who is your favorite teacher? Why?
- Describe someone you know who is a giving person.
- Who is the most patient person you know? How can you tell he or she is patient?
- In *Horton Hears a Who!*, Dr. Seuss says, "A person's a person, no matter how small." What do you think he meant by that?
- Have you met any new kids at school this year? How are they different from you? How are they like you?
- What personality traits do you feel you got from each of your parents?
- What are 3 things you can do to make other people happy that don't cost anything?
- What are 3 things you could do for a friend to make him or her happy?
- Have you ever volunteered? What did you do? What did you enjoy or learn?
- Talk about a person you admire who fought for the rights of others.
- Do you think it is possible to change the world?
- Do you think it is possible to change yourself?
- How have you changed over the past year?
- How has the world around you changed this year?
- What is a book that influenced you in an important way?
- What is one of your favorite movies? Why?
- What do you want to be when you grow up?
- If you could make money doing whatever you love to do, what would it be?
- What do you like most about being part of this family?
- What is the kindest thing you've ever done?

You'll notice that some of these topics focus explicitly on virtues like kindness, patience, giving, courage (sticking up for someone being bullied), and justice (fighting for the rights of others). Currently, our Center for the 4th and 5th Rs (www.cortland.edu/character) is partnering with the University of Leeds in England (www.narnian virtues.leeds.ac.uk) on a character education project that has middle school students reflecting on and putting into practice six virtues exemplified by characters in C. S. Lewis's *Chronicles of Narnia*: wisdom, love, integrity, fortitude, self-control, and justice (six of the ten essential virtues we discussed in chapter 5). We've asked families in the project, as one of the home activities, to choose, for dinner discussion, questions related to those six virtues. Your family might also wish to discuss them.

Wisdom

- What is a good decision you made recently?
- What is an important decision you are trying to make? Who do you ask for advice when you have to make an important decision?

Love

- What is a good deed you could do this week for someone?
- Why do some kids cyberbully? What can schools, kids, and parents do to try to stop cyberbullying?

Integrity

- How could you explain to someone who cheats why it's wrong?
- Why is having a reputation for being honest important?

Fortitude

- Where does courage come from? How can you develop it?
- Who do you admire because of their courage?

Self-Control

- Most people say self-control is their weakest virtue. Why is self-control so hard?
- How can you avoid becoming addicted to anything— including your smartphone?

Justice

- Why do many people have much more money than they need and others not enough? How much poverty is there in our country and the world (google this), and how could it be reduced?
- Why do most middle and high school students say that their peers don't respect other students? What could be done to increase respect among students?

Vary the format.

To keep things interesting, experiment with different kinds of dinner discussions. When our younger son, Matthew, was a 1st grader, he would get impatient when he had to wait for his turn to comment on whatever the topic was. He proposed that we have more of what he called "jumping in" topics. Anyone could propose a topic—sports, movies, school, friends, games, superheroes, whatever—and anyone, in any order, could say anything (even a one-word association) that came to mind. We had fun with that.

A mom described a dinner discussion activity her family enjoyed:

During the week, each family member cut out a picture from the newspaper or downloaded one from the Internet and posted it on the refrigerator. On Friday, everybody brought his or her picture to the table, and the rest of the family tried to guess who was in the picture and what it was about. This kept the family in touch with what was happening in the world.

Once, I came home from Singapore with a box of laminated cards called "Knowing Me, Knowing You." On the back of each card were three questions, such as: "What is one thing you wish your family could do more of?" "If I gave you a thank-you card right now, who would you send it to—and why?" "What are three major problems faced by teenagers today?" We invited each person at the table to draw a card from the box, and then choose one question from the card to respond to. Your family can write your own questions on strips of paper, put them in a Dinner Qs Jar, and have each person draw three and choose one to answer.

Dilemmas for Dinner

Moral dilemmas are another way to change up the dinner-discussion format—one that can create stimulating conversation and foster the development of moral reasoning. Dilemmas can come from current events, history, the advice column in your paper, or family members' own experiences. The Family Dinner Project offers dilemma-style topics in a category it calls "Pickles and Predicaments." Here's one that made worldwide news at the time and touches on many ethical issues still worth considering.

A Hero's Fall from Grace

(Posted on January 22nd, 2013 by Amy; abridged here)

Once upon a time, a young man from Texas beat cancer and went on to win the prestigious Tour de France cycling race seven times. He was lauded a hero. Then, last week, the fairy tale came to an end.

   After nearly a decade of vehemently defending himself against accusations that he took performance-enhancing drugs to win, Lance Armstrong came clean. He admitted to Oprah Winfrey that *yes*, he took a variety of illegal substances during his racing years, and even bullied his friends and teammates into keeping quiet. Armstrong blamed a "ruthless" desire to win "at all costs," especially after his fight against testicular cancer. . . . Those of us who believed in the Lance Armstrong fairy tale now feel disappointed and betrayed. Yet his fall from grace offers us an opportunity to consider our own beliefs about winning, cheating, lying and forgiveness.

   Amy went on to post questions for teens and younger kids, which included:

1. Lance Armstrong told Oprah that he "viewed it as a level playing field where most everybody doped." Have you ever done something you knew wasn't right because everybody else was doing it, or because you really wanted to win? Does that make it okay to cheat?

2. The Armstrong story isn't only about lying and cheating, but about bullying people—his friends and former teammates. Which is his worst offense: bullying, cheating, or lying about cheating? Why?

3. As a cancer survivor, Armstrong created the Livestrong Foundation, an organization committed to empowering and educating cancer patients. . . . A doctor from the Dana Farber Cancer Institute argues that Armstrong remains a hero because he raised a lot of money to fight cancer and help people.

What do you think? Should his efforts to fight cancer over-shadow his other actions?

4. Lance said that he would like to run in the Chicago Marathon when he turns 50, yet he is banned from all US government-sanctioned events, including cycling and marathons. Now that he has confessed, do you think he should be forgiven and allowed to compete again? Why or why not?[5]

Among other things, the Lance Armstrong story offers a chance to think about the meaning of forgiveness and justice and what each requires. Is it possible to forgive someone (not harbor resentment, anger, or any ill will toward them) and still believe that, as a matter of justice, the person should be held accountable for his actions and experience fitting consequences for his offense or crime? Ask your kids to find other in-the-news dilemmas to bring to the table. Common Sense Media is a source of challenging moral situations in the news, with suggested questions for discussion.

4 Steps to a Good Decision

In the Narnian Virtues project I previously described, we provide moral dilemmas for families to discuss and a 4-step process for trying to reach a good decision:

1. *Choices and consequences:* What choices does the person have in this situation? What are the consequences that each choice might have for the person and for others—now and in the future?
2. *Virtues:* What virtues are involved in this decision?
3. *Seeking advice:* Who should the person go to for help in making this decision?

4. *Best decision:* What seems like the wisest decision—keeping in mind the choices, the possible consequences, the virtues involved, and advice the person might get from parents, teachers, and wise persons?

This 4-step decision-making process was very helpful to our family in dealing with a moral dilemma after I got a visiting professorship that took us to Boston when Mark and Matthew were 11 and 5, respectively. At Mark's new school, his 6th-grade teacher did cooperative learning projects from which Mark made two friends—Wayne and Doug. But trouble was around the corner.

After school one afternoon, Mark, Wayne, and Doug came into our apartment, said a quick hello to Judith and me, and disappeared into Mark's bedroom. They came out about ten minutes later, and Mark saw them to the door. At dinner, Mark looked troubled. He said slowly, "There's this kid . . . who has a moral dilemma." He paused and took a deep breath. I said, "Mark, is that kid you?"

He then told us what had happened that afternoon. As he, Wayne, and Doug were walking home from school, Wayne spotted a package in someone's mailbox. He grabbed it and said, "Let's go!"—he told Mark they'd done this before—and they ran to our apartment building. They came into our apartment with the stolen package under Wayne's jacket, and opened it in Mark's bedroom. It contained two gold-plated medallions. "Oh, cool!" Wayne said. Mark said he replied, "Yeah, but I think we'd better take them back. Stealing is against the Ten Commandments." He said Wayne just shrugged and said, "Well, I'm not very religious." Wayne and Doug then each pocketed one of the medallions and went home.

We thanked Mark for telling us the truth and coming to us for advice. Now we faced a moral dilemma as a family: What should we do? For the next hour, we had the most intense family discussion we'd ever had. Stealing someone's mail is a federal crime.

What made the situation hard for Mark—and us—was that Wayne and Doug were his first friends in his new school, and now he was in the position of getting them in big trouble.

We used the step-by-step process of thinking through a moral problem—what were our choices, the likely consequences, and so on. Doing nothing was obviously not an option. Mark might keep Wayne and Doug as friends, but that wouldn't get the stolen property back to its rightful owner, and Wayne and Doug might continue to steal from people's mailboxes. Mark could try again to talk Wayne and Doug into returning the medallions, this time giving new reasons ("Did you know it's a federal crime to steal from mailboxes?" "Would you like it if somebody ripped off packages from your family's mailbox?"). But we didn't think that would work.

We considered calling Wayne's and Doug's parents. That would probably get the medallions returned, and the parents would know that Wayne and Doug had been stealing and could do something about that. But there was no telling how the parents would handle the situation. Doug had told Mark that his father had a violent temper.

Another option was to talk directly with Wayne and Doug and ask them to return the medallions anonymously. That wouldn't get them in hot water with their parents, and it might have a positive effect on their future behavior. And if they stopped stealing, Mark could give their friendship another chance.

What virtues were involved in this situation? At least these:

- Integrity, which had been violated by the boys' stealing another person's property and concealing it from us when they brought it to our apartment.
- Responsibility as citizens to report a crime.
- Love—wanting to help Wayne and Doug stop stealing, and wanting Mark to have friends at school but ones who had good character.

- Justice—getting the property back to its rightful owner and preventing other people from having things stolen from their mailboxes.
- Courage—for us to take some kind of action to solve the problem, however uncomfortable that might make things for Mark.

Whose advice should we seek? Although Mark had sought our advice, as parents we didn't consider seeking the advice of anyone outside our family about how to handle this situation. In retrospect, I think that we should have. We could have asked the school counselor what he or she would recommend. The counselor would likely have said that the parents needed to know that their sons had been stealing from people's mailboxes. The counselor might have facilitated a meeting with the parents.

In the end, we decided to try talking directly with Wayne and Doug. I wrote each of them a letter and put it in a sealed envelope that Mark gave to them the next day in school. The letter said it had been very hard for Mark to tell us about the medallions because he didn't want to get them in trouble—but that what they had done was very wrong, and we'd like them to bring the medallions back to our apartment after school, wrap them up, and return them to the owner's mailbox with an anonymous note of apology. Doug showed up after school with both of the medallions. Wayne didn't come, and no longer had anything to do with Mark but didn't make trouble for him. Mark and Doug remained friends.

Talk About Friends

The conversations we have with our kids should give priority to the subject of friends. Our children's choice of friends matters a lot. Mark's experience with Wayne and Doug was a clear example of that. We know how important friends are in a kid's life. Kids without friends are lonely, tend to do less well academically, and are more at risk of being bullied. If there's nobody at school you can count as a friend, school is not a happy place. When Mark made two friends at his new school, we were very glad for him. But what happened with Wayne and Doug was a reminder that the wrong kind of friends can spell trouble.

How can you get to know your children's friends? One way is to have them to the house and then hang around so you can observe and listen. Another is to listen to them when you're driving them somewhere. Kids in the back seat of a car tend to forget an adult is present.

It's also important, as much as possible, to try to know something about the parents of your children's friends. When we were trying to decide how to deal with the mailbox theft, Mark mentioned that Wayne said he had no father at home and that his mother usually didn't know where he was or what he was doing. That was important to know. Kids without supervision are much more likely to get into trouble.

We want our kids to know that friends have an influence. It's human nature to be influenced by the people we hang around with. That's why people say, "You become like the company you keep." Studies of peer influence find that both boys and girls tend to take on the attitudes of their "reference group" regarding social behaviors.[6]

How should we respond as parents if we think that a particular friendship is not good for our child? It's a mistake to stay silent. Here is a father who wishes his parents had said something:

When I was 15, I hung around with a kid who was not a good influence on me. I got into some trouble that I don't think I would have gotten into otherwise. At the time, I could tell my parents weren't happy about my being friends with this kid, but they never said anything to discourage it. They probably thought it wouldn't have done any good. But I wish they had tried—it might have made a difference.

If we don't think a particular friend is a good influence, we owe it to our child to be honest with them about that. We can sit down and say, in a respectful and loving way:

Look, I can't tell you who to be friends with. Friendship is a personal thing—you have to like and enjoy each other. But parents have a responsibility to guide their kids, even when it comes to friends. So if I think a friend is not having a good effect on you and I'm concerned about that, I have to be honest with you—out of love. You might not even be aware of how that person is affecting you.

Then you can mention a specific concern you might have. ("Hank's language is a little rough. I'm also concerned about the disrespectful way he talks about girls.") If you've previously commented on positive things you like about their friends, that will make them more receptive when you express a concern. If you notice what you think is a negative influence, give a specific example ("Your language is getting to sound a bit like Hank's"). Kids may deny that any change in them is due to their friend, but you will have sensitized them to the possibility that this is happening.

If friends are leading our kids into behavior that is harmful to themselves or others, we have to say we can't, in good conscience, permit the friendship to continue. That will be hard to hear, and we have to help our kids understand that we are doing this because we love them. If kids persist in refusing to stop associating with someone whose influence is harmful, family counseling may be the next step.

We can increase the chances that our kids will find good friends by encouraging them to participate in church youth groups, Scouts, 4-H, and other youth groups where they can connect in wholesome ways with kids who share their values and interests. If we're fortunate, we'll count among our own friends other parents who share our basic values and who have kids around the same age as ours. Often, the kids of the two families end up being good friends, and the families' shared values are thereby mutually reinforced.

What else can you do to help your child choose friends who will be a good influence, not a bad one? Keep a conversation about friendship going. At the dinner table, and in one-on-one conversations, discuss questions like:

- What are the qualities of a true friend? What is a "false friend"?
- What qualities do you admire in a current good friend? How have those qualities influenced you?
- How do you think you may have had a good influence on a friend?
- Have you ever had a friend who was a bad influence? How did you deal with that? (*Here's a chance for us to share a story about a time when a friend had a bad influence on us—and what we learned from that.*)
- What makes a friendship last? What makes it end?

The chapter on friends in Sean Covey's book for teens, *The 6 Most Important Decisions You'll Ever Make*, has lots of good stories and insights. It can be a bridge to talking about a particular friendship issue with your child.

There's a lot to talk about with your kids while they are still at home. Conversation about things that matter is too important to leave to chance. Make it part of your family culture. Your kids are likely to remember your efforts with fondness and gratitude.

CHAPTER 12

Cut the Complaining!

10 Ways to Teach and Practice Gratitude

O N A SATURDAY AFTERNOON, you take your three kids to a movie they've wanted to see, then to their favorite hamburger spot for dinner, followed by ice cream. When they get home, they want to watch a movie on Netflix. When you tell them you think they've had enough screen time for the day and you'd like them to do something else, they complain that they have nothing to do.

What parents haven't had an experience like this with their kids? It's frustrating for at least 3 reasons: (1) when we do things for our children, it's natural and reasonable to expect them to express thanks and disappointing when they don't; (2) when they aren't thankful but instead complain, that puts both us and them in a bad mood (since complaining almost always makes a person feel worse, not better); and (3) being ungrateful and complaining is inconsiderate, self-centered behavior—the opposite of kindness. Kindness means thinking of others and acting in ways that contribute to their happiness; complaining certainly doesn't do that. If you've been trying to make kindness part of your family culture and there's still a lot of complaining, it's time to take further steps to teach and practice gratitude.

Complaining is common kid behavior—indeed, common human behavior. What can you do to change it and gradually replace it with "an attitude of gratitude" in your family? Let's look at some gratitude-nurturing strategies that can help.

1. Cultivate the virtues that support thankfulness.

Gratitude depends on two other virtues: a positive attitude (seeing the good) and fortitude (coping with adversity). We won't feel thankful unless we have a mind-set to recognize the positive things in our lives for which we should be grateful. When my wife and I find ourselves in a negative frame of mind, one of us will say, "Let's do positives," and we take turns remembering the positive things that have happened that day (and there are always positives, even on the worst days). We can teach our kids to do the same.

Fortitude, the inner toughness that enables us to endure pain and suffering, requires a realistic view of life. Many kids think life should be easy—free of frustration, disappointment, and heartache—and are unhappy when it's not. The virtue of fortitude begins with understanding and accepting a basic truth: Life is difficult. With our help, kids can learn to be grateful even for life's difficulties—and the opportunities they provide to grow in wisdom and strength of character.

2. Discuss the positives of being positive.

About a decade ago, at the end of his first year as our college's new president, Dr. Erik Bitterbaum addressed the honors graduates. He said, "I'm going to tell you five things that will help you in your life. The first is to be a positive person. As our college prepares for the future, we're looking to hire positive people. We can't afford to hire negative people. Positive people lift up those around them. Negative people drag others down. So be a positive person in whatever path you pursue."

This isn't just one man's opinion. UCLA's John Wooden, the winningest men's coach in any college sport, considered "enthusiasm" one of the two cornerstones of his 21-values pyramid of success. Enthusiasm is an asset in all areas of life. Project a positive attitude in a job application, and you're more likely to get an interview. Project a positive attitude in the interview, and you might very well land the job. As a family, share your observations and experiences with other people: What kind of people do you like to be around? What kind of people appear to be most successful?

3. Teach that your attitude is always a choice.

The writer Anne Husted Burleigh observes, "Gratitude, like love, is not a feeling but an act of the will. We choose to be thankful, just as we choose to love." The author Charles Swindoll says, "[W]e have a choice every day regarding the attitude we will embrace for that day. . . . We cannot change the past. We cannot change the fact that people will act in a certain way. We cannot change the inevitable. . . . I am convinced that life is 10 percent what happens to me and 90 percent how I react to it. And so it is with you. We are in charge of our attitudes."[1]

Do you agree? Are being grateful and having a positive attitude always something we can choose if we want to? Discuss that as a family. What does your own experience teach you? What has helped you stay positive and thankful even during tough times?

4. Share stories about being positive and grateful when life is difficult.

Even if it's true that our attitude is always a choice, the fact remains that when life is difficult, gratitude can be difficult. So it's important to share stories with our kids about people who have chosen a positive attitude and gratitude in the face of great adversity. John Perricone, a former student of mine and an award-winning high school teacher, describes his approach to teaching in his book *Zen and the Art of Public School Teaching.* At the beginning of his courses, he speaks to his students about three people who have significantly influenced his own philosophy of life. One of them is a student named David.

> When David was 16, his mother died of cancer. When he was 17, his father was struck and killed by a drunk driver. Six months later, his oldest brother was killed in a freak trucking accident. Three months after that, his youngest and only remaining brother took his life because of his overwhelming grief. If ever in my life I met a person who would have been justified in slamming the door on life, it was David. But he took this miserable hand of cards that was dealt him and decided this was what he had to work with. He went on to get his Master's Degree in psychiatric social work where he specialized in grief counseling—in helping others cope with what he had, through no choice of his own, become an expert in. When David talked to you, he was totally present in that moment because he had learned that the things we often assume are permanent in our lives—such as our families and our friends—can slip through our hands in a second. David is one of the greatest teachers in my life.[2]

In his book, *With Love and Prayers: A Headmaster Speaks to the Next Generation,* F. Washington Jarvis, an Episcopal priest and head for thirty years of Boston's Roxbury Latin School for boys, shares the following talk about gratitude that he gave at a morning assembly:

> If there is any secret to happy living, I believe it is in living thankfully. . . . Right now sitting amongst you . . . are boys with alcoholic parents, boys from dysfunctional families, boys living in situations where they are physically and/or

psychologically abused, boys living with parents who are dying painfully or whose parents have died. . . . A boy whose mother was dying a hideous and painful death a few years ago said to me: "I'm grateful . . . I may be able to bring her some small comfort by something I do or say each day." No bitterness. No "Why me?" No entitlement to a trouble-free life. . . .

Life entitles you . . . to nothing. . . . If you want to be happy, you will find happiness not from dwelling on all you do not have in life and feeling bitter about it. You will find happiness by dwelling on all that is good and true and beautiful in your life and being thankful for it.[3]

5. Count your blessings.

We're told that the way to be happy is to "count our blessings," but how do you actually do that? As a family, make a list of the things you tend to take for granted. If you do this over dinner, you could think about everyone at every stage whose work went into the meal you are eating—the farmers and harvesters, the truck drivers, the grocery store staff, up to the cook. As a follow-up activity, try this from Hal Urban's *Life's Greatest Lessons* (and check out his website and blog at www.halurban.com): Write across the top of the page "I am thankful for . . ." Under that make three columns. Label the first one "People"; under that, list all the people you are thankful for. Label the second column "Things"; under that, list all the material things you're grateful for. Label the third column "Other"; under that, list anything else you are thankful for (possibilities that Hal would suggest to his high school students: freedom, education, friendship, love, peace, intelligence, abilities, health, talents, God, particular experiences, beauty, and kindness).

For the next twenty-four hours, read each of these three lists four times: (1) when you wake up, (2) after lunch, (3) after dinner, and (4) before going to sleep. Then share as a family: What was good about doing this? What did you learn from it? Hal says that the day after doing this with his high schoolers, their body language was different when they came into class. "There were more and bigger smiles; eyes were open wider; they were more alive. Thankfulness does wonders for the soul."

6. Appreciate family members.

Find the natural opportunities in family life to express appreciation. In our family we would sometimes start dinner or a family meeting with a round of "appreciations." Each of us would express our appreciation for whatever other family members had done for us that week (you could mention more than one thing). It didn't take long but always produced a lot of good feelings.

Marthe Seales, my longtime associate at our Center for the 4th and 5th Rs, shares this story: "When I was growing up, my mom worked very hard to prepare nutritious, homemade dinners made from scratch for our family of ten every day. She baked homemade bread each week and prepared the vegetables that we harvested from our garden. I think there may have been a time when she felt we kids didn't fully appreciate all the work this entailed, so she began a 'compliment the cook' tradition that ended dinner. We each said something positive about what we liked the most. At the very least we would say, 'Thank you for dinner, Mom.'"

Or try the "appreciation chair." Each day during the week, a different family member takes a turn sitting on it. Everyone else tells that person why they appreciate them and expresses their gratitude for kindness shown or help given by that person during the past year. Our younger son Matthew's family does a variation of this: When it's someone's birthday, family members take turns at dinner saying things they admire and appreciate about the birthday person.

7. Take the "no-complaints challenge."

Since complaining is the number one enemy of a spirit of thankfulness, we need to confront that head on. A fun and challenging way to do that is to take the "no-complaints challenge": go twenty-four hours without complaining about anything. Ask family members to predict whether they'll be able to do it. Keep a rubber band around one wrist and change it to the other wrist each time you slip and complain, or keep a list of each time you complain. Hal Urban, the creator of this activity, says that when he did this with his school students, it took twenty-three years before he finally had a student who was able to go the whole twenty-four hours without a single complaint. Her strategy: "Every time I was about to complain, I thought of something I should be thankful for."

After the twenty-four hours are up, discuss as a family: How did we each do? What made this hard? What did we learn from it? Does complaining make us feel better—or worse? As a follow-up activity, consider taking the 21-day challenge described in Will Bowen's *A Complaint Free World: How to Stop Complaining and Start Enjoying the Life You Always Wanted*. (You can get a complaint-free bracelet from acomplaintfreeworld.org.)

8. Be "gratitude proactive" as a parent.

Think ahead. Anticipate situations where you would like your kids to express gratitude instead of complaining, and then help them plan to do that. Remember the anecdote at the start of the chapter about taking kids to a movie, then for burgers and ice cream—and having them complain when they got home because they couldn't watch a movie on Netflix? Before the outing, the father could have been proactive by saying, "Okay, guys, when we get home today, I'm going to ask you, 'What were some things we did today that you're thankful for—and why?' So be thinking of that, okay? It will make a nice end to the day. And when we get home, instead of more screen time, I'm sure Mom would appreciate it if you ask if there's anything you can do to help."

9. Take the fear out of failure.

Of the many difficulties we face in life, few are more challenging than failure. In an increasingly competitive world, many young people feel tremendous pressure to achieve—and never to fail. Rachel Simmons, a leadership development specialist at Smith College's Wurtele Center for Work and Life, says, "For many of our students—those who have had to be almost perfect to get accepted into a school like Smith—failure can be an unfamiliar experience. So when it happens, it can be crippling."[4] To one degree or another, this is true for most of our kids. How to stay positive in the face of failure?

A new initiative at Smith, called "Failing Well," aims to "de-stigmatize failure." Here's how the Wurtele Center for Work and Life explains this:

> Failing Well is a set of programs dedicated to the discussion of failure, risk taking and mistakes. . . . [O]ur mission is to increase student resilience by teaching, telling stories, and opening a campus conversation about failure. When you can fail well, the world opens up to you. There's no challenge you can't pursue, no risk you can't take, because you know how to get back up when you're knocked down. . . . When you can fail well, your self-worth doesn't ride on your success. . . . When you can fail well, you have the courage to ask for help when you need it—and leverage every resource available to get the job done. You have the ability to be vulnerable about your limits, and authentic with your peers—and forge powerful networks as a result. Failing well is a skill.

Says a junior at Smith: "On our campus, everything can feel like such a competition. We get caught up in this idea of presenting an image of perfection. So to see these failures being talked about openly, I felt like, 'OK, this is OK, everyone struggles.'"[5]

Discuss failure with your kids. How have you coped with it in your life? How can they? How can they help their friends when they're struggling with failure? That's an important opportunity to be kind.

10. Say gratitude prayers.

If you're a praying family, encourage your child to pray a prayer of gratitude as soon as he or she wakes up. For example: "Thank you, Lord, for the gift of this day. Thank you for the gift of my life. Help me to be thankful all day long." Encourage kids to begin their personal prayer time with prayers of thanksgiving. Say grace before meals, at home and when you're eating out. Make thanksgiving a regular part of bedtime prayers. Discuss this statement from St. John of the Cross: "One prayer of thanks when things go badly is worth a thousand when things go well." Why do you think he said that? What enables us to give thanks even when things go badly?

~

Expressions of thanks cost nothing but do much to lift our spirits, improve the family atmosphere, strengthen relationships, and make it easier to practice the other virtues, including kindness. Our mental health and our relationships suffer in the absence of gratitude. The more we can do as parents to promote gratitude in our family life, the better. You'll never regret making gratitude a priority in your home.

CHAPTER 13

Using Stories to Teach Kindness and Other Virtues

S TORIES—WHETHER TOLD, READ, or shown—are one of the oldest ways of teaching virtues. Through the ages, cultures around the world have used stories to pass on a moral and spiritual heritage. Stories teach by attraction rather than compulsion; they invite rather than impose. They capture the imagination and touch the heart. They stay in the moral memory. How can we use stories— good books, inspiring movies, stories in the news, stories from our childhood and generations past—to bring virtues to life for our children and help them take hold in their hearts and character?

Ever since they were 9 years old, our twin granddaughters, Joan and Mary, have read and reread the 1940s classic *The Hundred Dresses* by Eleanor Estes. It's a book with memorable lessons about peer cruelty, not judging by appearances, and the regrets that come from missed opportunities to be kind to someone others are treating badly. Mary and Joan have often asked if they could borrow our copy and take it home. They and their younger sister, Clare, even repeatedly acted out the story—an indication of how much it captivated them.

The Hundred Dresses tells the story of Wanda Petronski, a poor, quiet girl who always wears the same faded blue dress to school. She has no friends. The other girls, led by the popular Peggy, constantly tease Wanda about her one dress. Finally, one day Wanda blurts out she has a *hundred* dresses at home—all different colors! After that, the girls' teasing becomes merciless. Maddie—Peggy's best friend—wishes she and the others would stop being so mean to Wanda, but Maddie doesn't have the courage to say anything.

The time comes for the annual art contest conducted each spring by their teacher. On the day the winner is to be announced, the children enter their classroom amazed to see one hundred beautiful drawings of dresses—each different—displayed on the walls. They were all drawn by Wanda, the teacher explains, but she is not present to receive the first prize. The teacher then reads a letter from Wanda's father:

Dear Teacher:
My Wanda will not come to your school any more. Jake also. Now we move away to big city. No more holler Polack. No more ask why funny name. Plenty of funny names in the big city.

Yours truly,
Jan Petronski

After Wanda moved away, Maddie had a sick feeling in the pit of her stomach. She felt like a coward. If you read this story with your children, you could ask at this point, "What are some ways Maddie could have helped Wanda? Suppose she wanted to be friendly toward Wanda but still stay friends with Peggy—how might she have done that?"

In the following box is the true story of a boy named Pascal. As a 2nd grader he at first joined in the teasing of a classmate, but then the cruelty got worse and he had to decide what to do. I encourage you to read and discuss Pascal's story with your children.

You can also share a time when you were a kid and saw others picking on someone—and how you responded. If you didn't do anything to help, or somehow took part in the bullying, you can share your feelings about that too. Our children and grandchildren can benefit from the mistakes we made and what we learned from them. I still wince when I think of mindlessly calling an overweight boy on our Little League baseball team "Fats" because that's what everybody else called him.

Pascal's Story: Standing Up to Bullies

In his book *The Men They Will Become*, Harvard pediatrician Eli H. Newberger tells the story of Pascal. When Pascal was a sophomore on his high school's wrestling team, the juniors and seniors would beat up the new freshman members as part of initiation, push them into lockers, turn out the lights, and violently shake the lockers.

Pascal was upset by this. One day after practice, he went up to the team's captain, a senior who was considerably bigger than he was. Pascal said to him, "I don't think initiation is a smart thing to do. We're losing kids. They're quitting."

The captain called him "pussy" and other names. But the hazing stopped for a few days. Then it started again. Pascal confronted the captain. They exchanged words. Pascal told him, "If you're going to hurt these kids, you're going to have to hurt me first." The hazing stopped.

Where did Pascal get that kind of compassion and courage? His parents said that when he was in second grade, the boys in his class picked on a kid named Joshua. Joshua was overweight, didn't smell good, and stuttered. On the playground, kids called him names and pinched him. Pascal told his parents about this and sheepishly admitted he had sometimes joined in the name-calling.

Then kids began throwing rocks at Joshua. That really bothered Pascal. He decided to ask his parents what he should do. They said he had to stick up for Joshua. Pascal's first response, his father remembers, was, "But, Dad, gee, I don't know . . . the other guys . . ." But his parents persisted. They said: "Look, if you go against your friends by doing the right thing and they make fun of you, they're not really your friends. Whether it's hard or not, this is the right thing to do."

Pascal's parents expressed confidence that he could do it. The next day on the playground, he told the other kids to lay off Joshua. Although Pascal had previously been well-liked by these kids, they called him "Joshua lover." But after that, they left Joshua alone.

Food for Thought

What Pascal did at 15 to stop hazing on his high school wrestling team was no fluke. At age 7, he had stood up for Joshua. Of course, not every kid can effectively confront bullies, but they can still help. Bullied kids interviewed by the Youth Voice Project say that it's a big help when other kids just say something supportive to them, invite them to sit with their group in the cafeteria, or take them to an adult who can help. What's important is that bystanders become "upstanders" who do *something*. What would you be willing to do if you saw someone being picked on?

Narnian Virtues

Let me tell you a bit more about the Narnian Virtues character education project that I described briefly in chapter 11 (www.narnianvirtues.leeds.ac.uk). It encourages schools to partner with parents in an effort to help children understand and apply 6 universal virtues: wisdom, justice, fortitude, self-control, love, and humility. The stories we're using are from C. S. Lewis's much-loved *Chronicles of Narnia*, which depict a universe where moral choices have significant consequences. Sixth graders read *The Lion, the Witch and the Wardrobe*; 7th graders, *Prince Caspian*; and 8th graders, *The Voyage of the Dawn Treader*. We also make use of relevant excerpts from other literature—classics such as *Little*

Women and *Lord of the Flies* and contemporary novels like *The Hunger Games*—that depict both virtue and vice.

Reading good books doesn't automatically make us better people, so we've devised various ways to help children relate the Narnia stories to their own lives. As they read and discuss each of these novels, we ask them to identify the virtues and vices shown in particular passages. We ask them to think of a time when, in their own lives, they've shown the same virtue or character flaw. You might consider doing the same with you child as you read a story, and share a time when you showed that virtue or flaw.

We've found English schoolchildren in our Narnia classrooms to be surprisingly forthcoming in their self-examinations. One 11-year-old boy said, "This project gets you thinking, like, 'Oh no—I've probably been doing that most of my life,' and it makes you think about how you can change it." Another boy said, "Edmund [in *The Lion, the Witch and the Wardrobe*] showed deceit by lying to his siblings. I've shown deceitfulness when lying about breaking something—I blamed it on someone else. I wouldn't do that again." These children are acquiring a "virtues vocabulary" that enables them to look at things from a moral point of view. An 11-year-old girl said, "Before Narnia I wouldn't have had a clue about what vices and virtues were. But now you're, like, 'Oh, what virtue is that character showing?' It's quite fun to think about it."

We know it's not realistic to expect kids to improve in all six Narnian virtues at the same time, so at the start of each school year we ask every child to choose just two of the six virtues to focus on—and then to make a Virtue Improvement Plan (VIP) for working on their two personal target virtues. To help them decide on their target virtues, we have them do a "My Character" self-assessment and discuss it with their parents. Note that we've constructed this self-examination to allow a child to say that they show a particular virtue at least some of the time *and* that they would like to exhibit that virtue more often. That makes this "look in the mirror" a positive experience—an opportunity to identify one's character assets—and not just a self-critical experience focused on identifying areas for improvement.

MY CHARACTER

Please check all the statements below that describe you. If both statements for a particular virtue are true—that you show that virtue some of the time, but would like to show it more often—then check both statements.

Wisdom

_____ I show good judgment and make good decisions.

_____ I'd like to show better judgment and make good decisions more of the time.

Love

_____ I show kindness toward everyone in my family and toward people outside my family.

_____ I'd like to be kind more of the time.

Fortitude

_____ I overcome difficulties and failures and don't give up when the going gets tough.

_____ I'd like to show greater determination to keep trying when the going gets tough.

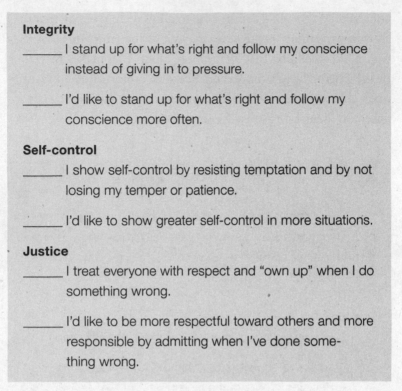

Integrity

_____ I stand up for what's right and follow my conscience instead of giving in to pressure.

_____ I'd like to stand up for what's right and follow my conscience more often.

Self-control

_____ I show self-control by resisting temptation and by not losing my temper or patience.

_____ I'd like to show greater self-control in more situations.

Justice

_____ I treat everyone with respect and "own up" when I do something wrong.

_____ I'd like to be more respectful toward others and more responsible by admitting when I've done something wrong.

After discussing their completed "My Character" with parents and getting their suggestions for which virtues to focus on, the child chooses two to work on over the whole fall term. We ask them to make their VIP with their parents and have a weekly conversation with at least one parent to discuss how they're doing. We provide a template that includes what we consider the necessary components of an effective plan. (See the sample template for a self-control VIP.)

I'd encourage you to help your child make a similar plan for whatever virtue they'd like to work on. You might also consider doing one for yourself, so that your child has a partner in this character journey. You'll be better able to guide their efforts—you'll have more sympathy and patience—if you're taking on the same kind of self-improvement challenge. Ideally, everyone in the family (who's old enough) would be working on a self-chosen target virtue.

VIP for Self-Control

Virtue	Challenges I've faced	Strategies I'll try	What happened
SELF-CONTROL	1. Losing patience when Kate is doing something to annoy me.	1. Ask her nicely to stop. If that doesn't work, say, "Would you please stop—or should I get Mom?" 2. Count to 20 to keep my temper. 3. Ask a parent to ask her to stop.	1. Asking nicely didn't work. But saying "Should I get Mom?" usually did. 2. I usually forgot to count. Once, I did lose my temper and yelled at her. 3. One time I did have to get Mom. Kate was mad at me for telling, but I had asked her to stop.
	2. Spending too much time on PlayStation.	1. Write out an agreement with Mom and Dad for when I can be on each day and how long. 2. Set the timer. 3. Lose it for the next day if I don't keep the agreement.	1. Mom and I made an agreement. Setting the timer helped. 2. Once, I went fifteen minutes over and lost it for the next day. But it was fair because I had agreed.

One mother spoke of her son's progress in self-control as a result of his VIP: "He realized that playing on his PlayStation was taking over his life. . . . Now he manages his time exceptionally well on that."

To make the most of reading time, I suggest choosing, as much as possible, books like the Narnia novels that entertain and teach good values at the same time. *Brightly Books* (www.readbrightly.com) recently ran a helpful article titled "Children's Books That Show Kids the Goodness in the World," on good picture books for young readers.[1] In Appendix B, I've recommended character-rich books for different developmental levels that I think your kids and you will enjoy.

Of course, you can talk about a good book with your child even if you don't read it together. Says one mom, "I read to our two younger ones, but I can't keep up with my nine-year-old daughter's reading. So in the car we talk about what she's currently reading or whenever we can find a few minutes. It works."

Watch and Talk About Good Movies

A good movie, documentary, or docudrama, like a good book, can teach important lessons about life and character. Good movies have a special power to inspire and stay in our imagination. As with books, our kids will get the most value out of a good movie if we spend at least some time talking about it together. Questions we liked to ask our kids about movies (and now the grandchildren): "What was your favorite part?" Then, "What lessons do you think the movie taught?" After the kids shared their thoughts, we'd give ours.

When our son Mark was a high school senior, he and I watched a two-part television movie on Raoul Wallenberg, the Swedish diplomat who was personally responsible for saving thousands of Jews from the Holocaust. After the show, we had a good discussion about why some people have a deep respect and caring for their fellow human beings and why others, like the Nazis, appear to have no regard for human life and dignity.

Amazing Grace is another film that dramatically depicts the contrast between those who feel responsible for the welfare of other people and those who treat certain categories of human beings as if they were subhuman. The movie tells the story of British Parliament member and antislavery crusader William Wilberforce. Sustained by friends, his faith, and his commitment to human rights, Wilberforce persevered for twenty years, despite defeat after political defeat, to finally end four hundred years of British slave trading. We also learn of Wilberforce's love for nature and animals and how he helped found the Society for the Prevention of Cruelty to Animals.

Amazing Grace can also serve as an occasion for discussing the still underreported and much-neglected problem of human trafficking, including sexual trafficking, in our country and around the world. Globally, an estimated twenty-five million persons are caught up in the nightmare of human trafficking; in the United States, according to the state department, 300,000 persons are victims of human trafficking each year. Two of our teenage grandchildren recently heard a presentation by a woman who heads a San Diego–based organization, Children of the Immaculate Heart, that helps minor girls who are survivors of trafficking and alerts young people to the dangers. Documentaries on global and US human trafficking include *Call + Response, Not My Life, Tricked: The Documentary,* and *The Abolitionists.* To learn what you can do to help, check out "15 Ways You Can Help Fight Human Trafficking," websites such as innocentsatrisk.org, and books such as *A Crime So Monstrous* by historian Benjamin Skinner.

For recommendations of many more movies with memorable role models and strong character themes, visit teachwithmovies.com, which also lists movies *not* recommended for kids. Michele Borba's

Building Moral Intelligence also has an appendix listing good books and movies. Here are some of my favorite films and the virtues they highlight:

- *The Miracle Worker* (Annie Sullivan's determination to find a way to teach language to 7-year-old Helen Keller, who is blind, deaf, and mute)
- *A Man for All Seasons* (integrity)
- *Gandhi* (the power of nonviolence)
- *Chariots of Fire* (friendship, quest for excellence, fidelity to principle)
- *The Spitfire Grill* (sacrificial love, forgiveness)
- *The Chronicles of Narnia: The Lion, the Witch and the Wardrobe* (loyalty, sacrifice, and courage)
- *The King's Speech* (loyalty, hope, courage)
- *42* (Jackie Robinson's courage and determination in being the first African-American to play Major League baseball)
- *Selma* (depicting the moral vision and courage of Martin Luther King Jr. and others who led the 1960s civil rights movement)
- *Sounder* (family love, resilience in the face of racism)
- *Hoosiers* (determination, humility, redemption)
- *Sense and Sensibility* (devotion to family, kindness, authentic love versus infatuation)
- *Up* (love, marriage, friendship, and kindness)
- *The Incredibles* (strong family themes)
- *Cinderella* (Disney's live-action portrayal of the heroine's dignity, kindness, and courage in the face of cruelty)
- *Wonder* (family, love, courage, friendship, and kindness)

Ask your friends who have children, "What are your top five favorite movies for watching with your kids—and why?" and keep a running list. For dozens of recommended movies for school-age kids, preteens, and teens, as well as links to character-centered "inspirational videos," check out 10kids.com.[2]

Also keep an eye out for stories of kindness and courage in the news. The *New York Times* op-ed columnist Nicholas Kristof is a regular source of reports—accompanied by short videos[3]—on extraordinarily kind and courageous work being done around the world.

Storytelling

Some years ago I had the pleasure of observing a 6th-grade teacher in Clovis, California, by the name of Tim Kent. Shortly before lunch, he sat on the edge of his desk and said to his students, "Would you like to hear a story?" Their eyes brightened, and he continued:

> This is a story about W. C. Fields. He was a comedian, and he lived in this part of central California. When he was dying, he was very uncomfortable. He couldn't sleep; he hadn't slept for nights. His wife knew he loved to go to sleep to the sound of the rain falling on the roof. But it hadn't rained in weeks. So one night, she took the garden hose and stood outside his bedroom, spraying water on the roof to make the sound of rain. He fell asleep—and that night, he died in his sleep.

You could hear a pin drop; the children were clearly touched by the story. Then Tim Kent added a simple comment: "That's a story about love. She did that because she loved him."

After his students had gone to lunch, he said to me: "That's my main way of teaching character—the told story. I get them from things I read, the Internet, my grandfather, my own life experience. Every story teaches a lesson about character, about life."

As Tim Kent discovered, there's something particularly powerful about *telling* a story. Telling a story makes it personal; it comes through us, to the listener, as a kind of gift. Many teachers have discovered the emotional bond that storytelling creates with their students.

When is the last time you told a story to one of your children? They'd love to hear stories from when you were a kid. How were things different—maybe easier in some ways, harder in others—when you were growing up? What jobs did you have to do? What was school like? What was a time you were really scared? A time when you got in trouble but learned an important lesson? A time when some kind person did something for you that you'll never forget? A time when you helped someone who really needed it?

Pick a time or situation that feels natural and when you won't be competing with a screen—such as a walk together, playing or working outside, over a meal or snack, or after bedtime reading. Your kids will remember the stories you tell them.

～

These are some of the ways we can use stories as a tool for teaching virtue. Ask everyone in the family to keep an eye out for good stories—and to share them.

CHAPTER 14

Schools That Cultivate Kindness

I'm working very hard to teach my children to be good persons.
I need to know that the school is backing me up.

—A MOTHER

W E CAN DO a great many things to form our children's character in the family. That's where the foundation is laid down. A parent's socializing influence is there from the very beginning and endures throughout a child's growing years. The emotional bond between you and your child deepens the impact of your values and example. Parents are also uniquely positioned to surround their child with a spiritual heritage that provides a vision of life's meaning and ultimate reasons to lead a good life.

But schools also matter. Consider how many hours your kids spend at school each week—interacting with their teachers, coaches, and friends; hearing messages and seeing examples that— you hope—will promote kindness and respect but sadly, in too many cases, do not. Each day, the range and sheer number of human interactions your children observe and experience at school considerably exceeds their experiences at home. So, in the big picture of what influences your child's growth in virtue, the quality of character education at their school is very important. You want what's happening at school to support, not undermine, what you are trying to teach at home.

Let's look at how schools across the country, at every developmental level, are cultivating kindness, respect, courage, honesty, and the other essential virtues. In a school of character, these virtues are modeled, upheld, discussed, celebrated, personalized, and practiced in every part of school life—from the caring and example set by adults to the relationships among students, the handling of discipline and conflicts, the content of the curriculum, the instructional process, the rigor of academic standards, the ethos of the environment, and the partnership with parents. Character education is everything that happens in a school. Every child, every parent, deserves a school where the kids are learning to be smart *and* good.

Let's Be Courteous, Let's Be Caring

Before bullying became a national concern, Henry Winkelman Elementary School, on Chicago's North Shore, had the kind of culture that can easily breed peer cruelty. Put-downs and fights among students were a problem. Kids would "smart off" to teachers and other adults in the building, saying, "I don't have to listen to you!" The school served an extraordinarily diverse community. More than forty different languages were represented among its families, who were Irish, Italian, Asian, African-American, Brazilian, Mexican, Indian, Pakistani, and Greek. There was also a high level of economic diversity. Some kids came from homes on welfare, while others arrived in limos.

Winkelman's test scores were well above the norm; it was student behavior they were concerned about. The principal and faculty decided that to deal more effectively with the behavioral challenges, they needed a schoolwide character education program. At the start of the new year, they launched a project they called Let's Be Courteous, Let's Be Caring.

I visited Winkelman three years later; by then its character-education initiative had won a Chicago-area award. When I walked into the school lobby, the first thing I saw was a giant display defining courtesy and caring in terms of concrete, observable school behaviors. "Courtesy" was defined as (1) saying please, thank you, you're welcome, and excuse me; (2) being a good listener; (3) waiting your turn; (4) acting politely everywhere; and (5) discussing problems. "Caring" was defined as (1) sharing; (2) respecting others' feelings; (3) following rules; (4) working cooperatively; and (5) being a good friend. This was a big first step toward creating a unified school culture based on clear norms, illustrated with behavioral examples that everybody could understand.

Next came a bigger challenge: how to bring these new expectations to life in every classroom. On the first day of school in September, all teachers asked their students, "What rules do we need that will help us show courtesy and show caring in our classroom?" In this way, kids learned to see rules as the expression of something deeper—shared values. When a student didn't follow one of the class rules they had made together, a teacher would take the child aside and ask quietly, "Did that behavior show courtesy?" "Did it show caring?" In this way, students learned to use those standards to reflect on their own character and conduct.

Parents were asked to make a conscious effort to foster these qualities in family life. Then, at the parent–teacher conferences in October, the teachers said, "We're emphasizing courtesy and caring at school, but we need your help at home." At weekly school assemblies students performed skits on courtesy and caring, or invited speakers from the community to come in and talk about them. Finally, every Winkelman student in grades first through sixth was asked to do community service, working with the elderly or the physically handicapped. Children were learning to care by giving care.

The school recognized acts of good character through Winkelgrams, bright yellow, preprinted, 5 x 8 message forms that anyone could use to write a note of appreciation to anyone else. There were stacks of Winkelgrams everywhere. On the day I was there, the principal had just sent a Winkelgram to a 4th-grade girl who had helped a 2nd grader when she fell on the playground: "Dear Lori, Thanks for being a super person and helping somebody in trouble. Mrs. Sechrist." A class of 2nd graders wrote Winkelgrams to the school custodian thanking him for his help on a special classroom project.

Winkelman's school culture and student behavior steadily improved. When I visited, parents said fights were now very rare. When I ate lunch with the kids in the cafeteria, they told me that if you forgot your lunch, someone would always give you some of theirs. A veteran teacher who had taught in several Chicago-area schools and came to Winkelman after it started its character program said that Winkelman students showed "an unusually high level of respect for teachers and each other." Three years after beginning its Let's Be Courteous, Let's Be Caring program, Winkelman was selected to receive a Chicago-wide award for excellence in both academics and character.

The National Character Education Movement

Given the importance of character in our personal and public lives, the character education movement is arguably our country's most important educational reform. There are lots of turnaround stories like Winkelman's, where schools facing poor student behavior, low academic achievement, low faculty morale, or all of these and more, decide to put character first. These schools create a shared sense of purpose and identity—based on character. They typically reap the rewards in the form of better academic performance and better interpersonal behavior. The nation gets better citizens in the bargain.

To give you another picture of a "character first" classroom, let me take you from Chicago to rural West Virginia, where Deb Austin Brown has taught for more than thirty years, first as a kindergarten teacher and now as a 6th-grade teacher. (She's also written two very good handbooks—*Growing Character* and *The Success Strategies*—describing exactly what she does with her students.[1]) Many of the kids in the school where she now teaches come from the town's trailer parks. Most come from a home with no father figure.

When you enter Deb Austin Brown's classroom, the first thing that catches your eye are the words printed in very large letters high on the wall behind her desk: OUR DECISIONS DEFINE US. On the first day of school, she explains to her students what those words mean:

> Each day we make dozens of decisions—big and small. We create our character by the decisions we make. Even our smallest decisions add up in big ways to determine the kind of person we become. Decisions to be kind or to be cruel, to be respectful or disrespectful, to do our best work or not do our best—all of these decisions shape our character and shape our lives.

Those are big ideas about character that all of us can teach our kids. Families and schools should speak with one voice: "We create our character by the choices we make. Make good choices."

Next, Mrs. Brown talks to her class about the Golden Rule and what kindness and respect look like and sound like. Then she asks, "What do you want from me as your teacher this year—what makes a good teacher?" Hands shoot up. She records her students' ideas on chart paper, takes them home, and uses them to create her teacher pledge. The next morning, she reads her pledge to the students, signs it in front of them, posts it on the wall, and promises she will do her best to live by it.

Here's how her pledge read last year:

- I will listen to each of you and care about what you have to say.
- I will speak in a soft, respectful voice.

- I will treat everyone fairly, with no favorites.
- I will grade and return papers in a timely manner.
- I will help every student who asks for help.

That afternoon, she asks her students, "What makes a good class?" She leads them in generating a list of student behaviors that will make their classroom a good place to be:

- I will listen when my teacher and classmates are talking.
- I will be kind and helpful to classmates and not leave anyone out.
- I will complete my assignments and turn them in on time.
- I will try to do the right thing—even when it is hard.
- I will not lie, cheat, or take things that do not belong to me.

After each student signs the student pledge, it is posted on the wall next to her teacher pledge.

Every day begins with a morning meeting in which students share good news (like the birth of a baby sister) and sometimes sad news (someone's dog got hit by a car). And every Friday, Mrs. Brown gives her students the same homework assignment for the weekend, aimed at forging a strong partnership with parents:

1. Read for twenty minutes each day! (Kids report what they actually do read.)
2. Have fun and spend some time with your family!
3. Do a good deed!

On Mondays, she asks the children to share the good deeds they did in their families over the weekend. She comments, "By the end of the school year, we have charts all over the room listing hundreds of good deeds the kids have done."

One year, early in December, 11-year-old Drew disclosed to the group in morning meeting that he had been a bully at his previous school. "I was a punk," he said. "I used to make little kids cry." Deb Brown says:

> We were all surprised. We had not seen any evidence of this from Drew. I think our classroom's emphasis on character had given him a chance to make a new start. I think deep down, kids want to be good. They all want attention. They all need love. A lot of them don't know how to get it.

Drew said that in Mrs. Brown's classroom, "it was easier to be kind." Drew later moved on to other schools but kept in touch with Mrs. Brown. He says he never went back to his bullying ways.

Why Cooperative Learning Matters

Schools that do character education well ensure that students have regular opportunities for high-quality collaborative learning. More than a hundred studies show that having students work in teams of two, three, or four—when it's designed correctly to make sure there's both *interdependence of effort* (everyone has an essential part to play) and *individual accountability* for learning (at the end, everybody takes a test or produces some other evidence of learning)—increases academic motivation and learning, promotes respect for the ideas and talents of others, reduces prejudice, and gives students necessary practice in the teamwork skills needed in the twenty-first-century workplace.[2]

American schools, reflecting American culture, often foster competition more than they teach cooperation. One study found that students in highly competitive classrooms were likely to act more aggressively toward their peers. By contrast, in classrooms that made greater use of cooperative learning, students were more likely to be kind and helpful toward classmates.[3]

Why Student Voice Matters

Schools of character give students voice—an opportunity and responsibility to help shape the culture of the school, just as kids in a family can help to shape its culture through family meetings. As one high school student leader put it:

> For students, it's very important that their voice be heard. It gives them a chance to tell the school what they think. There would be a major difference in a school's moral character if students were just given the chance to express themselves. This would show students that administrators and teachers respected them, and students would be more likely to show respect in return.

In our center's *Smart & Good High Schools* study of twenty-four award-winning high schools, we describe how these schools give their students a voice and responsibility in creating a culture of excellence and ethics. (You can download this study from our website: http://www2.cortland.edu/centers/character/high-schools/). One way they do that is simply to ask their students, "How can we improve our school?"

A Hudson, Massachusetts, school superintendent recounted how each year, his district's high school devoted a half day to having the entire student body participate in small-group, student-led discussions of school improvement. One of the first issues identified was the lack of integration of new students. As a result of increased immigration, about 15 percent of the student body were now coming from countries such as Brazil, Portugal, Mexico, and Guatemala. To address the feelings of isolation these new students felt, the student body established a program called Friends, in which students volunteered to buddy with students from other countries.

Our *Smart & Good* study found that some high schools have redesigned their student governments to function as a representative democracy. Student delegates serve as representatives of their class-rooms, seek input from their constituency on any given issue, and report back to them. At Troup County Comprehensive High School in LaGrange, Georgia, the redesigned student government is called the leadership team. It consists of nine groups of ten students—two elected representatives from each second-period English class. Through this participatory school-wide process, the leadership team in its first year developed—and the school adopted—an honor code that covered not only lying, cheating, and stealing, but also bringing drugs or weapons to school and all forms of bullying.

Troup High School's Honor Code

1. I will be honest in all my actions.

2. I will treat others in the same way I want to be treated.

3. I will extend kindness and respect to all.

4. I will treat our school building and other people's property with care.

5. I will strive for a spirit of pride in all our school programs.

6. I will have the courage to report bullying in any form and the possession of drugs or weapons on our school campus.

7. I will uphold this honor code and exhibit these same behaviors when I represent our school off campus.

When we visited Troup High School at the start of the school year, the principal was presenting the leadership team with a new challenge: "This past year we've seen many more incidents of drugs being reported and wallets and purses being turned in with their contents intact. But we still have incidents of disrespect and theft. We need your input to continue to improve our school: What can we do to promote and recognize honor code behaviors?"

On the eve of World War II, the distinguished social psychologist Kurt Lewin published a study, still cited today, showing that peer scapegoating is greatest in groups characterized by an "autocratic atmosphere." In autocratic groups, power is exercised unilaterally, top down, in a way that gives group members little or no voice.[4] By contrast, Lewin found that scapegoating and peer disrespect are lowest when there is a "democratic atmosphere" that provides many opportunities for all group members to make their voices heard.

~

All schools inevitably affect the character of their students by everything they do. The question is whether a school will do character education well—as thoughtfully and systematically as it undertakes math, science, and any other area of the academic curriculum. Wherever your child's school is in its character-education journey, you and other parents can encourage it to make character development a high priority and to take advantage of the resources on best practices.

Just some of what's available to schools: Harvard's Making Caring Common project (https://mcc.gse.harvard.edu/), led by professor Rick Weissbourd; Marvin Berkowitz's Center for Character and Citizenship (www.characterandcitizenship.org) and its Leadership Academy for Character Education; the *Journal of Character Education*; national organizations such as Character.org and Character Counts!; our center's website, cortland.edu/character;

and any number of how-to books. Mine include *Educating for Character, Character Matters,* and (with Matthew Davidson) *Smart & Good High Schools.* Hal Urban's *Lessons from the Classroom: 20 Things Good Teachers Do* is a treasure trove of easy-to-use classroom strategies.[5] Kevin Ryan and Karen Bohlin's *Building Character in Schools* is another book I routinely recommend.[6] Galit Breen's *Kindness Wins* is well described by its subtitle: *A Simple, No-Nonsense Guide to Teaching Our Kids How to Be Kind Online.*[7] Matthew Davidson's Institute for Excellence and Ethics (www.excellenceandethics.org) can help your child's school assess to what extent its character initiative is having the desired impact and how it can be strengthened. Schools can also point parents toward a new online resource, www.familiesofcharacter.com.

I would also encourage you to communicate in writing that you care at least as much about character as academics. And take the trouble, now and again, to drop a note or email to a teacher or the principal to express appreciation for something the school or your child's classroom has done to promote good character.

If your children can be in a kind, respectful, character-building school environment for the many hours they're not with you, then what you're doing at home will be honored and supported. That will be a blessing for your children and for you.

CHAPTER 15

How to Help Your Kids Avoid the Dangers of a Hypersexualized Culture—and Find True Love

It's to get the likes. Everything's about the likes.
—NINA, AGE 14, EXPLAINING WHY
GIRLS POST NUDE PHOTOS

S O FAR WE'VE LOOKED at three significant cultural changes that make the work of raising kind, respectful, and responsible children more challenging than ever: an angry and increasingly violent political culture; a culture of entitlement that fosters self-centeredness on the part of kids and slows their progress toward adulthood; and a screen-driven culture that impoverishes family relationships, disrupts children's healthy brain functioning, and fosters among teens (especially girls) a fragile sense of identity and susceptibility to anxiety and depression.

Let's look now at a fourth cultural challenge: a hypersexualized environment that sexualizes our children at ever younger ages, normalizes extreme behavior, and is now exacerbated by ubiquitous pornography and social media's promotion of sexual attitudes that are the opposite of respect for the self and others. How can we help our children make good decisions about romantic relationships and maximize their chances of finding real love? I'll share some strategies and resources (including the "True-Love Character Test") that our center has used in its character education work with parents and schools, and I'll describe some recent positive developments on college campuses. There's a lot of bad news out there about the sexual culture, but there's some good news too.

How Social Media Sexualizes Our Children

The 2016 bestseller *American Girls: Social Media and the Secret Lives of Teenagers* by award-winning journalist Nancy Jo Sales turned an unnerving light on the hypersexualized world that American adolescents are now growing up in.[1] She visited ten states and talked to more than two hundred girls and reports in detail how they think about sex, their bodies, the hookup culture, how to attract the attention of boys, and how to stay plugged into the latest hot thing on social media.

Sydney, one of the girls interviewed by Sales, attends a public school in New York City. She used to go to a private school, but her father was laid off and the family could no longer afford the tuition. At her private school, she says she wore a uniform. At her public school, she "couldn't believe what the girls wear. They wear, like, tube tops, bandeaux, and those high-waisted short-shorts that show all your butt cheeks. But if you don't dress like that, you're considered weird, and you will get shunned."

Sales asked her how this way of dressing in school had become the norm.

"Everything on TV and websites tells you to look like this," Sydney said. "They say this is how to get a guy. Everything is based off looks and how many likes you get. So a lot of girls post pictures with literally nothing on, or bikini shots. . . . Girls see that and want to compete for more likes and hotter pictures."

Sydney described boys' response to all of this: "[G]uys judge girls so much by the kind of photos they have up. Like on Ask.fm they say your name and ask, like, 'smash or pass' [whether someone wants to have sex with you]. And boys answer 'smash' or 'pass.' It makes you feel awful. I hate it."

What is the current boy–girl social scene like? Sales asked.

"There's no such thing as dating anymore," Sydney said. "The way people get together is they hook up at a party and he'll ask for her number. . . . It all starts with hooking up. There are a lot of parties [typically in houses where the parents aren't home]. . . . [T]he guys try to hook up with as many people as possible."

"At one party?" Sales asked.

Sydney said, "Yeah. The boys have lists and stuff. This kid in my grade has this list of ninety-two girls he's hooked up with."

Sales asked if that ever seemed awkward, hooking up with more than one person at the same event?

"[I]t's not considered a big deal," Sydney said. "The 'in' thing for girls to do is to really just go nuts at parties, just go insane. They feel the more they drink and the crazier they act, the more guys will come to them."

At a mall in LA, Sales talked with 16-year-old Melissa and her friends. Melissa said, "My friend, she was VC-ing [video chatting] this guy. . . . He sent so many nudes to her, but she wasn't trusting he wouldn't show her pictures to other people. So she Skyped him and showed him nudes that way. He took a screenshot without her knowing it. He sent it to so many people and the entire baseball team. . . . He still has it and won't delete it."

Sales asked why girls sent nudes, or posted provocative pictures of themselves, if they knew they could be spread around.

"More provocative equals more likes," one girl said offhandedly.

Sales wanted to understand, why are girls complicit in this very self-undermining aspect of social-media culture? Again and again, she heard the same explanation. As one 14-year-old girl put it: "[I]t's just to get attention. It's to get the likes, everything's about the likes."

At a mall in Williamsburg, Virginia, Sales asked a group of girls if there is a difference in how a girl is seen for sending nudes, versus boys.

"Oh, yes," they said.

"A girl who sends naked pictures, she's a slut," one girl explained. "But if a boy does it, everyone just laughs." Same for sex. Girls talked about this double standard as if it were just a fact of life.

One of the ostensible aims of the sexual revolution was to fight misogyny. But if *American Girls* is an accurate account, sexism is back with a vengeance. Reviewers of *American Girls* say things like, "If you have a teenage daughter, read this book—and have her read it, too." Good advice. But we should obviously read and discuss it with our sons as well. We should ask them, "What percentage of the boys at school, would you say, think like this about girls? Why, in your opinion? What percentage of the girls at school think this way about boys? Why?"

Our kids might not tell us just how bad it is, but that's okay; our goal should be to start a conversation—and keep it going. And in that process, to make it clear, beyond a shadow of a doubt, what our own views are: that the sexual attitudes prevailing on social media are demeaning and dehumanizing for both sexes. That viewing women as things is part of a sexual culture that includes scandalously high levels of sexual assault (an estimated one out of five women, according to the Centers for Disease Control and Prevention, is the victim of an attempted or completed rape in the course of her lifetime). That our bodies are part of who we are as a person. If you have religious faith, you can add that they are sacred, a gift of God.

You can point out that the hookup culture empties sex of dignity, beauty, and love. That living nonstop in a social media world that takes such attitudes for granted is a terrible way to prepare for a mature, loving, and committed relationship as an adult. That you don't want to carry into that relationship the memories and emotional baggage of debased, meaningless sex. That someday you may be married with children of your own and will want to teach them healthy attitudes toward sex. Now is the time to start developing those attitudes yourself.

How Porn Affects Our Kids: What the Research Shows

American Girls rightly calls attention to the role of pornography in promoting the sexual attitudes that dominate social media and encourage behavior like sexting. If kids are viewing Internet porn—as are more and more kids (mostly boys, but increasing numbers of girls as well), at younger ages—should we be surprised that they themselves are creating and posting what amounts to pornography? Periodically, the news will report a "sexting ring," in which nude photographs of teens are being circulated among wide groups of students. The girls in such photos strike a porn-star look, with glistening pursed lips and butts stuck out. These "amateur pornography sites," Sales says—kids call them "slut pages"—existed at every school she visited.

There are still some people who will say the jury is out on whether pornography is really harmful. That's a position that's increasingly difficult to maintain. In October 2015, the American College of Pediatricians issued *The Impact of Pornography on Children*, a review of the growing scientific literature on the damage done by pornography. In youth, the consumption of pornography is linked to increased rates of depression, anxiety, violent behavior, early sexual debut, sexual promiscuity, and higher rates of teen pregnancy. Children who have viewed pornography are more likely than those who haven't to sexually assault other children.

In the 1980s, well before Internet porn (when pornography was tame compared to today), two psychologists conducted an experiment in which college students and nonstudents from the community viewed pornographic material for six weeks.[2] A control group did not. Compared to the non-viewing group, those who viewed pornography for this length of time became more interested in extreme forms of pornography, considered rape less of a crime, were more likely to believe that promiscuity is normal, were more accepting of sexual infidelity, valued marriage less, and expressed less desire to have children. This experiment was ethically controversial because it exposed subjects to something that could harm them. But because of its inclusion of a control group, it provided experimental evidence that viewing pornography could *cause* significant changes in attitudes and values.

In 2012, the journal *Sexual Addiction & Compulsivity* published a research review, "The Impact of Internet Pornography on Adolescents," that analyzed dozens of studies from around the world, including countries as diverse as China, the Netherlands, the United Kingdom, and the United States.[3] Among the findings:

- The negative impact of Internet pornography on adolescent sexual attitudes and behavior appears to be a global trend.
- The more frequently teens view sexually explicit Internet material, the more they think about sex, the stronger their interest in sex, and the more they become distracted by their thoughts about sex.
- The more teens consume pornography, the more likely they are to approve of casual sex and to view women as sex objects.
- Girls tend to report feeling physically inferior to the women they see in pornographic material. Boys worry that they may not be able to perform as the men in pornographic films do.
- The more teens watch porn, the more likely some are to engage in high-risk sexual behaviors such as anal sex, sex with multiple partners, and sex while using drugs.

- When teens view pornography that depicts violence, they are more likely to become aggressive in their own sexual behavior. In a Canadian study, the more pornography boys consumed, the more likely they were to agree that it is acceptable to hold a girl down and force her to have sex.
- The more teens consume porn, the more likely they are to engage in delinquent behavior, become depressed, and have trouble forming close relationships with their parents and other caregivers.[4]

How to Talk to Your Kids About Pornography

The sobering research findings on porn's corrupting effects on adolescents should motivate us to be proactive and not wait until our kids are teens before addressing this issue. In the US and UK, the average age at which boys begin to access Internet pornography is now 11.[5] This means that some form of parental teaching about pornography is needed before the middle school years in an effort to prevent involvement and to establish a moral framework for discussing pornography should involvement occur.

If you have an elementary school–aged child, I recommend you consider reading your child the picture book *Good Pictures Bad Pictures: Porn-Proofing Today's Young Kids* by Kristen A. Jenson and Gail Poyner. Jenson blogs at *Protect Young Minds*; Poyner is a psychologist and a child and adult therapist who treats various disorders, including pornography addiction. The authors acknowledge that good parents want to protect their kids' innocence, but they point out a sad reality: "[C]hildren, all over the world, begin viewing hard-core Internet pornography long before their parents even consider discussing its dangers."

The tragic stories of individual children damaged by pornography illustrate the dangers. One girl, for her eighth birthday, got an Internet-abled device, which prompted her to do online searches for information about sex, which led to the violent world of hardcore porn. She became withdrawn and depressed until her mother discovered her involvement. A 7-year-old boy, after being shown a pornographic magazine by his older cousins, sought out more and more pornographic pictures and eventually developed an addiction to Internet porn that lasted for decades. After being molested by his foster sister, a 6-year-old boy became involved with Internet pornography, developed an addiction to it as a teen, and during his teen years molested his younger siblings while he hid his addiction.[6]

Good Pictures Bad Pictures is written in sensitive, gentle language (e.g., some pictures are good, like pictures of our family and friends; bad pictures show the private parts of the body that we cover with a swimsuit) that enables you to explain, with a minimum of embarrassment, what pornography is and what your child should do if he or she sees it. The books teach kids a 5-step CAN DO plan to use if they ever come across pornography: "Close my eyes; always tell a trusted adult; name it when I see it; distract myself; order my thinking brain to be the boss!"[7]

In a 2017 post for *Protect Young Minds*, Jenson alerts parents to five back-to-school dangers related to pornography: (1) *Smartphones.* Kids bring them to school and share XXX videos on the bus or playground. (2) *School computers.* Even innocent searches for images can bring up pornography. (3) *Library databases* link kids to pornographic books. (4) *Slang terms* spark curiosity and often lead to online searches and pornography. (5) *Sexualized conversations or behaviors* acted out by children who have viewed pornography or have been sexually abused. In one incident, a 3rd-grade girl overheard a classmate say that her father made her watch videos of naked people. Says the mother of the 3rd grader who overheard the comment: "Because we had discussed the dangers of pornography at home, she knew how to react. She told her teacher, and the school responded by addressing the needs of the student and putting a stop to the abuse."[8]

Parental vigilance is also needed regarding the homes our kids might be invited to by their friends. A mother of two girls, ages 11 and 6, says: "My children's friends come over to our house nearly every day. They feel safe here. But I don't allow my girls to go to other kids' houses, strict as that may sound. I don't know what the language there will be, what will be on the TV or laptop or video games, whether pornography will be on the coffee table, or whether Mom will have a boyfriend in the house." If you're fortunate to have friends whose values are similar to your own, you may feel more secure than this mother about letting your child go to other people's homes, but the larger point still holds: in today's moral environment, parental supervision is more important than ever.

As our children get older, the challenges posed by pornography are greater. If you don't go after it, it will come after you. For young people, especially young boys, the temptations and pressures will be immense. Thanks to the Internet, a universe of endless, ever-changing sexual stimulation, including real-time sex, is just a click away.

In high schools these days, boys will discuss at the lunch table the latest porn they've watched and ask each other what they've done or would be willing to do. A colleague who directed an ethics and character education center in Washington, DC, recounted a conversation initiated by an 8th-grade boy who spoke enthusiastically about all the pornography he watched with his friends. "All kinds of sex—oral sex, anal sex, group sex, you name it. His mind is full of this stuff. He says his favorite video is *Blacks and Blondes*. He says he and his friends play truth or dare, in which they perform on each other various sexual acts they've watched on porn."

If you have sons and they go to college, they will most likely be in an environment where about 70 percent of their peers will be watching porn on a regular basis. Surveys show that a steadily increasing percentage of girls and women are into pornography now too. Even if a girl doesn't watch pornography on her own initiative, chances are her boyfriend will try to get her to view porn with him and then do what they've watched. Many girls report feeling insecure about their bodies and say that they feel they have to act like porn stars.

Teenage girls today are under a great deal of pressure to be considered "sex-positive," which has been promoted by some feminists as a sign of sexual liberation. Feminists are divided on the issue of porn; many see it as deeply sexist and misogynist. "You can spin it any way you want . . . ," says Harvard Medical School psychologist John Chirban, "[w]ith porn, you're not looking at the meaning and value of a whole human being. Girls take away from it the message that their most worthy attribute is their sexual hotness."[9]

Porn's Misogynist Content

For us to fully appreciate the dangers posed by porn and the urgency of addressing this subject with our kids, we need to realize what they are watching if they view the hard-core pornography (called "gonzo" by the industry) that is now all over the Internet. The research findings we've looked at so far give us a picture of how viewing porn negatively influences the sexual attitudes and behavior of teens, but those findings don't tell us what Internet pornography actually *shows* our kids. As parents, we need to know that before we sit down to talk to our children.

To give you some idea of the content your kids may be taking in if they view Internet porn, let me draw from the book *Pornland: How Porn Has Hijacked Our Sexuality* by Gail Dines, a professor of sociology and women's studies at Wheelock College and a frequent commentator on television and radio programs.[10] You may find what she reports painful to read about; frankly, I find it painful to write about it and wish I didn't have to. But I think we owe it to our kids to be informed about what they and their peer group are likely to be exposed to—and in some cases become addicted to.

As a scholar who writes about sexual culture, Dines has been lecturing on pornography for more than two decades. She says she consistently finds that most women, and some men, have an idea of pornography that is twenty years out of date; what comes to their minds is often a *Playboy* centerfold. To show her audiences what contemporary pornography is like, Dines uses a PowerPoint presentation consisting of snapshots from popular porn sites. In the introduction to her book she writes: "I use words rather than pictures here, but I need to add that however extreme the scenes I describe sound, my descriptions are nothing compared to actually viewing porn."

To randomly sample pornographic images on the Internet, Dines began by typing "porn" into Google and clicking on some of the sites that appeared on the first page. Within seconds, she was directed to "hundreds of sites that depicted a whole range of sex acts." She reports: "Some of the most popular acts advertised and depicted during my quick search were: vaginal, anal, and oral penetration of a woman by three or more men at the same time; double anal, in which a woman is penetrated anally by two men at the same time; double vaginal, in which a woman is penetrated vaginally by two men at the same time; and bukkake, in which any number of men ejaculate, often at the same time, onto a woman's body, face, hair, eyes, ears, or mouth."[11]

As revolting as all that may be, it doesn't completely convey the misogynist attitude toward women being promoted by such sites. As one of many examples, Dines quotes the introductory text (edited slightly here) advertising a website offering a free porn search engine: "Do you know what we say to things like romance and foreplay? We say f—k off! We take gorgeous young bitches and do what every man would REALLY like to do. We make them gag till their makeup starts running, and then they get all other holes sore—vaginal, anal, double penetrations, anything brutal involving a cock and an orifice. And then we give them the sticky bath!"[12]

In *American Girls*, Sales takes note of the same brutality and contempt for the women portrayed in porn. "The words the porn industry uses to describe its videos tell the story: women are 'pounded,' 'railed,' and 'jackhammered,' called 'cunts,' 'sluts,' 'bitches,' and 'whores.'"

Sales writes, "A search for 'violent sex' on the Internet, turns up millions of results, including videos tagged 'violent rape porn' and 'cruel sex.'" The *Washington Post* reported on Rape Tube, a site that urges users to share what it called "fantasy" videos of sexual attacks. The *Post* found dozens of similar sites showing sexual attacks on drunken women, on lesbians, on schoolgirls.[13]

One study analyzed the content of Internet porn videos and found that most scenes in fifty of the top-rented Internet videos contained physical and verbal abuse of the female performers, with an average of twelve abusive acts per scene. The number of sexual partners in a scene ranged from one to nineteen. Gang rape and brutal and repeated anal sex were frequently featured.[14] Always, the female performers appear to be enjoying the abuse and humiliation. The porn industry's exploitation and abuse of women makes pornography not just a sexual issue but a social justice issue as well. We should point this out to our sons and our daughters.

If you find all of this hard to read, imagine it going into the mind and emotions of a 6- or 16-year-old—and, worse yet, staying there and affecting their character and how they think about sex. In a 2016 Middlesex University study of British 11- to 16-year-olds, conducted at the request of Anne Longfield, the Children's Commissioner for England, more than half the boys (53 percent) and four out of ten girls said they thought Internet pornography is a realistic depiction of sex. By the time they were 13 or 14, nearly half the boys (four out of ten) said they wanted to copy the behaviors they had seen.[15] These findings prompted Parliament to pass a law to protect minors by requiring pornographic websites to install age verification checks that do not permit anyone to view porn videos unless they register with a verification program.[16]

A pornographic culture is obviously the antithesis of a moral culture that promotes respect and kindness. We may work hard as parents to instill those virtues when our kids are children and then see it all put at risk when, as teens, they are drawn into a corrupting sexual culture. What can we say to them about why pornography is immoral and something they should avoid like the plague? Here are a few things:

1. Pornography treats people as objects to be used and abused for the sexual pleasure of viewers and the profit of the pornographers. Every person has human dignity and should never be disrespected or exploited.

2. Sex is meant to express and deepen love between people. Porn doesn't show love; it shows hate. It never includes the behaviors that are part of healthy, caring sexual relationships, such as intimate conversation, kissing, cuddling, and being responsive to each other's needs. In pornography, deviant, violent, and abusive sex is the norm.

3. The mind stores everything. Once you let pornographic images into your mind, you may not be able to get rid of them even if you want to.

4. Pornography changes the brain, like a drug. It can quickly become addictive and can take over your life. Because it changes what the brain finds sexually attractive, it can reduce your ability to have normal sexual relationships with real people.

With middle schoolers and up, I recommend sitting down with them and checking out two tailored-to-youth websites: fightthe newdrug.org and pornkillslove.com. Both were created by young adults who have launched a worldwide movement that uses science to educate people about how "porn harms the brain, the heart, and the world." They tell their story in a hopeful and uplifting three-minute video, *A Movement for Love*[17] (well worth watching). For young people who may already be hooked on porn and need help breaking free, the Fight the New Drug website offers the Fortify app with "a battle tracker and behavior analytics that will help you monitor your progress and avoid triggers."

Teach Boys How Porn Can Fry Their Brain

How does pornography affect our brain? Why is it being called "the drug of the twenty-first century"? Our kids need to know this, especially our sons. A clear explanation is given in the article "The Science Behind Pornography"[18] by Kevin Majeres, a psychiatrist and cognitive-behavior therapist at Harvard Medical School. He explains that when our sexual desires are not governed by our highest ideals, by the upper brain, "the animal instincts regarding sex come to dominate."

> Scientists have discovered that if you place a male rat in a cage with a receptive female, they will mate; but once done, the male rat will not mate more times, even if the female is still receptive. He loses all sexual interest. But if, right after he finishes with the first female, you put in a second receptive female, he will immediately mate again; and again a third, and so on, until he nearly dies. This effect has been found in every animal studied. . . .
>
> This explains why men use pornography. Pornography's power comes from the way it tricks the man's lower brain. . . .

Pornography offers a man an unlimited number of seemingly willing females; every time he sees a new partner, with each click, it gears up his sex drive again. . . . [T]he lower brain actually comes to prefer pornography to real sex . . .

The reason has to do with a chemical called dopamine. "Dopamine," Majeres explains, "is the drug of desire. . . . [W]hen someone clicks and sees a new pornographic image . . . he gets an enormous dopamine flood in his upper brain, causing a wild amount of electrical energy."

Each new [image] causes another flood of dopamine, time after time, click after click. . . . It's a dopamine binge. The brain's synapses (connections) do NOT like being overstimulated with dopamine, so they respond by destroying some dopamine receptors. This makes [the man] feel depleted, so he goes back to pornography, but having fewer dopamine receptors, this time it requires more to get the same dopamine thrill; but this causes his brain to destroy more receptors.

In other words, the brain, remarkably, "has a mind of its own." It doesn't like being overstimulated by a flood of dopamine, so it protects itself by shutting down dopamine receptors. "Guys start to find that they have to use pornography for longer and longer periods to have the same effect," Majeres says, "and they have to visit more and more sites."

What happens next is that men often turn to increasingly extreme forms of pornography, including violent and abusive porn, child pornography, and other things they would have found repulsive before. In *Pornland*, Gail Dines says she has interviewed many young men who are now hooked on the gonzo porn that demeans, debases, and brutalizes women. They say things like, "I never imagined that I'd be watching stuff like this or that I would need it to get sexually aroused." The problem is that they have altered their brains to need the extreme porn in order to get excited. "This," Majeres says, "is the number one reason not to get started with pornography."

Time's April 11, 2016, cover story, "Porn: Why Young Men Who Grew Up with Internet Porn Are Becoming Advocates for Turning It Off," brought widespread attention to another reason to stay away from porn: countless young men who have consumed lots of Internet pornography are finding themselves unable to have normal sexual activity with real human beings.[19] Some are speaking out in an effort to warn others.

A hopeful note: we should point out to our kids that because of the brain's plasticity, the neural rewiring caused by pornography can be reversed. Some are able to achieve this on their own by quitting porn cold turkey, but more find they need help from a counselor, therapist, or support group. Recovery programs include Sex Addicts Anonymous, based on the 12 steps originally used by Alcoholics Anonymous. A website recently developed by Majeres, overcomingcravings.com, provides seven modules that explain the nature of addictions, including pornography addiction, and how to overcome them by strengthening virtues such as reframing, patience, mindfulness, and self-control. The psychotherapist Peter Kleponis, in his book *Integrity Starts Here!,* lays out a pornography recovery program that includes self-knowledge, support and accountability, counseling, a spiritual plan, stress management, education about healthy relationships, and daily "virtue exercises" to build character strengths that protect against slipping back.

We should share with our teens the encouraging testimonies of people who have, with courage and the support of loved ones, overcome a pornography addiction and gone public with their stories. Nick Willis is a champion long-distance runner and a national hero in New Zealand who won a silver medal in the 1500 meters at the Beijing Olympics. In 2016, he surprised fans with a Facebook post about his past addiction to pornography:

> I am 2.5 years porn free (and it feels AMAZING). Since I was a teenager, it had been a rollercoaster ride of shame and justification. . . . Not until I realized the true implications this had on my marriage and my ability to father could I finally break free.

Video Games and Other Misogyny Allies

Pornography may be the chief culprit in marketing misogyny, but unfortunately it has allies. Video games that feature sexualized violence are one. *Grand Theft Auto* (GTA), hugely popular among boys, is one of the worst offenders. The sociologist Matt Ezzell describes scenes from a video montage of *Grand Theft Auto IV*'s "The Ladies of Liberty City." It opens with images of women stripping, pole-dancing, and giving Niko, the protagonist, a lap dance. The next scene shows Niko shooting a woman in the street. Then he is shown picking up prostitutes. One offers to give him oral sex. He drives her to a baseball field. They have anal sex. He says, "Life is strange, don't you think?" She gets out of the car and walks away. As she does, he pulls out a gun and shoots her several times. She screams. He says, "Stay down or I will finish you off!"[20]

On the first day of *GTA IV*'s release, it sold a record 2.5 million copies in North America. That week I was doing a character education training for a high school in Atlanta. A member of the faculty told me that earlier that week she had asked one of her classes, "How many of you have the new *Grand Theft Auto*?" Most of the boys raised their hands.

As Gail Dines points out, messages like *Grand Theft Auto*'s shape the way boys develop their masculine identity. As boys turn into men, unless counterinfluences intervene, these messages are absorbed into their adult sexual identities. The more they are exposed to violence-against-women as entertainment, the more they are desensitized to it. Even if they don't perpetrate such violence themselves, they become more tolerant of its being perpetrated by others. It's no accident that when women report being sexually assaulted to men in positions of authority, these men often fail to take their reports seriously.

Misogynist music is also complicit. As gangster rap became a bestselling genre, it glamorized a view of women as "bitches" and "hos." By the 2000s, Sales says, "misogyny had become so unremarkable that rape jokes were mainstream comic fare." In 2012, when a female audience member heckled comedian Daniel Tosh, host of a popular Comedy Central show, for making a rape joke, he responded, "Wouldn't it be funny if that girl got raped by, like, five guys right now? Like right now?"[21] He subsequently drew criticism from some quarters, but many comedians defended him.[22]

We need to monitor the music our kids listen to. And when a comedian or anyone else treats rape like a joke, we need to make very clear why it's not. Better still, ask your child why it's not, and see if they can tell you.

Campus Rape: Lessons to Be Learned

The American Association of University Women estimates that one out of six women will be the victim of a rape or attempted rape during her college career. The stories of individual young women who have been victims of campus rape are what helped to bring greater media attention and then heightened college response to this problem. *Saturday Night: Untold Stories of Sexual Assault at Duke* is a prime example. A few days before fall break in October 2002, Duke University sophomore Emily Faulkner (not her real name) stayed up late one night in her dorm studying for a biology midterm.[23] Around 5:20 a.m., she walked down the hall to the bathroom. She noticed a young man in one of the stalls and assumed it was someone's boyfriend spending the night.

He grabbed her. Faulkner tried to defend herself with a penknife, but her attacker turned the knife against her, inflicting multiple wounds. He then sexually assaulted her. The incident shook the Duke campus. Female students began traveling in pairs or groups to bathrooms. With the encouragement of friends, Faulkner told her story in Duke's campus newspaper in November of that year and invited anyone else who had been affected by sexual assault to share their stories.

"I was shocked by the response," she says. "I heard from men, women, parents, friends of assault survivors. She and a group of other Duke students subsequently published *Saturday Night*. One woman wrote about being raped on the eve of graduation by a friend who had offered her a ride home. An African-American woman, raped by a classmate, said she decided not to report it because she felt it would reflect badly on the black community.[24]

In 2011, Liz Seccuro, who had been raped while a student at the University of Virginia, published a memoir, *Crash Into Me: A Survivor's Search for Justice*, that launched her personal crusade to call attention to the continuing problem of campus sexual assault. She says she was a naive UVA freshman when, during her first semester, she went with a friend to a fraternity party. Upon arrival, frat brothers gave Seccuro a punch that caused her to become immediately disoriented. Frat member William Beebe then pulled her into his room, ripped off her clothes, and brutally raped her. She awoke the next morning wrapped in a bloody sheet. Years later a subsequent criminal investigation found that two other fraternity brothers had raped her that night and that all three rapes took place before numerous onlookers. As Elayne Bennett recounts in her 2014 book *Daughters in Danger*, William Beebe would later serve time for his rape, but the fraternity's code of silence protected the other guilty parties.

Jean Leonard, director of Duke University's Sexual Assault Support Services when *Saturday Night* was published, commented: "Most, but certainly not all, students who are assaulted are assaulted early in their college careers. The first six weeks carry the highest risk for assault because you've got a new class of students who are eager to fit in and be accepted. They go to parties and are handed something in a cup, and before long, many have exceeded their limits or lost good judgment. Unfortunately, there are people who take advantage of that."[25]

The National Institute on Alcohol Abuse and Alcoholism estimates that seventy thousand college students are victims of alcohol-related sexual assault every year. Mary Eberstadt's book *Adam and Eve After the Pill: Paradoxes of the Sexual Revolution* coined "Toxic U" to describe the intersection of two negative campus trends—casual hookups and binge drinking. In *Smashed: Story of a Drunken Girlhood*, Koren Zailckas reports that over the past four decades, while male alcohol abuse has remained constant, there has been a three-fold increase in the number of women who get drunk ten or more times a month—leading to higher risks of depression, suicide, and sexual assault.

What is the takeaway for us as parents? One, I think, is that today's typical campus culture is a perfect storm of three forces facilitating sexual assault. First, pornography, consumed by college males as much as they imbibe beer, has been shown by researchers to increase the extent to which men believe rape myth ideology[26] (that women cause or enjoy sexual assault) and to increase sexual aggression in men.[27] Second, the campus hookup culture normalizes depersonalized sex—exactly the way porn treats women. Third, binge drinking disables moral judgment and glorifies reckless "out of my mind" behavior. Should we be surprised when inebriated college students, accustomed to depersonalized hookups and conditioned to be aroused by graphic depiction of violence toward women, don't take the trouble to get a yes before proceeding to the next stage of sexual activity?

Some colleges try, without much success, to discourage binge drinking (which half of 18- to 23-year-olds say they do at least once every other week[28]) and display posters all over campus telling students that "consent is sexy." But on your typical college campus, there's a thunderous silence when it comes to discouraging men from a steady diet of porn, or addressing the dangers of hookup sex. This means we are going to have to deliver those messages ourselves as parents.

We need to make sure our sons know that we consider the pornography industry horrifically exploitative and grossly immoral (be sure to have them log on to fightthenewdrug.org and pornkills love.com so they know the science documenting the damage porn does). We need to make sure they know we think getting blind drunk is morally irresponsible, that we consider rape an unconscionable crime for which the man is *always* morally responsible, that we hope they'll pursue real romance instead of hookup sex, and that they'll consider seriously the benefits of saving the ultimate intimacy for the ultimate commitment: the person with whom they want to spend their life.

We can encourage our daughters to join other women and men in speaking out against the violence and misogyny of pornography, to avoid parties and all other situations where there's excessive drinking, to find friends who have too much respect for themselves and others to participate in hookup culture, and to look for a guy with character. We should urge them not to put themselves at risk—for example, by being in someone's dorm room with the door closed or in any other situation that could turn dangerous. And when our daughters are still under our roof, we might have them learn some form of self-defense, something that will increase their self-confidence and contribute in a pinch to their actual safety.

We should also encourage our college-age sons and daughters to consider getting involved in movements that are urging students to make healthier sexual choices during their college years. One such movement gaining momentum is the Love and Fidelity Network (www.loveandfidelity.org), which began at Princeton University and now has chapters or a presence on thirty-nine campuses, including Brown, the Catholic University of America, Columbia, Harvard, Notre Dame, Stanford, Swarthmore, Yale, University of Virginia, University of Wisconsin–Madison, and University of California, Santa Barbara. Its goal is to promote a positive alternative to the hookup culture and promote "sexual integrity" aimed at fostering more respectful, more fulfilling romantic relationships.

Even before the Love and Fidelity Network was beginning to get traction, some campuses started using Valentine's Day to encourage students to reflect on the 3 Rs—"respect, responsibility, and romance." A common format has been to have a panel that addresses questions such as, "What kinds of relationships have the potential to lead to real love?" and "What kinds of relationships help you find the person you would like to marry?" Panels typically include student couples who are dating but not engaging in sexual intimacy.

Colleges in the twenty-first century are ostensibly committed to promoting respect for diversity, but the actual intellectual and moral life of a college is often characterized by a poverty of diverse perspectives. That is nowhere more the case than in the realm of sexual ethics. Long-term, the most effective way to combat a corrupt culture is to create and promote a more positive one. Colleges fight the current cheating culture by working to build a culture of academic integrity. They would do well to support an anti-porn culture and to promote respect between the sexes and a vision of romance that is more challenging and ennobling than "be sure to use a condom." To get a sense of the values and virtues driving the countercultural Love and Fidelity Network movement, you can look up their "Top 10 Ways to Live Out Sexual Integrity Amidst the College Hookup Culture."

Teach the "True-Love Character Test"

Deep down, all of us want to be loved. We all want genuine intimacy—to be known and valued for the person we are. And most young people, even in today's hypersexualized world, still dream of being happily married—of finding someone with whom they would like to share their life. When I'm invited to high schools, conferences, or churches to talk to teens about romantic relationships, I always ask at the start: "How many of you would like to get married someday?" The great majority of the hands go up. "How many of you would like to have children?" Again, most raise their hand. UCLA's annual *American Freshman* survey has consistently found that about three-quarters of entering college freshmen say "raising a family" is for them an "essential" or "very important" life goal.[29] That finding, despite shifts in other values, hasn't changed in the more than forty years UCLA has been doing the survey.

Marriage and parenting are two of the most challenging responsibilities that any of us will ever take on. Both have a profound effect on our happiness. Both have a far-reaching effect on the social health of a society. Both require good character. In talking to teens, I stress the importance of knowing the character of a romantic partner as early as possible in the relationship. I give them a copy of the "True-Love Character Test," a tool I've developed as an aid to standing back and taking stock of the character of another person to whom you might be attracted. I introduce this test by saying:

A truly loving relationship, one based on mutual respect and caring, requires good character. This test will help you look objectively at the character of a person you are romantically attracted to or involved with—and decide whether it is wise to pursue that relationship. Even one character problem in an important area may be a sign that a relationship isn't healthy and may bring you unhappiness.

To drive home the point that character deficiencies can spell big trouble for a relationship, I share the story of a young woman I once counseled, at her mother's request. Caitlyn was 19 and engaged to a young man who was extremely possessive and jealous, had a hot temper, drank heavily, and got into bar fights when he'd had too much to drink. Given all these danger signals, I tried to get her to reconsider her intention to marry this guy. I asked her if she could tell me three qualities she admired in him, and he in her. She couldn't name any but insisted that they loved each other.

They went ahead with the marriage, and it was a disaster. Soon after, he became even more possessive and took to hitting her when he was drunk. Once, he pushed her down part of a flight of stairs. Caitlyn fled in terror to live in another city, where she secured an order of police protection.

One out of ten high school girls has been the victim of dating violence. Four out of five girls in physically abusive relationships continue to date their abuser.[30] Looking at a relationship through a character lens can help young people avoid such relationships. A tool like the True-Love Character Test helps a young person ask, "Is this really someone I really want to be with?"

As I walk my listeners through the questions I challenge them, saying, "Think not just about the character of the person you're involved with but also about your own character. If somebody used this test to evaluate you, how would they answer these questions?"

True-Love Character Test

1. Does this person treat me with kindness and respect?	YES	NO
2. Is this person kind and respectful toward people in general?	YES	NO
3. Does this person ever shove, shake, hit, threaten, verbally abuse, or in other ways bully me?	YES	NO
4. Is this person self-centered, always expecting to get his or her own way?	YES	NO
5. Does this person bring out the best in me?	YES	NO
6. Do I feel happy after spending time together?	YES	NO
7. Does this person respect my values, including my sexual values, and never pressure me to do something I think is wrong?	YES	NO
8. Does this person get angry a lot?	YES	NO
9. Become violent when angry?	YES	NO
10. When we disagree, does this person try to understand my feelings and work things out?	YES	NO
11. Does this person apologize when he or she has done something wrong?	YES	NO
12. Is this person able to forgive and make up after an argument?	YES	NO

13. Does this person use illegal drugs or abuse alcohol?	YES	NO
14. Does this person use pornography?	YES	NO
15. Can I trust this person to tell me the truth?	YES	NO
16. Does this person keep commitments and fulfill responsibilities?	YES	NO
17. Does this person make poor decisions?	YES	NO
18. If faith is important in my life, does this person share or at least respect that?	YES	NO
19. Would I be proud to call this person my husband or wife?	YES	NO
20. Would this person be a good role model for my children—an example of good character? Would I want my kids to grow up to be like him/her?	YES	NO

After reading aloud all the test questions, I say: "If a person gets low marks on this test, don't waste time on that relationship. Don't think, 'Maybe I can change him or her,' or 'Maybe things will be better after we're married.' People who have serious character deficiencies are very often *worse* after they get married."

Recently, on the way out of a school assembly where I had presented the True-Love Character Test, a boy said to me, as he stuffed the test into his backpack: "Hey, thanks for this. It's a pretty good checklist to see where you are. I'm actually going to discuss it with my parents."

Teach the Emotional Dangers of Premature Sex

We need to help our kids understand that for human beings, sex is about more than the body. Our entire person is involved. That's why sex has uniquely powerful emotional and spiritual consequences. To give parents and teachers a resource for addressing this dimension of human sexuality, our center devoted an issue of our education letter to "10 Emotional Dangers of Premature Sexual Involvement."[31] Health education teachers have told us they give it out every semester in their classes. They say they see kids, especially girls, reading it as they walk down the hall.

To illustrate the 10 emotional dangers, we use true stories from the lives of teens. Many teens are weary of hearing warnings about pregnancy and STDs. Despite that, we still have to teach them the facts about those potentially life-changing consequences and the evidence that condoms reduce but don't eliminate those dangers. But stories about the human heart—stories dealing with the emotional side of sex—go under kids' defensive radar, because they speak to their hearts. Not every kid has contracted an STD or experienced pregnancy, but everybody knows how it feels to be hurt emotionally. Stories from the lives of young people are the best way we can convey an important truth: "There is no condom for the heart."

Let me share just two sample stories. The first is about a 14-year-old girl and illustrates, among other things, the dangers of getting involved with someone older. The National Longitudinal Study of Adolescent Health found that among 12- to 14-year-olds, only 13 percent of same-age boy–girl relationships involved sexual intercourse. But if the partner was two years older, the probability of sexual involvement doubled. Here is one 14-year-old's story:

Sandy, a bright and pretty girl, asked to see her 9th-grade health teacher, Mr. Bartlett, during lunch period. She explained that she had never had a boyfriend, so she was excited when a senior asked her out.

After they dated for several weeks, he asked her to have sex with him. She was reluctant, but he persisted. She was afraid of appearing immature and losing him, so she consented.

"Did it work?" Mr. Bartlett gently asked. "Did you keep him?"

Sandy replied: "For another week. We had sex again, and then he dropped me. He said I wasn't good enough. There was no spark."

She continued: "I know what you're going to say. I take your class. I know now that he didn't love me. I feel so stupid."[32]

Depression is another emotional consequence that frequently follows premature sexual involvement. The National Longitudinal Study of Adolescent Health found that sexually active teens are two and a half to four times more likely than virgin teens to be depressed or have suicidal thoughts.[33] Two-thirds of teens who have had sex say they wish they had waited.[34] One study found that among adolescent girls, depression is *not* consistently followed by sexual activity, but sexual activity *is* frequently followed by depression.[35] A study in the journal *Pediatrics* found that the attempted suicide rate for sexually experienced girls between 12 and 16 was six times higher than for girls who had not had sex.[36]

Boys are also at risk for depression following sexual involvement and the breakup that nearly always follows. I remember a high school counselor, just before I was about to speak to the students about making wise sexual decisions, taking me aside to say, "Be sure to talk about boys. I had a boy in my office this morning who was an emotional wreck because his girlfriend broke up with him. They had been sexually involved." It made me think of Brian's story:

I first had intercourse with my girlfriend when we were 15. I'd been going with her for almost a year, and I loved her very much. She was friendly, outgoing, charismatic. We'd done everything but have intercourse, and then one night she asked if we could go all the way. A few days later, we broke up. It was the most painful time of my life. I had opened myself up to her more than I had to anybody, even my parents. I was depressed, moody, and nervous. I dropped out of sports. My grades weren't terrific. I didn't go out again until I got to college. I've had mostly one-night stands. I'm afraid of falling in love.[37]

As parents, we worry about many areas of our children's decision-making where the wrong choices can carry a high cost. But we sense—correctly, I think—that they are most vulnerable, most at risk emotionally as well as physically, in the sexual domain of their lives. Besides discussing the dangers of premature sex, it's important to talk to our kids about the benefits of saving sex for a truly committed love relationship. Here are 6 rewards of waiting:[38]

1. Waiting will make your relationships better. You'll spend more time getting to know each other.
2. Waiting will increase your self-respect and gain you respect for having the courage of your convictions.
3. Waiting means a clear conscience (no guilt) and peace of mind (no regrets).
4. Waiting will help you find the right mate—someone who values you for the person you are.
5. By practicing the virtues involved in waiting—such as self-control, modesty, and genuine respect for yourself and others—you're developing the kind of character that will make you a good partner.

6. By becoming a person of character, you'll be able to attract a person of character—the kind of person you would like to be the father or mother of your children.[39]

Here, too, a story can help. You could share with your teenager this girl's story from Sean Covey's *The 6 Most Important Decisions You'll Ever Make*:

My decision not to have sex wasn't difficult in middle school, but when I entered high school, it definitely became more of an issue. A lot more of my friends began to have sex with older guys.

I had the same boyfriend all the way through high school, plus my first year of college . . . , so instead of having to say no to a lot of people, I was just saying no to him. I must admit, I almost gave in a few times because I was sooooo sick of having the same conversation and argument over and over.

Sometimes, out of frustration, I would finally say, "Fine, whatever, I'll do it then!" But then I'd quickly think about it and say, "You know what? I'm not giving it to you and letting you ruin that experience for me since it will be out of sheer frustration that I'd be doing it!" . . . Fortunately, I finally realized it was a very unhealthy, immature relationship and I found the courage to end it.

I am 19 years old now, and there is not a day when I have regretted my decision to stay abstinent. . . . I have a new boyfriend who completely respects my decision . . . and we have a wonderful relationship.

If there is a girl out there who is struggling with the decision to remain abstinent or not, I would say . . . hold true to what you want for yourself. If your friends or boyfriend don't accept your decision or make fun of you, . . . they're not your friends anyway.

Here's my list of advantages for waiting:

1. I can give the person I marry a gift that no one else will ever have.
2. I've escaped the emotional trauma I've seen friends go through. . . .
3. I escaped a bad reputation.
4. I have learned a tremendous amount of self-respect.
5. I know my decision is pleasing to God and my family.[40]

Finally, we can encourage our children to consider marriage and family as life goals. This helps to foster a future orientation that contributes to better decision-making in the present. For all young people, understanding their sexuality and making decisions about this area of their lives is a key developmental task. In one sense, sex is deeply personal. At the same time, sex is intrinsically a moral matter with consequences for yourself and others. Parents make a difference here, as in every other aspect of a child's development. Mothers who clearly communicate to their teens that they disapprove of early sex have kids who delay sexual involvement.[41] Fathers who convey that message and are emotionally close to their children have the same effect.[42]

So, do all that you can to help your children make decisions that will help them avoid the dangers of the current sexual culture and lay the foundation for their future happiness. Help them learn to apply virtues like good judgment, respect, kindness, self-control, responsibility for their actions, and the courage to resist peer pressure in this crucial area of their lives. They need good guidance from those who love them. Teach them that learning to bring self-discipline to their sexuality is a way to develop their character and prepare themselves for a deep, loving relationship as an adult.[43]

Appendix A

Character Quotations for the 10 Essential Virtues

Character quotations offer memorable observations about the meaning and importance of the virtues in our lives. They can be used in different ways to stimulate discussion, deepen understanding, and foster positive aspirations. I've provided some of my favorite quotes here for each of the 10 essential virtues, qualities of good character that are affirmed by cultures around the world. Choose the ones you think are appropriate for the ages of the children in your family. Here are some of the ways you can use them:

- Post a different quotation each week on the refrigerator or on a wall near your dinner table and discuss it over a meal.
- Focus on the quotations for a particular virtue until you've gone through most or all of them.
- To stimulate thinking and discussion, you can ask:
  - What does this mean to you? How would you put it in your own words?
  - What do you like about this quote? Is it true? How do you know?
  - How does it relate to your own experience?
  - If you were to do one thing this week to put this quote into practice, what would it be?

1. WISDOM

Practical wisdom is the ability to do the right thing, at the right time, for the right reason.
—John Bradshaw

We cannot do right unless we first see correctly.
—Richard Gula

Each of us is engaged in a lifelong search for wisdom and for a life worth living.
—F. Washington Jarvis

Wisdom is . . . the right use of knowledge. To know is not to be wise.
—Charles Spurgeon

Knowledge without goodness is dangerous.
—John Phillips

The life which is unexamined is not worth living.   —Plato

Wisdom is the quality that keeps you from getting into situations where you need it.   —Doug Larson

Whatever is true, whatever is honorable, whatever is right, whatever is pure, whatever is lovely, whatever is of good repute, if there is any excellence and anything worthy of praise, let your mind dwell on these things.
                                                          —St. Paul

2. JUSTICE

There are two kinds of injustice: harming another, and failing to protect another from injury when we can.   —Cicero

Civilization is a method of living and an attitude of equal respect for all people.   —Jane Addams

Injustice anywhere is a threat to justice everywhere.
                                            —Martin Luther King Jr.

Whatever is hateful to yourself, do not to your fellow man.
                                                        —The Torah

More than anything else, [goodness] is about how we treat other people.
                                                     —Dennis Prager

Grant that I may not criticize my neighbor until I have walked a mile in his moccasins.   —Native American saying

Resistance to tyranny is obedience to God.   —Susan B. Anthony

I am only one, but still I am one. I cannot do everything, but still I can do something.   —Edward Everett Hale

A person's a person, no matter how small.   —Dr. Seuss

He who is cruel to animals becomes hard in his dealings with men.
                                                  —Immanuel Kant

3. FORTITUDE

Character cannot be developed in ease and quiet. Only through the experience of trial and suffering can the soul be strengthened . . .
                                                   —Helen Keller

Energy and persistence conquer all things.   —Benjamin Franklin

If there is no struggle, there is no progress.   —Frederick Douglass

You must do the thing you think you cannot do.   —Eleanor Roosevelt

Courage is rightly esteemed the first of human qualities . . . because it is the quality which guarantees all the others.
                    —Winston Churchill, paraphrasing Dr. Samuel Johnson

I learned that courage was not the absence of fear but the triumph over it.
                                                    —Nelson Mandela

If you want peace, you don't talk to your friends. You talk to your enemies.
                                                    —Moshe Dayan

It is curious—curious that physical courage should be so common in the world, and moral courage so rare.   —Mark Twain

4. SELF-CONTROL

Either we rule our desires, or our desires rule us.   —Proverb

No person is free who is not master of himself.   —Epictetus

Never go to excess, but let moderation be your guide.   —Cicero

It is not the mountain we conquer, but ourselves.
                                                    —Sir Edmund Hillary

When angry, count ten, before you speak; if very angry, an hundred.
                                                    —Thomas Jefferson

[T]here's only one corner of the universe you can be certain of improving, and that's your own self.   —Aldous Huxley

Discipline yourself, and others won't need to.   —John Wooden

Self-respect is the fruit of self-discipline, the sense of dignity grows with the ability to say No to oneself.   —Abraham Joshua Heschel

If you are patient in one moment of anger, you will escape a hundred days of sorrow.   —Proverb

First keep the peace within yourself, then you can also bring peace to others.   —Thomas à Kempis

Only a virtuous people are capable of freedom.   —Benjamin Franklin

5. LOVE/KINDNESS

We are made kind by being kind. —Eric Hoffer

Kind words do not cost much. Yet they accomplish much.
—Blaise Pascal

I can live for two months on one good compliment. —Mark Twain

Kindness consists in loving people more than they deserve.
—Joseph Joubert

Be kind, for everyone you meet is fighting a hard battle.
—Ian MacLaren

Forgiveness is an act of the will, and the will can function regardless of the temperature of the heart. —Corrie ten Boom

Have I not destroyed my enemy when I have made him into my friend?
—Abraham Lincoln

Speak not a word by which anyone could be wounded.
—Hindu Proverb

Do all the good you can, by all the means you can, in all the ways you can, in all the places you can, to all the people you can, as long as ever you can.
—John Wesley

You can never do a kindness too soon, for you never know how soon it will be too late. —Ralph Waldo Emerson

God has been very good to me, for I never dwell upon anything wrong which a person has done. If I do remember it, I always see some other virtue in the person. —St. Teresa of Avila

If we really took seriously the injunction to "Love your neighbor as yourself," would we not make every effort to avoid gossiping about others and calling attention to their faults, given how sensitive we are to such things said about us? —Fr. Gabriel of Mary Magdalane

Be kind whenever possible. It is always possible. —Dalai Lama

Let no one ever come to you without leaving better and happier.
—Mother Teresa

6. POSITIVE ATTITUDE

Live as if you were to die tomorrow. Learn as if you were to live forever.
—Mahatma Gandhi

When people are laughing, they're generally not killing one another.
—Alan Alda

Most folks are about as happy as they make up their minds to be.
—Abraham Lincoln

I have learned from experience that the greater part of our happiness or misery depends on our dispositions and not on our circumstances. We carry the seeds of the one or the other about with us, in our minds wherever we go.   —Martha Washington

Every problem is an opportunity in disguise.   —Chinese Proverb

The greatest discovery of my generation is that human beings can alter their lives by altering their attitudes.   —William James

Anyone who has never made a mistake has never tried anything new.
—Albert Einstein

Find something you're passionate about and keep truly interested in it.
—Julia Child

A bad attitude is like a flat tire. You can't go anywhere until you change it.
—Anonymous

Whether you think you can or think you can't, you're right.
—Henry Ford

7. HARD WORK

Whatever you are, try to be a good one.
—William Makepeace Thackeray

Nothing ever comes to one, that is worth having, except as the result of hard work.   —Booker T. Washington

Opportunity is missed by most people because it is dressed in overalls and looks like work.   —Thomas Edison

The impossible takes just a little longer to accomplish.
—Wilma Rudolph

I challenge you to show me one single solitary individual who achieved his or her own personal success without lots of hard work.

—John Wooden

[T]he best prize that life offers is the chance to work hard at work worth doing.   —Theodore Roosevelt

There is no easy way to learn difficult things.   —Joseph de Maistre

Whatever we hope ever to do with ease, we may first to do with diligence.

—Samuel Johnson

Genius is 1 percent inspiration and 99 percent perspiration.

—Thomas Edison

The secret joy in work is contained in one word—excellence.

—Pearl S. Buck

The best preparation for tomorrow is to do today's work superbly well.

—William Osler

If you are called to be a street sweeper, he should sweep streets even as Michelangelo painted, or Beethoven composed music, or Shakespeare wrote poetry. He should sweep streets so well that all the hosts of heaven and earth will pause to say, "Here lived a great street sweeper who did his job well."   —Martin Luther King Jr.

8. INTEGRITY

I hope I shall always possess firmness and virtue enough to maintain (what I consider the most enviable of all titles) the character of *an honest man*.   —George Washington

Hold yourself responsible for a higher standard than anybody expects of you.   —Henry Ward Beecher

Do not cut your conscience to fit the year's fashions.

—Catherine Cookson

Right is right, even if everyone is against it, and wrong is wrong even if everyone is for it.   —William Penn

Conscience in the soul is the root of all true courage. If a man would be brave, let him learn to obey his conscience.   —James Freeman Clarke

[T]ruth is the only safe ground to stand upon.

—Elizabeth Cady Stanton

If you tell the truth, you don't have to remember anything.

—Mark Twain

If it is not right, do not do it. If it is not true, do not say it.

—Marcus Aurelius

Our character is what we do when we think no one is looking.

—H. Jackson Brown Jr.

Be who you are and say what you feel, because those who mind don't matter and those who matter don't mind.   —Dr. Seuss

There is no better test of a man's integrity than his behavior when he is wrong.   —Marvin Williams

Nearly all men can stand adversity, but if you want to test a man's character, give him power.   —Abraham Lincoln

9. GRATITUDE

Gratitude is not only the greatest of the virtues, but the parent of all the others.   —Cicero

When you rise in the morning, give thanks for the light, for your life, for your strength. Give thanks for your food and for the joy of living.   —Tecumseh

No duty is more urgent than that of returning thanks.   —St. Ambrose

The happiest people in the world aren't the ones who have everything. The happiest people are the ones who are the most thankful for what they do have.   —Ruth Urban

Man invented language to satisfy his need to complain.   —Lily Tomlin

When I started counting my blessings, my whole life turned around.

—Willie Nelson

When it comes to life, the critical thing is whether you take things for granted or take them with gratitude.   —G. K. Chesterton

At times our own light goes out and is rekindled by a spark from another person. Each of us has cause to think with deep gratitude of those who have lighted the flame within us.   —Albert Schweitzer

If the only prayer you ever say in your entire life is thank you, it will be enough.   —Meister Eckhart

10. HUMILITY

Humility is the foundation of all the other virtues. Hence, in the soul where this virtue does not exist, there cannot be any other virtue except in mere appearance.   —St. Augustine

Humility is the essential virtue, because pride blinds us to all of our faults.
                                              —David Brooks

Addicted to being right . . . it is the most common character flaw of all.
                                              —Louis Tartaglia

Humility is not thinking less of yourself, it is thinking of yourself less.
                                              —Rick Warren

A person wrapped up in himself makes a very small bundle.
                                              —Benjamin Franklin

Talent is God-given. Be humble. Fame is man-given. Be grateful. Conceit is self-given. Be careful.   —John Wooden

In the course of my life, I have often had to eat my words, and I must confess that I have always found it a wholesome diet.
                                              —Winston Churchill

These are a few ways we can practice humility: Speak as little as possible of one's self. Accept contradictions and correction cheerfully. Pass over the mistakes of others. Accept insults and injuries. Accept being forgotten and disliked. Be kind and gentle even under provocation. (abridged)
                                              —Mother Teresa

And if he finds he has made a mistake, then he must not be afraid of admitting the fact and amending his ways.   —Confucius

Appendix B

Books That Teach Kindness and Other Virtues

This is just a small sampling of the many books that help teach kindness and other virtues. Most are fiction, although the books for 12 and up include a number of biographies. See my *Raising Good Children* and *Books That Build Character* by William Kilpatrick, Gregory Wolfe, and Suzanne M. Wolfe for more extensive annotated bibliographies of both fiction and nonfiction books with strong character themes. My colleague Joy Mosher provides a helpful bibliography of picture books that teach kindness, respect, and perspective-taking in her article "Children's Literature and Character Development."[1] To keep up with new releases, use *Brightly* (www.readbrightly.com).

I think it's helpful to discuss the character issues in a story and make connections with your child's experience and your own, but do this in a way that feels natural and doesn't turn story time into a "lesson." A good book will do its own work in a child's moral imagination. And remember that in addition to the wholesome values a good book can bring to life, reading to or with your child is one of those "connective rituals" that deepens the parent–child relationship—your most important asset for nurturing virtues.

PICTURE BOOKS (4 YEARS OLD AND UP)

My First Ever and Best Story Collection (see also Charlie and Lola animated TV series)
Joy Berry's *Help Me Be Good* series—28 books, each on a different bad habit
Laaren Brown and Lenny Hort, *Children's Illustrated Jewish Bible*
Tomie dePaola, *Book of Bible Stories*
Peter Golenboch, *Teammates*
Thomas Locker, *The Boy Who Held Back the Sea*
David Wisniewski, *The Warrior and the Wiseman*
Susan Wojciechowski, *The Christmas Miracle of Jonathan Toomey*
Pearl S. Buck, *Christmas Day in the Morning*
Wendy and Harry Devlin, *Cranberry Thanksgiving* and *Cranberry Christmas*
Sandra Dutton, *Dear Miss Perfect: A Beast's Guide to Proper Behavior*
Miriam Young and Arnold Lobel, *Miss Suzy* (and sequel)

Stephen Kellogg, *Johnny Appleseed: A Tall Tale*
Dr. Seuss stories: *The Grinch*; *The Lorax*; *The Sneeches*; *Horton Hatches the Egg*; and *Horton Hears a Who!*
Bill Peet, *The Wump World*
Jean Giono, *The Man Who Planted Trees*
Taro Yashima, *Crow Boy*

CHAPTER BOOKS (8 TO 12 YEARS OLD)

Kate DiCamillo, *Because of Winn Dixie*; *The Miraculous Journey of Edward Tulane*; and *The Tale of Despereaux*
Louisa May Alcott, *Little Women*
Katherine Applegate, *Wishtree*
Frances Hodgson Burnett, *The Secret Garden*
Carol Ryrie Brink, *Caddie Woodlawn*
Eleanor Estes, *The Hundred Dresses*
Mary Mapes Dodge, *Hans Brinker and the Silver Skates*
Esther Forbes, *Johnny Tremain*
Deborah Wiles, *Each Little Bird That Sings*
Elizabeth Speare, *Sign of the Beaver*; *The Witch of Blackbird Pond*; and *The Bronze Bow*
John Flanagan, The Ranger's Apprentice (series)
L. M. Boston, *The Children of Green Knowe*
Brian Jacques, *Redwall* (series)
L. M. Montgomery, *Anne of Green Gables*
C. S. Lewis, *The Lion, the Witch and the Wardrobe*. Volume 1 of the 7-volume *Chronicles of Narnia*.
R. J. Palacio, *Wonder*
Scott O'Dell, *Island of the Blue Dolphins*
Rosa Parks, *Rosa Parks: My Story*
Eric Knight, *Lassie Come Home*
Laura Ingalls Wilder, *Little House* series
Focus on the Family's Radio Theater: *Little Women*; *Anne of Green Gables*; *The Secret Garden*; and *Chronicles of Narnia* (www.focusonthefamily .com/radio-theater)

CHAPTER BOOKS (12 YEARS OLD AND UP)

Chaim Potok, *The Chosen*
Eric P. Kelly, *The Trumpeter of Krakow*
Marguerite de Angeli, *The Door in the Wall*
Richard Adams, *Watership Down*
J.R.R. Tolkien, *The Fellowship of the Ring*
William Armstrong, *Sounder*
Robert Newton Peck, *A Day No Pigs Would Die*
C. S. Lewis, *That Hideous Strength* (Space trilogy, Book 3)

Mark Twain, *Adventures of Huckleberry Finn*
Willa Cather, *My Antonia*
Baroness Emmuska Orczy, *The Scarlet Pimpernel*
Harper Lee, *To Kill a Mockingbird*
Robert Bolt, *A Man for All Seasons*
Charles Dickens, *David Copperfield*
John Steinbeck, *The Grapes of Wrath*
George Orwell, *Animal Farm*
Sigurd Undset, *The Master of Hestviken*
Mary Ann Shaffer and Annie Barrows, *The Guernsey Literary and Potato Peel Society*
Mildred D. Taylor, *Roll of Thunder, Hear My Cry*
Elizabeth Goudge, *The Dean's Watch*
Anne Frank, *The Diary of a Young Girl*

BIOGRAPHIES

Albert Marrin, *Hitler*
Albert Marrin, *Stalin: Russia's Man of Steel*
Russell Freedman, *Lincoln, a Photobiography*
Helen Keller, *The Story of My Life*
Patricia Reilly Giff, *Mother Teresa: Sister to the Poor*
Rick Bennett, *Jessie Owens: Champion Athlete*
Stephen Krensky, *George Washington: The Man Who Would Not Be King*
Catherine Clinton, *Harriet Tubman: The Road to Freedom*
Susan Sloate, *Clara Barton: Founder of the American Red Cross*
Louise Quayle, *Martin Luther King, Jr.: Dreams for a Nation*
Melba Pattillo Beals, *I Will Not Fear: My Lifetime of Building Faith under Fire*

Appendix C

Family Projects That Foster Kindness and Purpose

1. KINDNESS PROJECTS

My colleague Michele Borba's book, *UnSelfie: Why Empathetic Kids Succeed in Our All-About-Me World*, includes a chapter on kindness with 10 easy-to-do family projects that promote kindness at home and beyond. Just three of them:

A Family Kindness Box. Have all family members look for kind deeds that *others* do; write or draw the kind act on a slip or sheet of paper and drop it in a Kindness Box (an old shoe box with a slit in the top will do). Then read and discuss the notes during a family meal or other gathering.

Choose a Caring Cause. Match your child's passion with a good cause. After a boy's mom survived cancer, he got his soccer team to send daily email greetings on hospital computers to child cancer patients. The kids who received them were delighted. (*A variation:* Together, choose a cause each year that you think worthy of supporting as a family. Decide how each family member will contribute.)

Teach Bucket-Filling. Read Carol McCloud's wonderful picture book, *Have You Filled a Bucket Today?* The message: Everyone carries an invisible bucket on hold good thoughts and feelings. When your bucket is filled, you're happy. When it's empty, you're sad. We can all be bucket-fillers—inside and outside our family—by saying and doing kind things.

Another good source of family kindness projects is Debbie Tenzer's *Do One Nice Thing: Little Things You Can Do to Make the World a Lot Nicer.* One example:

Eight-year-old Brandon Keefe proposed to his classmates that they donate books they no longer needed or wanted to poor schools that needed books. His mom then founded BookEnds.org. Through events they have organized, more than 140,000 student volunteers have collected used books, which are then delivered to needy schools and youth organizations. So far, more than 1.5 million books have been given away, and more than 400,000 at-risk kids have received them.[1] (For many more stories like this, check out www.DoOneNiceThing.com.)

2. 100 LIFE GOALS

Psychologist William Damon, director of Stanford University's Center for the Study of Adolescence, writes in *The Path to Purpose* that parents and teachers must help young people find a particular purpose for their lives—a personal vocation or calling that gives their life meaning and direction. Having a sense of purpose, research shows, contributes to success in school and work and success in relationships.[2]

Some young people find a sense of purpose in their religious faith—from their belief that a loving God has put them on this earth to use their gifts to make the world a better place. Others may find their sense of purpose simply in the conviction that everyone has a responsibility to use their talents to make a positive difference in the world. All young people, whatever their source of meaning, need to feel that their lives matter, not only to themselves but also to others.

What will help our children find their vocation in life? School can help—especially if it includes exposure to different kinds of careers and helps in matching one's talents and interests to possible careers. So do internships and service opportunities that provide hands-on experience. It helps to interview and even job-shadow people in the line of work that you might be considering. Thinking about being a college professor? Actor? Engineer? Marine biologist? Musician? Talk to some people who are doing it—about what they find fulfilling and what they don't. Want to pursue your passion but not sure that it will pay the bills? Talk to someone who has done that. Talk to someone else who has a day job and pursues his or her passion on the side.

There's no substitute for actual work experience. The more experience kids can get doing different kinds of jobs, the better. When our first son had a paper route, for example, he had a real responsibility; people were expecting their paper to be delivered on time, every day. And when kids have a job, they're earning their own money, which then gives them a chance to learn to spend, save, and contribute to good causes wisely. Remember to check out Ron Lieber's book, *The Opposite of Spoiled*, on raising kids who are both generous and money-smart.

It's also important for us to talk openly and often to our kids about the work and service we do. What makes it rewarding? What helps us put up with the hard parts in order to experience the satisfaction of applying ourselves, doing our work well, and making a difference to those who benefit from our labors?

100 Goals is an activity intended to help young people develop a sense of purpose and begin to formulate life goals to which they'd like to aspire. It was developed by Hal Urban, the award-winning teacher and popular author who raised three sons on his own and whose work I've recommended earlier in the book. In his book *Lessons from the Classroom*, he describes this activity as one his high school students found valuable. I've done it with teachers and parents in my character-education course, and I've recommended it to faculties and families.

Your teenage children, I think, are more likely to do this activity with a seriousness of purpose if you do it, too, and you share your lists of 100 goals when you've finished them. Goals can be as small as fixing a neglected flat tire on your bike and as big as getting married or changing the world in some way. Here's how this activity works:

100 Goals

1. Over the next two weeks, write at least 100 goals you'd like to achieve in your lifetime. (For kids 12 and under, you could reduce that to 50.)
2. Divide them into categories such as these; add others if you wish.
   - education
   - career
   - family
   - learning
   - reading
   - service to others
   - fun/adventure
   - creating/making/building
   - self-improvement
   - spiritual growth
   - things you'd like to own
   - US travel
   - foreign travel
   - major accomplishments
3. To prime the pump, brainstorm together about possible goals for these various categories.
4. After you write the 100 goals, select the ten that are the most important to you. Write them in any order.
5. Then choose your #1 short-term goal and your #1 long-term goal.
6. Share your choices from steps 4 and 5 with family members, explaining why your top ten goals are each important to you and how you chose your top two.

After family members have shared their goals, they can support each other's efforts to attain them. Says one of Hal's former students, who went on to be a pre-med student at UC Santa Barbara:

> I still have my goals posted years later, and I look at them every day, just like Dr. Urban encouraged us to do. One of my goals was to run the 100-meter hurdles in 18 seconds. I really didn't think I could do it, but every day he encouraged me and asked about my progress. And I finally did make my goal.

Of course, life often has a way of disrupting "the best-laid plans of mice and men." Much of what happens to us is not under our control. As we mature, our goals may change, along with our philosophy of life. Many people come to believe that a life of purpose is not about pursuing our dreams but rather about responding to what we feel challenged or called to do in the circumstances we find ourselves in at the moment. We can come to find fulfillment less in what we achieve than in being faithful to our calling. That has been the path for many people who have done much good. It may be the path for most of us.

That said, for many young people an activity like "100 goals" can be very helpful—in reflecting on what goals in life are worth pursuing. Hal Urban said he got letters every year from former students who would send him a copy of their 100 goals with the ones checked off that they had already attained. "If it hadn't been for this assignment," wrote one boy, "I wouldn't have even dreamed of a lot of these goals let alone achieved them."

Notes

Introduction: What Would You Do?

1. Thanks to Bill O'Hanlon, author of *Do One Thing Different: Ten Simple Ways to Change Your Life* (New York: Quill, 2000), for this story.
2. James Stenson, *Compass: A Handbook on Parent Leadership* (New York: Scepter, 2003).
3. Anne Frank, *The Diary of a Young Girl* (New Dehli, India: Grapevine India Publishers, 2015).

Chapter 1: Why Kindness Matters

1. Joel Lovell, "George Saunders's Advice to Graduates," *The 6th Floor*, nytimes.com blog (July 31, 2013), https://6thfloor.blogs.nytimes.com/2013/07/31/george-saunderss-advice-to-graduates.
2. Beth Elfrey, *Magnificat* (February 2015).
3. Martha McVeigh, *Magnificat Lenten Companion* (2013).
4. The story of Daniel DeLoach and his sister, Kathleen DeLoach Benton, is told by Stephen Post and Jill Neimark in their book *Why Good Things Happen to Good People: The Exciting New Research That Proves the Link Between Doing Good and Living a Longer, Healthier, Life* (New York: Broadway Books, 2007).
5. Post and Neimark, *Why Good Things Happen*.
6. "Looking with Kindness and Finding Wonder: A Chat with R. J. Palacio," *Brightly*, http://www.readbrightly.com/looking-kindness-finding-wonder-chat-r-j-palacio.
7. "Looking with Kindness and Finding Wonder."
8. Lara Aknin, J. Kiley Hamlin, and Elizabeth W. Dunn, "Giving Leads to Happiness in Young Children," *PLoS One* 7, no. 6 (2012). This study is summarized by Delia Fuhrmann, "Being Kind Makes Kids Happy," *Greater Good Magazine*, August 1, 2012.
9. Stephen G. Post, "Six Ways to Boost Your Habit of Helping," *Greater Good Magazine*, March 15, 2011, https://greatergood.berkeley.edu/article/item/six_ways_to_become_more_altruistic.
10. Post and Neimark, *Why Good Things Happen to Good People*.
11. For a review of research on how parents affect children's moral development, see Marvin W. Berkowitz and John H. Grych, "Fostering

Goodness: Teaching Parents to Facilitate Children's Moral Development," *Journal of Moral Education* 27, no. 3 (September 1998): 371–91. See also David Streight, ed., *Parenting for Character: Five Experts, Five Practices* (Portland, OR: Center for Spiritual and Ethical Education, 2008); my review of the literature, "Do Parents Make a Difference in Children's Character Development?" is available on our center's website: https://www2.cortland.edu/dotAsset/4e26603a-86bb-4c2a-b111-d590dc 4e1dce.pdf.

12. See, for example, Paul Barton and Richard Coley's report *The Family: America's Smallest School* (Princeton, NJ: Educational Testing Service, September 2007).

13. Berkowitz and Grych, "Fostering Goodness"; see also Thomas Lickona's *Raising Good Children: Helping Your Child Through the Stages of Moral Development* (New York: Bantam Books, 1983) and *Character Matters: How to Help Our Children Develop Good Judgment, Integrity, and Other Essential Virtues* (New York: Touchstone, 2004); see also William Damon's *Greater Expectations* (New York: Free Press, 1995) and Streight, *Parenting for Character.*

14. Samuel P. Oliner and Pearl M. Oliner, *The Altruistic Personality: Rescuers of Jews in Nazi Europe* (New York: Free Press, 1988).

15. Perry London, "The Rescuers," in J. R. Macaulay and Leonard Berkowitz, eds., *Altruism and Helping Behavior* (New York, Academic Press: 1970).

16. London, "The Rescuers."

Chapter 2: Does Our Culture Cultivate Kindness?

1. Associated Press, "Doctor Shoots 7 in NYC Hospital," *Cortland Standard*, July 1, 2017.

2. For a fuller discussion of the interplay of character and culture, see Thomas Lickona, "Introduction," in Kevin Ryan, Bernice Lerner, Karen E. Bohlin, Osamu Nakayama, Shujiro Mizuno, and Kazunobu Horiuchi, eds., *Happiness and Virtue Beyond East and West: Toward a New Global Responsibility* (Tokyo and Rutland, Vermont: Tuttle Publishing, 2011).

3. Anna North, "The Scope of Hate in 2017: This Week in Hate," *New York Times*, June 1, 2017.

4. Sadie Gurman and Russell Contreras, Associated Press, "Report: More Than Half of Hate Crimes in US Go Unreported," *Cortland Standard*, June 19, 2017.

5. North, "The Scope of Hate in 2017."

6. North, "The Scope of Hate in 2017."

7. Nina Burleigh, "Trump Era Political Violence Deterring Democratic Candidates," *Newsweek*, June 12, 2017.

8. Rebecca Shabad, "Republican Receives Threat After Shooting, Warning 'One Down, 216 to Go . . . ,'" CBS News, June 14, 2017, https://www .cbsnews.com/news/republican-receives-threats-after-alexandria -shooting-warning-one-down-216-to-go.

9. Kimberly Hefling and Jesse J. Holland, Associated Press, "Racism a Lingering Problem Among Collegiate Millennials," Cortland Standard, April 4, 2015.

10. Benjamin Weiser, "Swastikas, Slurs, and Torment in Town's Schools," New York Times, November 7, 2013.

11. Beatrice B. Whiting and John W. Whiting, Children of Six Cultures: A Psycho-Cultural Analysis (Cambridge, MA: Harvard University Press, 1975).

12. J. E. Grusec et al., "Household Work and the Development of Concern for Others," Developmental Psychology 32, no. 6 (November 1996): 999–1007.

13. Elizabeth Kolbert, "Spoiled Rotten: Why Do Kids Rule the Roost?" The New Yorker (July 2, 2012).

14. Kolbert, "Spoiled Rotten."

15. James B. Stenson, Compass: A Handbook on Parent Leadership (New York: Scepter Publishers, Inc., 2003).

16. Quoted in Kolbert, "Spoiled Rotten."

17. Kolbert, "Spoiled Rotten."

18. "How Schools Can Reduce Cheating: An Interview with Don McCabe," excellence & ethics (SUNY Cortland: Center for the 4th and 5th Rs, Winter 2011).

19. Kolbert, quoting Hara Estroff Marano, A Nation of Wimps: The High Cost of Invasive Parenting (New York: Crown Archetype, 2008).

Chapter 3: Kids' Capacity for Kindness—and Cruelty—Is There from the Start

1. Felix Warneken and Michael Tomasello, "Altruistic Helping in Human Infants and Young Chimpanzees," Science 311, (March 3, 2006): 1301–3.

2. Alfie Kohn, The Brighter Side of Human Nature: Altruism and Empathy in Everyday Life (New York: Basic Books, Inc., 1990).

3. Paul Bloom, "The Moral Life of Babies," The New York Times Magazine (May 5, 2010).

4. For a famous experiment demonstrating what conditions create and reduce inter-group hostilities, see Muzafer Sherif et al., The Robbers Cave Experiment: Intergroup Conflict and Cooperation (Middletown, CT: Wesleyan University Press, 1988).

5. WHO, "Risk Behaviours: Being Bullied and Bullying Others," in C. Carrie et al., eds., Social Determinants of Health and Well-Being Among Young People (Copenhagen: WHO, 2012), 191–200.

6. B. Vossekuil et al., *The Final Report and Findings of the Safe School Initiative: Implications for the Prevention of School Attacks in the United States* (Washington, DC: US Secret Service, 2002).

7. E. C. Brown et al., "Outcomes from a School-Randomized Controlled Trial of Steps to Respect: A Bullying Prevention Program," *School Psychology Review* 40, no. 3 (September 2011): 423–43. See also M. M. Ttofi and D. P. Farrington, "Effectiveness of School-Based Programs to Reduce Bullying: A Systematic and Meta-Analytic Review," *Journal of Experimental Criminology 7* (2011): 27–56.

8. Suzet Tanya Lereya et al., "Adult Mental Health Consequences of Peer Bullying and Maltreatment in Childhood: Two Cohorts in Two Countries," *The Lancet Psychiatry*, June 2015, Vol. 2, 524–31.

Chapter 4: How to Create a Positive Family Culture: 6 Key Principles

1. Berkowitz and Grych, "Fostering Goodness."

2. Conrad Baars and Anna A. Terruwe, *Healing the Unaffirmed: Recognizing Emotional Deprivation Disorder*, Rev. ed., Suzanne M. Baars and Bonnie N. Shayne, eds. (Staten Island, NY: St. Pauls/Alba House, 2002).

3. Christiaan Barnard, *One Life* (Capetown, South Africa: Timmins, 1969).

4. William Damon, *The Moral Child: Nurturing Children's Natural Moral Growth* (New York: Free Press, 1988).

5. William Doherty, *Take Back Your Kids: Confident Parenting in Turbulent Times* (Notre Dame, IN: Sorin Books, 2000).

6. Diana Baumrind, "Authoritative Parenting for Character and Competence," in David Streight, ed., *Parenting for Character: Five Experts, Five Practices* (Portland, OR: Council for Spiritual and Ethical Education, 2008).

7. Baumrind, "Authoritative Parenting."

8. K. A. Moore and J. Zaff, "Building a Better Teenager: A Summary of What Works in Adolescent Development," *Child Trends Research Brief*, November 2002, www.childtrends.org.

9. Institute for Youth Development, *America's Youth: Measuring the Risk* (Washington, DC: Institute for Youth Development, 2002).

10. James Q. Wilson, "Raising Kids," *Atlantic Monthly*, October 1983.

11. Berkowitz and Grych, "Fostering Goodness"; see also Sheila Stanley, "The Family as Moral Educator," in Ralph Mosher, ed., *Moral Education: A First Generation of Research and Development* (New York: Praeger, 1980), 341–55.

12. Catherine Musco Garcia-Prats and Joseph A. Garcia-Prats, *Good Families Don't Just Happen: What We Learned from Raising Our 10 Sons and How It Can Work for You* (Holbrook, MA: Adams Media Corporation, 1997), 59.

13. Ron Lieber, *The Opposite of Spoiled: Raising Kids Who Are Grounded, Generous, and Smart About Money* (New York: Harper, 2015). Lieber's

book describes not only how to handle chores, allowance, and charitable giving but also how to teach other aspects of financial responsibility in a way that develops character traits that are "the opposite of spoiled." For a quick summary of his helpful tips, go to www.fatherly.com/love-and -money/how-to-raise-a-kid-whos-financially-savvy-and-grateful-at-the -same-time/.

14. For a list of age-appropriate personal and family responsibilities, see http://10kids.com/Erik/wordpress/wp-content/uploads/2016/09 /Age-GP.pdf)

15. Andrew Mullins, *Parenting for Character: Equipping Your Child for Life* (Lane Cove, Australia: Finch, 2005).

16. Christine I. Celio, Joseph Durlack, and Allison Dymnicki, "A Meta-Analysis of the Impact of Service-Learning on Students," *Journal of Experimental Education*, 2011, Vol. 334, no. 2, 164–181.

17. Michael Clark, "Bridging the Gap-Practical Application: A Realistic Approach for Strength and Conditioning Coaches to Deal with Steroids," *National Strength & Conditioning Association Journal* 10, no. 2 (April 1988), 28–30.

18. Centers for Disease Control and Prevention, "Youth Risk Behavior Surveillance—United States, 2015," *Surveillance Summaries* 65, no, 6 (June 10, 2016).

19. Adapted from G. T. Sewall, *Learning About Religion, Learning From Religion: A Guide to Religion in the Curriculum and Moral Life of Public Schools* (New York: American Textbook Council, 1998).

20. L. J. Bridges and K. Anderson Moore, "Religious Involvement and Children's Well-Being: What Research Tells Us (and What It Doesn't)," *Child Trends Research Brief*, September 2002.

21. John M. Wallace, Jr. and David R. Williams, "Religion and Health-Compromising Behavior," in J. Schulenberg, J.L. Maggs, and K. Hurrelmann, eds., *Health Risks and Developmental Transitions During Adolescence* (New York: Cambridge University Press, 1997), pp. 444–468.

22. Kent M. Keith, *Jesus Did It Anyway: The Paradoxical Commandments for Christians* (New York: G. P. Putnam's Sons, 2005).

Chapter 5: 10 Essential Virtues That Help Kids Be Kind

1. Berkowitz and Grych, "Fostering Goodness"; see also my book, *Raising Good Children*.

2. Martin Luther King, Jr., March 14, 1964, Thinkexist.com, http://thinkexist.com/quotes/martin_luther_king,_jr.

3. Roy F. Baumeister and John Tierney, *Willpower: Rediscovering the Greatest Human Strength* (New York: Penguin Books, 2011).

4. Mayo Clinic, "Mayo Clinic Study Finds Optimists Report a Higher Quality of Life Than Pessimists," *Science Daily*, August 2002.

5. Viktor E. Frankl, *Man's Search for Meaning* (New York: Washington Square Press, 1984; orig. 1946), 135.
6. Gretchen Rubin, *The Happiness Project: Or Why I Spent a Year Trying to Sing in the Morning, Clean My Closets, Fight Right, Read Aristotle, and Generally Have More Fun* (New York: HarperCollins, 2009).
7. John Wooden, *Wooden: A Lifetime of Observations and Reflections On and Off the Court* (Lincolnwood, IL: Contemporary Books, 1997).
8. Wooden, *A Lifetime of Observations*.
9. David Callahan, *The Cheating Culture: Why More Americans Are Doing Wrong to Get Ahead* (New York: Houghton Mifflin Harcourt, 2004).
10. For two decades of research on cheating in high school and college, see Donald L. McCabe et al., *Cheating in College: Why Students Do It and What Educators Can Do About It* (Baltimore: Johns Hopkins University Press, 2012).
11. Robert Emmons, *Gratitude Works!* (San Francisco: Jossey-Bass, 2013).
12. Jeffrey Froh and Giacomo Bono, *Making Grateful Kids: The Science of Building Character* (West Conshohocken, PA: Templeton Press, 2014).
13. C. S. Lewis, *Mere Christianity* (New York: HarperOne, 2001), 125.

Chapter 6: Respect and Fairness

1. David Isaacs, *Character Building: A Guide for Parents and Teachers*, 2nd ed. (Portland, OR: Four Courts Press, 2001).

Chapter 7: Discipline: What's in Your Toolbox?

1. This research, conducted by the psychiatrist Steven Wolin, is summarized in Bill O'Hanlon's book *Do One Thing Different: Ten Simple Ways to Change Your Life* (New York: Quill, 2000).
2. Judith Martin, *Miss Manners' Guide to Rearing Perfect Children* (New York: Penguin, 1985).
3. Mike Males, "This Is Your (Father's) Brain on Drugs," *New York Times*, September 17, 2007.
4. Males, "This Is Your (Father's) Brain on Drugs."
5. Robert Epstein, "Let's Abolish High School," *Education Week* (April 4, 2007).
6. Y. Shoda, W. Mischel, and P. K. Peake, "Predicting Adolescent Cognitive and Self-Regulatory Competencies from Preschool Delay of Gratification," *Developmental Psychology* 26, no. 6 (November 1990): 978–86.
7. Doherty, *Take Back Your Kids*.
8. Cynthia Ulrich Tobias, *You Can't Make Me (But I Can Be Persuaded): Strategies for Bringing Out the Best in Your Strong-Willed Child* (Colorado Springs: WaterBrook Press, 2002).

9. Fabiana Santos, "How to Defuse a Child's Tantrum with One Question," Catholic Education Resource Center (May 7, 2017), www.catholic education.org/en/marriage-and-family/parenting//how-to -defuse-a-child-s-tantrum-with-one-question.html.

10. Stanley Turecki, *The Difficult Child* (New York: Bantam Books, 2000).

11. Carolyn Zahn-Waxler, Marion Radke-Yarrow, and R. M. King, "Childrearing and Children's Prosocial Initiations toward Victims of Distress," *Child Development* 50 (1979): 319–30.

12. Rainer Dobert and Gertrud Nunner-Winkler, "Moral Development and Personal Reliability: The Impact of the Family on Two Aspects of Moral Consciousness in Adolescence," in Marvin Berkowitz and Fritz Oser, eds., *Moral Education: Theory and Application* (Hillsdale, NJ: Lawrence Erlbaum Associates, 1985), 147–73.

13. For a review of such research, see Alfie Kohn, *Punished by Rewards: The Trouble with Gold Stars, Incentive Plans, A's, Praise, and Other Bribes* (Boston: Houghton Mifflin, 1999).

14. Felix Warneken and Michael Tomasello, "Extrinsic Rewards Undermine Altruisitic Tendencies in 20 Month-Olds," *Developmental Psychology* 44, no. 6 (November 2008) 1785–8.

15. Jonathan Haidt, "Wired to Be Inspired," *Greater Good Magazine*, March 1, 2005, http://greatergood.berkeley.edu/article/item/wired_to_be _inspired.

Chapter 8: Family Meetings

1. Sheila Stanley, "The Family as Moral Educator."

Chapter 9: Getting Control of Screens

1. Yolanda Reid Chassiakos et al., "Children and Adolescents and Digital Media," report from the American Academy of Pediatrics, *Pediatrics* (October 2016), http://pediatrics.aappublications.org/content/early/2016 /10/19/peds.2016-2593

2. Common Sense Media, *Zero to Eight: Children's Media Use in America 2013*, October 28, 2013, https://www.commonsensemedia.org/zero-to-eight -2013-infographic.

3. Chassiakos et al., "Children and Adolescents and Digital Media."

4. Common Sense Media, *The Common Sense Census: Media Use by Tweens + Teens*, November 3, 2015, https://www.commonsensemedia.org /the-common-sense-census-media-use-by-tweens-and-teens-infographic.

5. Chassiakos et al., "Children and Adolescents and Digital Media."

6. Chassiakos et al., "Children and Adolescents and Digital Media."

7. Chassiakos et al., "Children and Adolescents and Digital Media."

8. Common Sense Media, "The Common Sense Census: Media Use by Kids Age Zero to Eight 2017," https://www.commonsensemedia.org/research /the-common-sense-census-media-use-by-kids-age-zero-to-eight-2017.

9. Jane Anderson, M.D., "The Impact of Media Use and Screen Time on Children, Adolescents, and Families," American College of Pediatricians report, November, 2016, https://www.acpeds.org/the-college-speaks /position-statements/parenting-issues/the-impact-of-media-use-and -screen-time-on-children-adolescents-and-families.

10. Ben Sasse, *The Vanishing American Adult: Our Coming-of-Age Crisis— and How to Rebuild a Culture of Self-Reliance* (New York: St. Martin's Press, 2017).

11. Anderson, "The Impact of Media Use."

12. Victoria L. Dunckley, "Electronic Screen Syndrome: An Unrecognized Disorder?" *Psychology Today*, July 23, 2012, https://www.psychology today.com/blog/mental-wealth/201207/electronic-screen-syndrome -unrecognized-disorder.

13. Victoria L. Dunckley, *Reset Your Child's Brain: A Four-Week Plan to End Meltdowns, Raise Grades, and Boost Social Skills by Reversing the Effects of Electronic Screen-time* (Novato, CA: New World Library, 2015).

14. Dan J. Siegel, "An Interpersonal Neurobiology Approach to Psychotherapy," *Psychiatric Annals* 36, no. 4 (April, 2006), 248.

15. Dunckley, *Reset Your Child's Brain*.

16. Anderson, "The Impact of Media Use."

17. Susanna Schrobsdorff, "Teen Depression and Anxiety: Why the Kids Are Not All Right," *Time*, November 7, 2016, http://time.com/magazine/us /4547305/november-7th-2016-vol-188-no-19-u-s/.

18. Schrobsdorff, "Teen Depression and Anxiety."

19. Schrobsdorff, "Teen Depression and Anxiety."

20. Schrobsdorff, "Teen Depression and Anxiety."

21. Rachel Lewis, "Suicide Rate for Teen Girls Hits 40-Year High," *Time*, August 4, 2017, http://time.com/4887282/teen-suicide-rate-cdc.

22. Schrobsdorff, "Teen Depression and Anxiety."

23. Cindy Eckard, "Growing Up in a False Reality," *Psychology Today*, May 20, 2017, https://www.psychologytoday.com/blog/mental-wealth/201705 /growing-in-false-reality. See also www.screensandkids.us.

24. Eckard, "Growing Up in a False Reality."

25. Adam Alter, "Why Our Screens Make Us Less Happy," TED Talk, https:// www.ted.com/talks/adam_alter_why_our_screens_make_us_less_happy.

Chapter 10: How to Help Your Kids Develop Good Habits (and Break Bad Ones)

1. Aristotle, *The Nicomachean Ethics*, trans. David Ross (New York: Oxford University Press, 2009).

2. Paul C. Vitz and Philip P. Scala, "Evaluating a Short Curriculum for Teaching Altruism," unpublished study, Department of Psychology, New York University. Available from Paul C. Vitz, The Institute for the Psychological Sciences, Suite 511, 2001 Jefferson Davis Highway, Arlington, VA 22202.

3. Daniel Lapsley, "The Development of Moral Identity," in Larry Nucci, Tobias Krettenauer, and Darcia Narvaez, eds., *Handbook of Moral and Character Education* (New York: Routledge, 2014).

4. Ogden Lindsley, "Precision Teaching: By Teachers for Children," *Teaching Exceptional Children*, 1990, 22 (3).

5. Richard O'Connor, *Rewire: Change Your Brain to Break Bad Habits, Overcome Addictions, and Conquer Self-Destructive Behavior* (New York: Hudson Street Press, 2014).

6. Michael Csikszentmihalyi et al., *Talented Teenagers: The Roots of Success and Failure* (New York: Cambridge University Press, 1993).

7. Thanks to my friend Michele Borba for this story.

8. Phil Stutz and Barry Michels, *The Tools: 5 Tools to Help You Find Courage, Creativity, and Willpower—and Inspire You to Live Life in Forward Motion* (New York: Spiegel & Grau, 2012).

9. Hal Urban, *Life's Greatest Lessons: 20 Things That Matter* (New York: Simon & Schuster, 2005). This book is available only at www.halurban.com.

10. Charles Duhigg, *The Power of Habit: Why We Do What We Do in Life and Business* (New York: Random House, 2012).

11. Sean Covey, *The 6 Most Important Decisions You'll Ever Make* (New York: Fireside, 2006).

Chapter 11: How to Talk About Things That Matter

1. Thanks to Kevin Hyland for this quote.

2. https://thefamilydinnerproject.org/4week-program/signup.

3. https://thefamilydinnerproject.org/conversation.

4. http://beautyandbedlam.com/conversation-starter-questions.

5. Amy, "A Hero's Fall from Grace," a *Family Dinner Project* post, https://thefamilydinnerproject.org/blog/conversation-of-the-week/a-heros-fall-from-grace.

6. D. L. Espelage, M. K. Holt, and R. R. Henkel, "Examination of Peer-Group Contextual Factors on Aggression During Early Adolescence," *Child Development* 74, no. 1 (January–February 2003): 205–20.

Chapter 12: Cut the Complaining!

1. Charles Swindoll, quoted in Jan & Dwight Trabue, *Parent Leaders: Effective Leadership Principles for Parents* (Tucson, AZ: Wheatmark, 2013).

2. John Perricone, *Zen and the Art of Public School Teaching* (Minneapolis: Free Spirit Publishing, 2005).

3. F. Washington Jarvis, *With Love and Prayers: A Headmaster Speaks to the Next Generation* (Boston: David R. Godine Publisher, 2000).

4. Jessica Bennet, "On Campus, Failure Is on the Syllabus," *The New York Times*, June 24, 2017.

5. Bennet, "On Campus, Failure Is on the Syllabus."

Chapter 13: Using Stories to Teach Kindness and Other Virtues

1. Denise Schipani, "Children's Books That Show Kids the Goodness in the World," *Brightly*, http://www.readbrightly.com/childrens-books-show -kids-goodness-world/?sid=302&mcg=526B0F58B82741AFE0534 FD66B0AA115&ref=PRH0563577803&aid=randohouseinc13256-20& linkid=PRH0563577803&cdi=526B1A5BFC824657E0534FD66B0A5A1A.

2. 10 Kids, "Family Movies," http://10kids.com/2016/10/06/family-movies/.

3. Nicholas Kristof, *The New York Times*, YouTube channel, https://www .youtube.com/playlist?list=PL1F5CE190342039B5.

Chapter 14: Schools That Cultivate Kindness

1. Deb Austin Brown, *Growing Character: 99 Strategies for the Elementary Classroom* (Boone, NC: Character Development Group, 2003); *The Success Strategies: 99 Timeless Strategies for Life's Journey* (Boone, NC: Character Development Group, 2010).

2. Marvin Berkowitz and Melinda Bier, "What Works in Character Education," *Journal of Research in Character Education* 5, no. 1 (2007): 29–45; available at www.characterandcitizenship.org; see also Robert E. Slavin, *Cooperative Learning: Theory, Research, and Practice* (Englewood Cliffs, NJ: Prentice Hall, 1990).

3. Jiyoung Choi, David W. Johnson, and Roger Johnson, "Relationships Among Cooperative Learning Experiences, Social Interdependence, Children's Aggression, Victimization, and Prosocial Behavior," *Journal of Applied Social Psychology*, 44, 2011, 976–1003.

4. Kurt Lewin et al., "Patterns of Aggressive Behavior in Experimentally Created 'Social Climates,'" *Journal of Social Psychology*, 1939, 10, 271–299.

5. Hal Urban, *Lessons from the Classroom: 20 Things Good Teachers Do* (New York: Simon & Schuster, 2005). This book is available only at www .halurban.com.

6. Kevin Ryan and Karen Bohlin, *Building Character in Schools* (San Francisco: Jossey-Bass, 1999).

7. Galit Breen, *Kindness Wins: A Simple, No-Nonsense Guide to Teaching Our Kids How to Be Kind Online* (CreateSpace Independent Publishing Platform, 2016).

Chapter 15: How to Help Your Kids Avoid the Dangers of a Hypersexualized Culture—and Find True Love

1. Nancy Jo Sales, *American Girls: Social Media and the Secret Lives of Teenagers* (New York: Knopf, 2016).
2. Dolf Zillman and Jennings Bryant, "Effects of Prolonged Consumption of Pornography on Family Values," *Journal of Family Issues*, 1988, vol. 9, no. 4.
3. Eric W. Owens, Richard J. Behun, Jill C. Manning, and Rory C. Reid, "The Impact of Internet Pornography on Adolescents: A Review of the Research," *Sexual Addiction & Compulsivity* 19 (2012): 99–122.
4. Owens et al., "The Impact of Internet Pornography."
5. Gail Dines, *Pornland: How Porn Has Hijacked Our Sexuality* (Boston: Beacon Press, 2010).
6. Kristen A. Jennings and Gail Poyner, *Good Pictures Bad Pictures: Porn-Proofing Today's Young Kids* (Glen Cove, NY: Glen Cove Press, 2014.)
7. Jenson and Poyner, *Good Pictures Bad Pictures.*
8. Kristen Jenson, "5 Back to School Dangers: Arm Your Kids Now!" Protect Young Minds, August 17, 2017, https://protectyoungminds.org/2017/08/17/5-back-school-dangers/.
9. Quoted in Sales, *American Girls.*
10. Dines, *Pornland.*
11. Dines, *Pornland.*
12. Dines, *Pornland.*
13. Sales, *American Girls.*
14. Robert J. Wosnitzer and Ana J. Bridges, "Aggression and Sexual Behavior in Best-Selling Pornography: A Content Analysis Update," paper presented at the 57th Annual Meeting of the International Communication Association, San Francisco, May 24–28, 2007.
15. Katherine Sellgren, "Pornography 'Desensitizing Young People,'" BBC News, June 15, 2016, http://www.bbc.com/news/education-36527681.
16. Jamie Rigg, "How the Digital Economy Act Will Come Between You and Porn," Engadget, May 3, 2017, https://www.engadget.com/2017/05/03/digital-economy.
17. Video: *Fight the New Drug—Who We Are & Why We Began This Movement for Love*, July 31, 2017, http://fightthenewdrug.org/video-fight-the-new-drug-a-movement-for-love/
18. Kevin Majeres, "The Science Behind Pornography," *Mercatornet*, July 22, 2016, http://www.mercatornet.com/articles/view/the-science-behind-pornography/18403
19. Belinda Luscombe, "Porn and the Threat to Virility," *Time*, April 11, 2016.

20. Summarized in Dines, *Pornland.*

21. Sales, *American Girls.*

22. Sales, *American Girls.*

23. This account is based on "The Silent Epidemic: Sexual Assault on Campus," *Duke Magazine*, March 31, 2005. http://dukemagazine.duke .edu/article/the-silent-epidemic.

24. "The Silent Epidemic."

25. "The Silent Epidemic."

26. Michael Flood, "The Harms of Pornography Exposure Among Children and Young People," *Child Abuse Review* 18, no. 6 (November/December 2009), 384–400.

27. Neil Malamuth, Tamara Addison, and Mary Koss, "Pornography and Sexual Aggression: Are There Reliable Effects and Can We Understand Them?" *Annual Review of Sex Research* 11 (2000): 45.

28. Christian Smith, *Lost in Transition: The Dark Side of Emerging Adulthood* (New York: Oxford University Press, 2011).

29. John H. Pryor et al., *The American Freshman: National Norms, Fall 2010* (Los Angeles: Higher Education Research Institute, UCLA, 2010).

30. Elayne Bennett, *Daughters in Danger: Helping Our Girls Thrive in Today's Culture* (Nashville: Nelson Books, 2013).

31. Thomas Lickona, "10 Emotional Dangers of Premature Sexual Involvement," The Fourth and Fifth Rs (Fall, 2007), http://www2 .cortland.edu/centers/character/images/sex_character/2007-Fall-red.pdf.

32. Bob Bartlett, "Going All the Way," *Momentum* 24, no. 2 (April–May, 1993), 36–9.

33. D. D. Hallfors et al., "Adolescent Depression and Suicide Risk: Association with Sex and Drug Behaviors," *American Journal of Preventive Medicine* 27 (2004): 224–30.

34. National Campaign to Prevent Teen Pregnancy, America's *Adults and Teens Sound Off About Teen Pregnancy: An Annual National Survey*, December 2003. Washington, DC, from http://www.teenpregnancy.org.

35. Hallfors et al., "Adolescent Depression and Suicide Risk."

36. D. P. Orr et al., "Premature Sexual Activity as an Indicator of Psychosocial Risk," *Pediatrics* 87, no. 2 (February 1991): 141–47.

37. Abridged from *Choosing the Best: A Values-Based Sex Education Curriculum* (Atlanta, 1993).

38. Thanks for the first three of these rewards of waiting from Kristine Napier's book, *The Power of Abstinence* (New York: Avon, 1996).

39. Thanks to Janet Smith for this point.

40. Adapted from Sean Covey, *The 6 Most Important Decisions You'll Ever Make* (New York: Fireside Books, 2006).

41. M. D. Resnick et al., "Protecting Adolescents from Harm: Findings from the National Longitudinal Study on Adolescent Health," *Journal of the American Medical Association* 278, no. 10 (September 1997): 823–32.

42. V. Guilamo-Ramos et al., "Paternal Influences on Adolescent Sexual Risk Behaviors: A structured review," *Pediatrics* 130, no. 5 (2012): 1313–25.
43. Thanks to my friend and colleague Kevin Ryan for this point.

Appendix B: Books That Teach Kindness and Other Virtues

1. Joy Mosher, "Children's Literature and Character Development," *The Fourth and Fifth Rs* (Fall, 2001), http://www2.cortland.edu/dotAsset /199292.pdf.

Appendix C: Family Projects That Foster Kindness and Purpose

1. Debra Gross Tenzer, *Do One Nice Thing: Little Things You Can Do to Make the World a Lot Nicer* (New York: Crown Publishing Group, 2009).
2. William Damon, *The Path to Purpose: Helping Our Children Find Their Calling in Life* (New York: Free Press, 2008).

Index